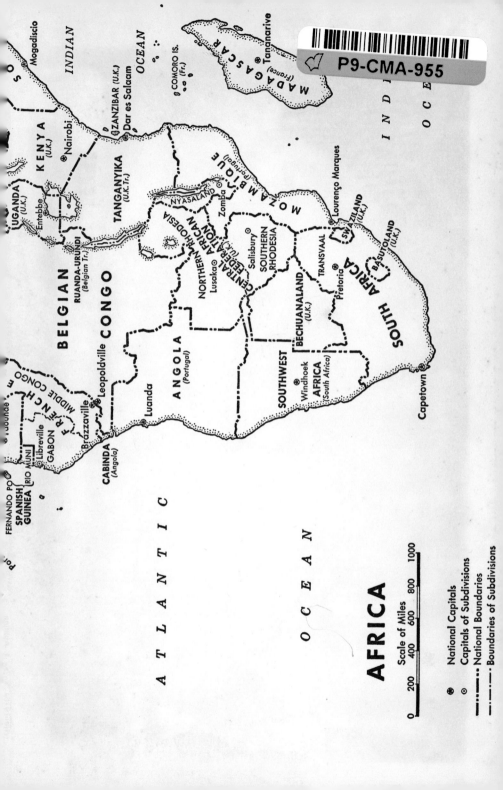

The Death of Africa

THE MACMILLAN COMPANY
NEW YORK · CHICAGO
DALLAS · ATLANTA · SAN FRANCISCO
LONDON · MANILA
IN CANADA
BRETT-MACMILLAN LTD.
GALT, ONTARIO

The Death of Africa

by

PETER RITNER

New York – THE MACMILLAN COMPANY – 1960

First Printing

Printed in the United States of America

The Macmillan Company, New York
Brett-Macmillan Ltd., Galt, Ontario

Library of Congress catalog card number: 60-7282

To
R. S. M.

Foreword

A version of the old Arabian Nights tale told me recently by my good friend Mr. Ed Fisher, the cartoonist and satirist, sums up my theme.

Somewhere off the Malabar Coast a poor Fisherman, hauling in his empty nets for the umpteenth time, caught a glimpse of a glittering object lodged in a knot of one of the ropes. He retrieved it, and after rubbing off the encrustations instantly recognized it for what it was, an otherworldly purple bottle containing a Djinn who had been condensed therein by Ormazd, Master of the Cosmos. The Fisherman shipped his oars, trimmed the little vessel, and smashed the bottle across one of the gunwales.

At once the gigantic, fiery-red Djinn leaped from the pieces and, wrapping a finger around the Fisherman's neck, began to strangle him like a boa constrictor.

"Stop! Please stop!" cried the Fisherman. "Do you know what you are doing? How can you be so ungrateful as to murder me when I have just freed you from eternal incarceration?"

"Ah," replied the Djinn, continuing to compress his liberator's throat. "There was a day when I should have agreed with you—but that day is long past. For nine hundred years I have lain imprisoned in that bottle. During the first three hundred years I vowed that the man who released me should command my powers for all time; I should make him Emperor of Creation, possessor of every lovely girl

vii

and shining jewel. No man came. During the second three centuries I had time to reflect on the superficiality and egocentricity of mankind. Why should I raise the specimen of such a race to a rank equaling my own? Granting his first three wishes should be enough for him. Still no man came. So for the last three hundred years I have burned with a consuming hatred of human frivolousness, and I have sworn to destroy the tardy scoundrel who finally sets me at liberty."

And he did.

The moral of our little story: When you deal with a Djinn, deal with him briskly and, if you can, while he is still in his bottle.

What the world, with insufficient apprehension, is now witnessing in Africa is the birth of a historical monstrosity whose whole future is mortgaged to its deformities. The parturition is already close at hand. African society has lost its coherence entirely, and its ability to defend itself from itself or from the impinging forces of the outside world. Nothing that happens there happens for the good. The old and the new—frequently the worst of both—are grafted onto each other higgledy-piggledy, so disastrously out of phase that what vigor or virtue accidentally inheres in either is destroyed before it has a chance to operate. Buffering mechanisms which normally shore up societies in crisis have broken down and given up. The deeds of good men are as likely to injure the society as to benefit it; hence, despair companions disappointment. After a few more years of this kind of thing it will be as impossible to conceive of living in the same world with Africa as it now is to conceive of living without her.

But a majority of Americans turns the same bland gaze on Africa that we spare for the other remote and exotic places of the world— a regard of benevolent and radically misplaced optimism. We are like the King of Siam in John Locke's parable, who believed every story the Englishman told him until his visitor described weather so cold that water changes to rock. That one was one too many for the Oriental monarch; ice overstrained his credulity, even as the notion of an inexorable, morbid, all-devouring impoverishment overstrains the credulity of the citizens of this bounteous Republic. We can barely compel ourselves to imagine Nature ravaging a society instead of collaborating with it. And so long as these remain our typical attitudes we shall never comprehend the fate that is swallowing up Africa, we shall never make heads or tails of what is occurring in this world of ours or the world of our children. Monstrosities do not cure themselves; they do not harken to reasonable persuasion; they do not prudently calculate their own self-interests; and they do not grow up to make good neighbors.

When I undertook this discussion of the realities of contemporary Africa I was conscious that the objectivity of the account would be adulterated by passionate convictions of mine that Something Must Be Done. I simply cannot bring myself to believe that Americans—my patient and generous countrymen—will stand idly by while another center of chaos in the world is created right under our noses. Our true and fixed strategic and moral interests are so plain in this area—our capabilities of achieving our ends so ample, the call on our resources so comparatively modest—that it is inconceivable to me that these interests may be betrayed on no better excuses than ignorance and indifference. But if I have failed to edit out every last bit of sermonizing along these lines, I think I have succeeded in keeping fairly clear of other melees of vituperation which are stultifying so much of the commentary on Africa these days, particularly in Africa herself. If we search the scene we can turn up an abundance of villains, but with the possible exception of the Afrikaner none who amounts to anything. The old soldier of colonialism has spectacularly faded away. African politicians have belied the appellation of "noisy boys" and have matured into surprisingly moderate, and even skillful, public administrators. Over most of Africa the white man's arrogance is confining itself to milder and milder surges of nostalgia. The principal industries are paternally supervised by government planners, whose object it is to shield the African and to integrate economic with social progress (whether they succeed in these aims is another story). Meddling American journalists and missionaries from the Anti-Slavery Society cannot poke into anything which is not already whirring and raging from internal fires. In short, it is quite impossible to pin the blame for uncorking the Djinn on the follies or sins of any group. History has uncorked Africa, and has delivered her over to a deformed and diseased evolution which is working itself up to a climax of destruction, a catastrophe of imbalance, a "mighty convulsion, which no mortal could make, and no mortal can stay," as Lincoln wrote of the Civil War—but a convulsion which we must nonetheless confront and treat with dispatch unless we want to see one more focus of hostility planted on the perimeter of our political and personal lives.

What justification is there for adding another essay to the lengthening shelf of serious works on Africa—many of which have been composed by men of greater experience of Africa and completer mastery of one or more of the pertinent academic specialties than I possess? An audience is the only excuse for anybody's book. It is my feeling that few of the new symptomatologies—a just characterization of the bulk of books on modern Africa—have been addressed to the right party, the only doctor who happens to be in the house: namely, the American voter. Consequently, the American voter has not had a fair chance to learn why he ought to do something, and what it is that he ought to do. Specifically, the ordinary American has not been told—or not told often enough—that colonialism's demise, and the independence movement which is spreading like a flush over the northern regions of Black Africa, has not materially affected one way or the other the progress of the cancer which is assaulting the tissues of African society. The Union of South Africa is an exception to many of the generalizations that can be imposed on Black Africa—and the Union's politics are certainly such as to corrupt and doom any attempt to get at deeper troubles there—but even in the Union the decay of the farms, and other maladies similar to this in nature, pose deadlier threats to the long-range settlement of Africa than the present, temporary bondage of African to Afrikaner. We are not grappling in Africa with a fracas to be pacified by the gestures of a conventional or constitutional formality. Nothing less than a full-scale social resurrection will turn the trick.

This approach has conditioned my method in one important respect. A man's views on the validity of generalization relate directly to his views on the much broader theme of historical determinism. That is to say, the extent to which you believe that grand events are created and guided by superpersonal forces like race, class, life-force, and so on, will largely decide the extent to which you lean on deductions from generalizations in describing lesser phenomena. And here I want to say—without taking the space to argue these abstruse points

—that I believe "historical determinism" to be an almost meaningless phrase, and that I agree with William Godwin that really to know any human act one must investigate the full complexity of the particular case. Nevertheless, it seems plain to me that societies vary tremendously in the degree to which generalizations can provide valid and useful insights into the things that interest us about them—on both the personal and mass levels. The example of Epictetus to the contrary, when a man is a slave he is almost invariably more "determined"—more susceptible of description by "class attitude," for instance—than a man who possesses a much wider spectrum of life-choices and in whom therefore the specifically human free-will factors count for a great deal more.

What does all this have to do with Africa? Simply that the specialist who concentrates exclusively on a half-dozen or so vying and merging traditions, tribes, and languages in the largely paleolithic hinterland of Africa may be tempted to overlook the "urbanization" of the society, the decay of the "agricultural sector," and other features of the Big Picture which have in fact enslaved the average African in a way that poverty, class-affiliation, or any other similar determinant can never enslave the average American. Every day in Africa the dominion of these "Big Picture" trends is expanding; I might even add that the "depersonalization" process implied in this expansion is one more sign of Africa's trouble. (Of course, the supersession of parochialisms by uniformities is a universal characteristic of the modern age, as the Coca-Cola Company can demonstrate for you—so one must exercise his own judgment in deeming this or that supersession healthy or sick.) In any case, African society is not going to reverse itself after the fashion of an old comic film sequence, with factories and towns melting back into the terrain, and medicine-men picking up their old rattles, so I have tried to focus here not only on the Big Picture but also the Big New Picture. But I do wish to caution my readers against the traps that all generalizations conceal—and against thinking of Africans as if they were indistinguishable molecules of a gas, ruled by Avogadro's Number.

A short note on the genesis of this essay. For the July 19, 1958, number of the *Saturday Review*, a weekly journal for which I labored more than six years, I wrote and produced a picture-and-story section on Africa about twelve pages in length. Although responsibility for the report was exclusively mine, I want here to acknowledge the assistance throughout of an African friend, Mr. Shadrach N. Okova, a Kenyan who at that time was studying for a degree in economics at Columbia University. Also, of course, I owe the usual debt to my fellow staffers. The project was an unusual one for our magazine, and we were gratified that it kicked up some dust in dusty quarters. Perhaps we were proudest of the public attack on us made from the floor of the House of Assembly in Capetown by Mr. Eric Louw, Minister of External Affairs of the Union of South Africa.

But from a personal point of view the most satisfactory flame of all was that enkindled in the breast of a young editor of the Macmillan Company, Mr. Emile Capouya, who managed not only to forgive the shortcomings of the *Saturday Review* presentation but also to talk his firm into sponsoring the trip and research of which the present effort is the result. When a man voluntarily takes on this kind of job—to trouble to understand what one is driving at, then singlehandedly to wrestle out of the way the various obstacles which prevent one from saying it more forcibly and accurately—that man has accumulated an account which cannot be discharged by any common thanks or dedication. All I can say here is that Mike Capouya, not I, is the *genius loci* of this book; I hope the roof doesn't leak.

Lastly, I want to express my gratitude to the scores of men and women who were so hospitable to me in Africa, and who by talking with me and showing me around—at great effort and occasionally risk to themselves—corrected as many as they could of the errors that were crawling into these pages. Of the hundreds of studies and texts consulted, I have noted at appropriate places those on which I depended most heavily. But I must acknowledge specially the debt owed by everyone who thinks about Africa to the English scholar William Malcolm, Baron Hailey, and particularly to his great work, *An African Survey*, revision of 1956.

Contents

Foreword   vii

1. Varieties of African Geography   1

2. Union of South Africa—1   27

3. Union of South Africa—2   47

4. Southwest Africa; The High Commission Territories   76

5. The Federation of the Rhodesias and Nyasaland   89

6. Portuguese Africa: Mozambique and Angola   111

7. The Belgian Congo   124

8. The French Community in Africa   152

9. East Africa   172

10. Ghana and Nigeria   205

11. The American Posture   232

12. What Is Going to Happen in Africa?   257

13. Conclusions in Search of a Program   274

Index   301

1. Varieties of African Geography

In itself, none of the slayers of the old Africa—the "developments" we read about in the newspapers—is a bad thing. And, in any event, it is pointless to fuss over private evaluations of the Technological Revolution, the sweep of which no one could hinder were he even to try.

Extracting precious metals out of rocks buried miles in the earth; transforming watersheds into dynamos; building railroads, highways, and ports to link up the regions of Africa with one another and with the outside world; erecting banks, suburbs, newspapers, schools, towns, churches, hospitals, and shops; the corollary paraphernalia of political administration—law-courts, jails, military barracks, the suppression of predatory tribes and encouragement of a common language—it is possible to regret the old Africa while apprehending the new one, but is it honestly possible to deprecate the fastening of human controls like these on Nature? Indeed, do not these controls beget a dimension of freedom which so far as we in the West are concerned is one of the chief justifications of history?

Nor has the colossal cultural collision between the old Africa and Technological Civilization been as all-demolishing a transaction as one might suppose. Certainly the African has withstood the onslaught without losing his biological grip. The Revolution in its

I

industrial aspect he could not of course resist, but unlike the American Indian and the Polynesian—who took one look at it and faded out of the picture—the African is holding on grimly to his share of the human future. He runs no risk of ending up an exhibit in an ethnological museum; his rate of increase compares favorably—if that is the proper term—with that of the rest of mankind.

And discrepancies in the temperament of Western Civilization itself have provided the African with a chance to evolve a personal response to modern history. Consider the spiritual and intellectual opportunities for self-assertion that open up to the African when the European has imported ideals, religions, and politics into the land along with engines. The European is not nearly so polished or coherent a philosopher as he is a mechanic. What is one European's legitimate aspiration is another's folly, and a third's vanity: the distinctions are subjected to analysis in famous books and the preachments of famous pastors, and combined with stern censures of the kind of behavior that Europeans tend to display in Africa. Because these contradictions are potential instruments of psychological self-defense, they make a powerful appeal to the African. He learns our languages so that he can unsettle our conventional ideas with the very contentions of our own most thoughtful and revered citizens.

It is useless to pretend neutrality in all this. This is "Progress"; and no matter how tremendously our Thoreaus belabor the idea of Progress we are thoroughly imbued with the conviction that a warm and well fed existence approximates more to God's plan than a life spent combing the desert for grubs and roots. But what in our wonderful national good fortune we sometimes forget is that the same drug which augments the strength of one individual, or even restores him to health, may coagulate the blood of another and kill him. It is not "things" like steel mills and river boats which constitute a soundly based Technological Civilization so much as the timing with which these things enter into relations of interaction and interconnection, with each other and with the pretechnological substrate. In America, Technology (and Progress) were fortunate in possessing generous dimensions of space and time in which gradually to knit together—by trial-and-error methods—a more or less non-self-conflicting social fabric. But Africa has had to absorb the implications of the germicidal properties of boiling water and of nuclear fission roughly within the same generation—and her political education has been similarly compressed. The phasing of the historical process has been totally different in her case from what it was in America's, and there are reasons for believing that this phasing as it exists in Africa is corrupting what should be good into something very evil.

To give only a few examples: Africa's population has begun to expand rapidly before her economy is mature enough to provide work and sustenance for the new recruits (or, to put the same idea another way, before science has learned how to compensate for—or capitalize on—her beggarly rations of natural resources). Fairly efficient governments began to rule Africans before Africans knew how to rule governments; Africans were denied the instructions of political history. Because during the colonial period these governments were nonresponsive and foreign-oriented they often sat on their hands when they should have been hard at work nipping troubles in the bud; in some cases these delays have complicated fantastically the job of ultimately rationalizing the African society. And to make matters worse, none of these lapses of the beat has slowed down the Africans' acquisition of new appetites and new ambitions.

In short, that aggrandizement of man's physical and mental powers which goes by the name of the Technological Revolution has come to Africa with a vengeance, and the bulk of Africans rejoice in it—or, at least, in the cosmetic side-effects now on view on their horizons. But what the Africans are experiencing is not the relatively homogeneous and manageable phenomenon-in-time that we Americans know as the Technological Revolution, but a sudden and unhealthy efflorescence in one sector of their lives at the expense of the others. This cannot fairly be termed Progress, for at the bare minimum Progress connotes material betterment. When in the modern era its components are drastically out of phase, when it throws the society into which it plunges into *danses macabres* of imbalance, the Technological Revolution most emphatically does not better men materially. Indeed, the African Technological Revolution bears no resemblance at all to the Western model except for prepotency—and this superpower is heading straight for convulsion and disruption of the new Africa beyond the worst nightmares of the old Africa of nomads and farmers which it crowded out.

The giant island of Africa bestrides the Equator, but the region under consideration in this essay—sub-Sahara Africa—lies principally in the Southern Hemisphere, extending roughly from latitude 10 degrees north (that of Addis Ababa and the Panama Canal) to latitude 35 degrees south (that of the Cape of Good Hope and the Argentinian capital of Buenos Aires).

The books tell us that Africa is a continent of superabundant physical charms—and so it is. It possesses three of the world's mightiest rivers; stupendous, impassable, moss-curtained rainforests; looming gray-and-green volcanoes, active and inactive, which rise out of limitless, cloud-pocked plains; the most enchanting menagerie of animals to be found anywhere on earth. But despite the popular conception of Africa as a synonym for the "tropics," the topography of Africa is dominated neither by jungles nor heavily-wooded, gorilla-infested hillsides, but by a gigantic raised plain, the Great Central Plateau, which unrolls like a carpet from one extremity of Black Africa to the other in various manifestations of grassland, scrub, bush, veld, and savanna.

Separated from the sea by a low-lying coastal belt which is narrow in most places, but which widens out along the Gulf of Guinea and in eastern and southeastern Africa, the normal altitude-range of the Plateau varies between 3,000 and 6,000 feet. Far to the south, the scrubby pasturelands of the Little and Great Karroos sustained the Afrikaner trekkers of the seventeenth and eighteenth centuries, when first they climbed up out of Table Bay to penetrate the unknown. Gradually the Karroos merge into another semiarid region (the Orange Free State) and enter the High Veld of 6,000 feet or higher (the Transvaal and Southern Rhodesia). West of this hospitable rolling country the plain slides down to the terrible deserts and pans of Bechuanaland, across the flatness of Southwest Africa, to meet the frontier of the South Atlantic at the rainless desolation of the Namib. Eastward, the High Veld frays out in the trees and hills of Mozambique.

North of the Transvaal and Southern Rhodesia the Plateau mounts into the highlands of Central Africa—where white men can live in comfort while enriching themselves—the ore-bearing ridges of Northern Rhodesia and the Katanga province of the Belgian Congo, the northeastern districts of Angola, the tea slopes of Nyasaland

and—pressing on to the north—the tiny, delightful trust state of Ruanda-Urundi, the majestic game plains of Kivu (Belgian Congo), western Tanganyika, and Kenya, and the lakes and farmlands of Uganda.

Northeast of the Kenyan highlands another desert supervenes before the Plateau achieves its climax in the great Plateau of Abyssinia, home of one of the world's most splendid peoples, whose magnificent escarpments shield them from the deserts of the south and the dust-choked littoral of the Red Sea. In the west, the hills of the Katanga dip down into the immense basin of the Congo River and its tributaries, of which the Belgian colony of the Congo is the locus; then the western limb of the Plateau commences to shred apart entirely in the marshes of Equator province (Belgian Congo), the forests of French Equatorial Africa and the Guinea coast, and the dry "Sudanese" regions of northern Nigeria and French West Africa.

Supreme as are the influences of the Plateau on African geography, they do not by themselves tell the whole tale. There are isolated highlands in eastern South Africa, Basutoland, and the Cameroons; there are the marvels associated with the bifurcated Rift Valley System of East Africa, which are boulevards of savanna —twenty miles across or more—dropped like trenches thousands of feet below the rim of the surrounding Plateau, geologically connected to the volcanoes in their vicinity and to the "pearls of Africa," the incomparable chain of lakes in their floors which runs from Lake Rudolf at the junction of the Sudan and Ethiopia to Lake Nyasa in the far south. Facing the Indian Ocean are the steaming lowlands of eastern Kenya and Tanganyika, the nomad-roaming deserts of Somalia and the Ogaden. At the southernmost tip there is the Cape, ecologically similar to Southern California, bathed by trade winds and decked with flowers. And everywhere on the continent the flora and fauna of plains, hills, and mountain sides are bound into self-reacting packets by immediate local determinants of altitude and rainfall; in some places, the environment changes every hundred feet or so, and in one day a man can saunter through six or seven different universes of animal and plant.

But it is the Great Central Plateau which is the battlefield of the African future, for to wrest a living from the Plateau is as tough a proposition as any race ever faced. Much of it is entirely unusable. Other vast regions are so dry that stockraising is the only practical form of food growing; overgrazing is a desperate, everpresent peril; and attenuation of the land's thin cover and depletion of the underground water constantly threaten to convert range into desert. In other parts there is rain enough, but it tends to come down all at once in one or two annual torrents, and then stream off—excavating as it goes—before the soil has absorbed much of the moisture; or the rains may fail for a season or two; again, if the structure of the soil and the water table are not painfully conserved, the pasture will degenerate into wasteland. In equatorial areas, denuding the land of its natural forest cover renders the ground equally defenseless against tropical downpours; soils already poor in nutrient minerals are leached of those which they have; intensive cropping of most kinds accelerates the rate of exhaustion; more often than not irrigation interferes critically with natural drainage; diseases peculiar to Africa prowl every furrow.

Africa is a pauper continent. She has no "black earth" realms, no pampas or Mississippi Valleys or Ukrainian steppes, where a supertolerant Mother Earth shrugs off human rapacity and ignorance, giving man a second, third, fourth turn at the pump. In Africa, Mother Earth smiles with a skeleton's grin.

This titanic and perverse Plateau, the shoulders of the peaks that punctuate it and the deserts and forests that fringe it, is the fatherland of the Negro race—which may, if one pleases, be broken down into the subraces of Negro proper, Bantu, Nilote (or Nilo-Hamite), Hamite, Bushman, and Hottentot. (In this essay we shall not explore these subclassifications, because they are based mainly on language differences, and the new Africa is characteristically learning the European languages to facilitate easier general communications.) For thousands of years the Negro was relatively isolated from the worlds of the Mediterranean and Europe by the great Saharan desert system and the ferocious natural watchdogs—climatological and bacterial—of his coast line. As a result of this semiprivacy Africa won a distinctive place in the library of romance, but even so the isolation was never an absolute one. Before Alexander the Great's conquest Egypt had been ruled for a time by a Negro dynasty from up the river; elephants and hippopotamuses fought in the games of the Emperor Trajan; and Sudanese Negroes served him and his imperial cousins of many eras as they had served the pharaohs.

Exploding Islam ruptured the ancient capsule of Mediterranean society in the seventh century, and not only Black Africa but Cyrenaica and Mauretania too passed out of the memory and computations of European politicians. But Islam's momentum washed across the dunes of the desert to the margin of the great Plateau; Moslem barterers and freebooters established rivaling merchant kingdoms that floated up, whirled for a century or two, and then burst like bubbles in the region where now lie the modern communities of the Mali Federation and northern Nigeria. Though the names of these states have been revived by contemporary African leaders, they are only dim historical shadows, yet still they account for a permanent Islamic deposit in West Africa which reaches across the continent to the Islamic communities on the east coast, down which Arabs have hunted from the Horn of Africa to Natal since before the days of the Prophet.

When Europe's sinews began to stir again in the Age of Exploration, it was the Portuguese who were in the vanguard with their expeditions down West Africa seeking a water route to the Indies. In 1487, in a little known and incredibly heroic feat of navigational resoluteness, the Portuguese sailor Diogo Cão forced his vessel eighty-five miles against the current up the huge Congo to the first cataract, just above the modern port of Matadi. Next year Bartholemeu Diaz, mariner and ivory speculator, discovered the Cape of Good Hope. Ten years later Vasco da Gama, on his voyage to India, charted one or more of the estuaries of Mozambique, and early in the new century the King of Portugal followed up these exploratory probes by sending trading agents to struggle up the Zambesi in search of half-mythical, putatively gold-heavy potentates in the interior.

Meanwhile, from the middle years of the fifteenth century, the coast bordering the Gulf of Guinea—the "Slave Coast"—had been receiving visitations from the nationals of other European states besides Portugal; and from the year 1510, when a regular slave commerce to the Caribbean was instituted, Spanish, British, French, Danish, Portuguese, Dutch (and American) supercargoes vied in supplying strong backs and arms to the sugar lands of the West Indies and the cotton plantations of the Old South—a traffic which was finally suppressed little more than a century ago. On the east coast the Arabs had from time immemorial operated yet another slave industry. While the European slaver was primarily a trader, depending on middleman chiefs to procure the African captives, the Arabs conducted their own slave harvests. Perhaps the acme of their system was achieved in the fabulous caravan industry of the Zanzibar raider Tippoo Tib. This precious scoundrel, who flourished in the waning decades of the last century and varied his crimes with a tour of duty as one of Leopold II's administrators of the Congo Free State, anticipated the Taylor system: his companies of Arabs, roaming the bush for years at a time, first hunted down hundreds of elephants, cached their tusks along the route, then dispersed to seize African villagers who now would transport themselves, plus the ivory, to the bazaar.

Students of the trade hesitate about estimating the total number of Africans who served as commodities during the four-hundred-odd years of slavery's heyday; perhaps there were 12 millions or more. But we should try to arrive at some conception of the social derangement involved in the industry. Briefly, in Africa the hostility of a mean and vicious Nature was magnified for a half-millennium by the hostility of crushingly superior and predacious alien civilizations. Though Western slavers more or less confined their operations to a small stretch of the Guinea Coast, this was at the same time the most populous part of Black Africa. For centuries the young people had to live like mayflies; for them it was murder, kidnaping, or flight; the middleman chiefs inured themselves to indescribable treacheries and cruelties; villages were incinerated wholesale, and those which somehow eluded this fate had to stand poised for instant dispersal; crops were laid low in order to enlist famine in the cause of commerce. Over and over again sprouts of resistance and indigenous civilization of which we know nothing must have been swooped down upon and wiped out. The land was scoured and rescoured until it came at last to possess its present-day texture—a sort of cultural plastic, infinitely tough but featureless.

Individually, the African was either an accomplice or a victim.

His home and his tribe were his hideouts; his religion was his narcotic; his survival was his fulfillment. As generation after generation slipped into oblivion—with no change in the climate of heat, blood, and terror—his psychology came to adapt to these conditions. The African came to value above all other things the springtime sprint—not away from Death and Pain, for these tutelaries were as familiar and remorseless as the African sun—but the sprint *toward* the muscular and sensual consummations of adolescence and young manhood. Once a certain content has been conferred on sheer survival, a man can face the hopeless future in a mood akin to tranquillity. Once a man is a man, life has lost the power to cheat his soul of all its portion of triumph and defiance.

Except at the Cape, the southern tip of Africa, where a cross-cutting mountain system plus a temperate latitude softens Africa, Europeans limited their permanent settlements during all these years to forts and posts associated with the slave and ivory trades. Even the colonization of the Cape was a comparatively tentative one until gold and diamonds were discovered in the Transvaal in the late 1860's. But in this and successive generations high and mighty Victorian Europe, galvanized by an eccentric vitality that recognized no physical or moral obstacles, mounted a full shock assault on Africa. Fanatic missionaries and explorers—young and old—trudged from the Niger to the Rifts seeking the source of a river, or elucidating the relations between a watershed and its discharges, or planting the Cross before the huts of unheard-of lake wizards. Year after year they would return, rotting with malaria and suppurations, until death liberated them from enthusiasm. In London and Paris Europe's shrewdest capitalists floated stock issues to finance companies building railroads into the African hinterland. When it was disclosed that these prodigiously dear constructions were leading not to bustling piazzas hungry for Lancashire textiles but to wider and emptier wastes of savanna, the bourses of Europe resounded to epic crashes and even louder burials of reputations. Finally, in the 1880's, the powers of Europe began their competition as to which among them could pour the most expenditure into the least promising terrain. Administration advanced up the river valleys across the bush until Frenchman met Englishman, German met Portuguese, in the heart of the continent, and it was necessary to summon the diplomats to adjudicate the dozens of boundary disputes. The coarse, scaly skin of Africa surrendered one secret after another until no secret remained; then she was bundled into parcels, and put in fee.

Civilization had truly come to Africa, but it was a civilization gravely flawed at the source, and in these flaws Africa found refuge wherein to await the hour of recovery.

At the turn of this century Europe ruled Africa with casual flicks of her power, but she was swiftly losing—if she had ever possessed—the power to rule herself. She was running at an increasingly critical internal temperature, and in 1914 came the inevitable spontaneous combustion. Two ghastly wars revolutionized the power ratio between Europe and non-Europe. Germany was struck from the roll of the colonial states altogether. No longer could English bankers lay their hands on credit and capital in unlimited quantities. When the government of France flitted to Vichy the old French Africa expired on the spot. Then came the full impact of World War II, with its great masses of capital pumped into Africa by the Allies in their need of her strategic bases and metals.

These were changes in the objective political situation, and other subjective changes had been occurring in the minds and hearts of the European, outgrowths of both the good and the bad sociopolitical movements of the Victorian epoch. For generations missionaries and schoolteachers had striven to teach that there was more to Western Civilization than greed and sadism. Now the British people themselves began to question the value of imperial dignities that rested on the shame of millions of colored people. (As always, the English classes had to obey the masses; and with perfect aplomb the Colonial Office opened the cell doors of nationalist chieftains one day and requested them on the next to form Queen's governments.) Starting in the 1920's, French parties of the left made a practice of training and subsidizing French African nationalists. America appeared on the scene during World War II, with her national faith in democracy that has survived uncounted idiotic self-betrayals. And the United Nations, dominated by sympathizers with non-self-governing peoples, inherited all but one of the former African mandates of the League of Nations.

The stage was set for Freedom. The medical phase of the Technological Revolution had fashioned a connected population, and inhabitants for the burgeoning new industrial concentrations. Colonial authorities had devised draft administrations around the modern postulate of the "nation." From a variety of origins the conceptions of equality, progress, and independence had permeated through the continent—and the leaders and techniques wherewith to strive for these things were also on tap. With less hubbub and fewer bleeding hearts than any sensible man could have predicted twenty-five years previously, the colonial episode began a quick-march to its natural close.

In 1940 the only free states in Black Africa were Liberia and Ethiopia. Now the situation is totally changed. In place of vast colonial empires ruled from the metropoles of Europe there are two new kinds of state, each one a radical departure from the prewar Africa: first, the independent African nation; second, the independent diehard white-dominated nation. Over the huge territory of its African empire, the British government has accepted the principle of independence—and is working actively toward that end—for every major ex-colony except Kenya, Nyasaland, and Northern Rhodesia. With the constitution of October 4, 1958, the twelve states of former French Equatorial Africa and French West Africa were delivered up to the perils and joys of total autonomy, free to choose their own political destinies. The Belgians have promised independence to the Congolese. Since 1945 more than 100,000,000 people in Africa have become "free citizens"—or very soon will become so. Only those Africans are left behind who are living in the Portuguese "overseas provinces" of Mozambique and Angola, a few negligible Portuguese and Spanish enclaves in West Africa, the temporarily stalled colony and protectorate of Kenya—*and* the white-dominated Union of South Africa and Federation of the Rhodesias and Nyasaland.

How agreeable it would be to report that the obsolescent but not-wholly-discreditable colonial experience is now definitively concluded, so that we all can turn from hackneyed political allocutions to more vital and arresting topics concerning Africa's health and welfare. But such a report—as everyone knows—would be all too premature. The racist regimes of the Union of South Africa and Southern Rhodesia—now reinforced by steely passions unknown

to even the worst of the old colonialisms—are more rigidly opposed
to African freedom today than they were fifty years ago. And
because of their industrial strength, these states constitute hinges on
which other relics of the colonial era, like the Portuguese colonies,
can swing almost indefinitely. Solve the riddle of South Africa and
the Rhodesias, and then perhaps mankind can lay the specter of
white *baas* and black *boy* forever. But this is a riddle wrapped in
dynamite—a Gordian knot to which no Alexander has yet addressed
himself.

Speedily as the new political era in Africa has overhauled the old
one, it has still limped disastrously far behind the thunderous progress
of the Technological Revolution.

It is probable, for example, that Africa is already overpopulated;
and permit me to digress for a period to investigate this important
idea. From the moment that population became controllable it became relative: that is to say, what is a convenient population density
for Society A may be overpopulation for B—and conceivably under-
population for C—and one man's judgment on it may differ from
his neighbor's. This view would have made nonsense in the days
when "starving margins," clipped by heaven-sent floods and epidemics, established a ratio between human fecundity and a land's
bearing capacity which was as unchallengeable—and in some cases
as immutable—as the stars. But when the human brain penetrated into
some of the secrets of diseases, improvements in the techniques of
food-getting, prevention of conception, and so forth—when we
learned to bend Nature a little in addition to being bent by her—
then we transferred the whole concept of population from the
column of phenomenon to that of policy.

In other words, competition for food is no longer the sole determinant of population shape, and in very lucky and advanced
countries like the United States it tends to disappear even as an
influence, being replaced largely by differential moral attitudes.
Of course, in less lucky or advanced communities the new powers
may barely have begun to mix it up with the old variables—and the
society's structure may be in a state of flux or even on the brink
of extinction. For instance, even when it acts at a distance of 1,000
miles from his own hut, the slightest pressure of population puts

the Eskimo of the Canadian Barrens out of business as an Eskimo—
because the herds of caribou on which he subsists *as an Eskimo*
require whole Siberias of tundra for their foragings and seasonal
migrations. And it is only because her people accept, or have resigned themselves to accept, lives of economic improvisation at
a very low level that India can support swarming cities of millions
despite a desperate poverty. Of course, in striking contrast to Es-
kimos and Indians is New York City, through which pass at high
velocity the currencies and trade goods of the entire world; and
in and around New York a population of office workers and their
families more numerous than the total population of any country
in Black Africa except Nigeria thrive at one of the highest living
standards known to history. (But we ought to notice that Sir Charles
Darwin, and those who agree with him, deride any general supposition that Technology has retired the "starving margin" method of
population control. With the world's population expanding at an
annual rate of about 2 per cent—and, particularly, with new techniques of food production falling behind the population increments
in the so-called "underdeveloped" areas—the neo-Malthusians con-
fidently prophesy the early re-establishment of the old mechanism
on a more monstrous scale than ever before.)

Thus, it would be convenient to possess something like an "index
of specific population," combining all of these factors—religious
values, bearing capacity of land, fertility, political structure, technological sophistication, and so on—with which to express an optimum population level for each community according to its own
spiritual and material desiderata. Such an index number would be
of limited utility, because of the transience of all the factors that
enter into it. Nevertheless, if we can imagine such an evanescent
index number we can understand the bases of the claim that Africa
is "overpopulated" even though her continental population density
is but slightly greater than one-third our own here in America.
When Africa's present conditions of culture, modernization, and aspiration change, then our index number would change too—and
when this happens "overpopulation" might cease to be a valuable
or significant description of one of her most crucial problems. But
at the moment it is.

In what does this overpopulation consist and how did it come about? To understand this let us sketch retrospectively the white man's modernization of Africa. As we know, one of the very first effects of the Technological Revolution is the bite into the death rate, the result of imposing political order and checking the depredations of pestilence. According to the 1958 United Nations Demographic Yearbook, Africa still has the highest birth and death rates of any of the continents, but the death rate has been so far brought under control that her over-all annual rate of increase is about 1.8 per cent (compared to 2.4 per cent for South America, 2.5 per cent for Southeast Asia). Of course, the population in some parts of Africa is growing much faster than this: French West Africa more than 3 per cent annually, Southwest Africa more than 4 per cent (in the latter case, immigration significantly supplements the natural increase).

Acting by itself this "medical effect" would in time transform African society out of all recognition, but it never acts by itself. Modernization alters the provenience of the African's life as well as its length. The African traditionally earns his livelihood by subsistence farming (a few tubers or grains on the doorstep), raiding and looting, or hunting—or a combination of two or more of the three. When the European came to Africa he circumscribed the hunting grounds of races like the Bushmen and exterminated their food animals. Raider or warrior tribes like the Matabele were defeated, domiciliated, and compulsorily introduced to agriculture—on land notably inferior in quality to that assigned the white settlers following on the soldiers' heels. Subtler influences went to work on the subsistence farmer—but, to cite only one, European administrations discouraged the random movements of an agriculture that depended on shifting its site of cultivation every two or three years.

Up to this point we have mentioned only automatic responses to the new ingredient in the situation, but now the positive policies and projects of the European begin to interact with and distort these responses. Despite the incorrigible deficits which the typical African colony racked up generation after generation, European governments never abandoned the hunt for ways to make them pay for themselves. How could the colonies accomplish this without contributing something salable to the world's markets—metals from beneath the surface or agricultural produce from on top of it? Over the years prospectors and businessmen established the fact that mining and cash cropping were indeed feasible profit-makers here and there, and the colonial authorities naturally dedicated themselves to exploiting them.

Sad to relate, they found—and it took them a long time before they would admit it—that it was almost impossible to balance their colonies' budgets without wrecking their societies. Before the population boom made it unnecessary over most of Africa, the mining and industrial enterprises lured or coerced their laborers off the land, leaving the agriculture of the continent in the hands of old men, women, and children. Even today there are sections of Mozambique where more than 85 per cent of the adult population is female; naturally, the society-dissolving consequences of this kind of imbalance ramify into areas other than agriculture. In encouraging the production of cash crops, even where the farming was left to African smallholders, as with the peanut and cocoa cultivators of West Africa, no attention was initially paid to the extra burdens being laid on the land. Like the soils of other hot countries, most African soils are exceedingly poor in many vital minerals like phosphorus and exceedingly delicate in their so-called "crumb structures." When they are intensively cropped (especially in demanding crops like peanuts), when their natural cover is removed and they are exposed to the sun, winds, and rains of the African climate, they deteriorate within a lifetime into worthless clays and sands. The old "shifting cultivation" system injured them severely too, but at least under this system a single plot might rest for a century or more, restoring itself with an overgrowth of scrub, while the tribe wandered on elsewhere. But this is a thing of the past.

When practical innovations like these began to intercombine dynamically—or, if you prefer, pathologically—it was no longer just the living who were impoverished, but the continent-in-time, generation upon generation of Africans unborn; and the more remote in time the generation, the more it is impoverished. A declining death rate and increasing social stability plant more people more firmly on the land. Land that was farmed intermittently is now farmed perennially, and by the weakest agriculturalists of the community. Forests and other cover of the reserves are lumbered off for profit or to clear the ground for cash cropping—years before Western agronomists have solved the problems of erosions, leachings, soil degradations, and so forth, years before Western governments have discovered the will to apply what restoratives they already possess. Scars and wounds begin to run together into a self-exacerbating ulcer; watersheds and provinces are irretrievably ruined —or at least condemned to a ruin that can be remedied only by the intervention of massive quantities of money, know-how, and patience. No time is granted the parsimonious Nature of Africa to recover and refresh herself. And yet more people, and still more people, must live in this ruin, among these gullies and stump farms, sucking the last ion of strength out of the land. The so-called "agricultural sector" finds itself in the fix that we can observe now in contemporary Africa—staring straight at Chaos.

Remember that this description of an impaled countryside is perfectly consistent with the other descriptions of Africa we are constantly shown nowadays. Raw, bright, new cities and universities, clamorous ports, gaily chattering women carrying baskets of produce on their heads to market, African miners holding the latest model in jackhammer—these are the pictures which old-timers and tourists alike are quick to spot and snap with their kodaks; more consequentially, no one disputes that they signify the great force transforming modern Africa. Statistics can be quoted *ad infinitum* to illustrate the sweep and speed with which Africa's economy is being revved up to the level of the international money world: Ghana's exports have quadrupled in value since the late 1930's; the Congo's have quintupled; Angola's have sextupled; since 1948 the annual value of the continent's mineral exports alone has tripled; Africa's "gross product" is estimated to be growing at an annual rate of 5 per cent. (But I must ask my readers to disparage these references to "gross product," because the best economists, like Professor S. H. Frankel, warn us that the Western terminology involved in its computation cannot meaningfully be applied to "underdeveloped" economies. Also, it is easy to exaggerate the dimensions of Africa's "boom"; in the years 1945 to 1958 the capital newly invested in Africa amounted to about $10 billions, one-quarter of America's *annual* budget for defense alone; of this $10 billions,

America contributed about $1½ billions. Again, this investment and the other symptoms of African prosperity were chiefly the result of an extraordinary period of high primary prices, a period now slackening off or terminating altogether.)

Nothing could be more foolish than to divorce interpretation of economic boom statistics from consideration of the social and even political reconstructions which are so intimately bound up with them. For example, the young laborers who clamber out of the African bush to work the new industries do not divide into the normal fractions of a Western industrial population. They do not form into an army of workers, a cadre of supervisors, and an executive suite, because the whole premise of African labor-economics differs radically from our own. The African is hired for his sweat—not for his participation in what we think of as the "economic process," at the levels either of enterprise or of consumption. He will not win promotion to the board of directors, marry the daughter of the boss, or earn the wages to purchase manufactures made from the copper he mines. He does not join a milieu which helps stimulate and regulate the industrial nexus. He does not take his place in the ranks of consumers, subsidizing secondary industries which partially cushion shocks to the primary industries. He does not appear as an investor (with a total annual per capita income less than the annual per capita sum—$90—which is saved and invested in the West, African thrift and acumen are imaginary quantities). He does not become the partisan of a political party which aims at modifying "laissez-faire capitalism" into "democratic capitalism." He does not plume himself on "middle-class" attitudes, studying how (rationally) to promote his own self-interest. He is permitted to be nothing but a proletarian, slavishly treading down the old Marxist trail—that fate which the African is powerless to repudiate for himself as we have done for ourselves. True, at this particular point in time he is a proletarian involved in the production of goods for which the West happens to have some use. But we are complacently informed (by stout non-Marxists) that some of the key industries of Africa depend on the cheapness of African labor for their profit margins, and that they will be lost to Africa the moment attempts to raise the African's standard of living begin to succeed.

In short, African cities are Potemkin cities, and the shiny new industries of Africa Potemkin industries. They work, but they work for decay instead of growth. Given a fall in primary prices, such as that which halved the price of copper in 1957, or a natural disaster such as Ghana's cocoa blight, the African "industrial sectors" are instantaneously cut off from their supply of nutriment like tumors from their pedicles, and left to fester helplessly as heaps of slums. Without savings, without adequate social services, the seasonal or chronic unemployment which immiserates the urban concentrations of Africa (with the exception of those of the Union, where other miseries make up for the want of this one) deepens the bias on which the economy has been reared from the beginning. These cities and these industries are not the embryos of a wonderful new Africa of the future, but merely beckoning mirages of what might be—faraway, and contingently animate, playthings of the overwhelming economies of America and Europe.

Despite all these observations, the facts that Africa's "gross product" is calculated to be increasing at an annual rate about double that of its population growth, that capital is coming into Africa at an annual rate of perhaps 15 per cent of this "gross product," and that authoritative studies indicate that there has been a steady rise in real per capita income over most of Africa in the past twenty years—all these statistics have confounded many friendly analysts into believing optimistically that a self-generating and progressive mechanism has now taken hold, and that from now on things will get better in Africa. At the risk of repeating ourselves, let us emphasize that nothing could be further from the truth. Put aside for the moment Professor Frankel's strictures on these indices as being founded on Western social and psychological assumptions rather than African, and accept them as rough-and-ready approximations. Then we have to admit, first, that per capita income in the United States, Europe, and Russia is rising at a far faster rate than that of Africa; therefore, to quote Professor Kuznets, "the *political* misery . . . the tension created by the observation of the much greater growth of other communities may only have increased." Secondly, this African growth is extremely lopsided (and compromised by its lopsidedness) with respect to current and imminent political probabilities; consider that 22 per cent of the continental "gross product" is represented by the Gross National Product of the Union of South Africa alone. Third, the observed increase in real per capita income is more than absorbed by (also observed) changes in the urbanized African's patterns of consumption.

When we arrive at this latter point we see that we have embarked on the mysterious seas of what economists call "measurement of satisfactions," but—unsteady as is our footing in these waters—if we venture out far enough in them we will perceive a truer image of what is really happening in Africa than can be conveyed by any naked statistics. To take a homely illustration: Africans in cities wear pants instead of skin. This is a modification of habits which is inevitable and uncontrollable, and which is therefore irrelevant to discussions of the *psychological* and *political* components of economic development. In other words, a man who feels that he *must* wear pants does not feel rich because he does in fact own one pair of pants. In the American Depression men owned pants, shoes, and even old Fords but they did not feel rich; they were out of work, resentful, and reflecting on revolution. Therefore, when an African population is in process of redistribution in the urban direction, it is perilous to attribute the price of pants to an increase in real income without appending a footnote to the effect that in his new surroundings the African will not tolerate being without pants— and, in addition, is exposed to almost equally compelling new cravings which he is not able to satisfy at all. A man is not grateful or contented who is permitted to subsist at *what he himself deems* a minimum level. (The fairly recent descent of this minimum level to a subminimum level, caused by rising living costs exceeding the rise in wages for most of Africa's cities, only puts pepper in this stew.)

In short, except for the special cases presented by advanced countries like the United States, it is worthless methodology to abstract the rate of capital accumulation from its place in the over-all description of a society. The case of Russia, where substantial, even spectacular gains in capital accumulation were registered in the last decade or so of the Czarist regime, might have provided us some instruction on this head. Africa can yield similar lessons. Her (relatively) high rate of capital accumulation—and the other indices of "growth" we have cited—are unquestionably signs of a rapid change in her economic structure; and the reality of this change can of course be confirmed by anyone who travels in Africa and looks at what he sees. But these indices are data, not principles of health; they do not by themselves cohere into a sound society; and, in fact, they reflect economic activity which is neither generous enough nor properly shaped and distributed to arrest or heal Africa's trouble.

Let us recapitulate the arguments of this chapter.

1. The rapidly waxing population concentrations of Africa are chiefly employed in producing primary goods like metals and cash crops. This "single-strap" kind of society is exceptionally vulnerable to damaging price fluctuations in the world's market places. These fluctuations do, in fact, occur. There are no middle class, no domestic African savings, no wealthy or sympathetic political government to qualify the resulting crises into buffered ebb-and-flow patterns. Hence the economic system does not meet the minimum standards of stability—and political stability is, naturally, a hostage to this economic instability.

2. One principal consequence of the decay of the "agricultural sector" has been the diversion of an increasing ratio of the increasing population into these population concentrations—accentuating their demonstrable instability. Also, despite a relatively low population density, enormous "rural" regions of Africa—for instance, most of French West Africa and the Union's Native Reserves—have turned into food importers. Once again, the factors of over-all strain and instability are augmented.

3. A rapidly growing population aggravates all other aspects of social imbalance, and profoundly modifies their character. There has been no significant rise in the level of the African diet, notoriously deficient in protein. There has been no significantly widespread program of African education. With the exception of pest control, there has been no significant program of research into Africa's primary environmental problems: soil reclamation and fertilization, irrigation, breeding of disease-resistant strains of livestock, and so on. There has been no significant evolution of an African middle class, which, using conventional economic and political weapons, might itself take the initiative for meeting and correcting some of these conditions.

4. No significant attempt has been made to "phase" the minimum aspirations of the politically awakened African into the dreary realities of his social and economic life. There is no conceivable way this could be done, nor would it be desirable to do it. But the "disphasing" will inevitably induce hit-or-miss renovations of Africa's political economies as her people try to bring them into harmony with their new appetites.

All these points superimpose on one another to make a dynamic pattern, like the conformation of a river that runs between banks which are rising and narrowing at the same time—therefore, the river races more deeply, swiftly, and turbulently as it nears its debouchment. This pattern is unfortunately not confined to Black Africa, but is the all too concrete historical reality which has captured perhaps 80 per cent of the people of the world. Many observers have caught sight of it and it is called by many names; we will briefly cite only three.

In her superb book *Algeria*, the French scientist Germaine Tillion has described the "pauperization" of the multitudes of French North Africa, but in addition to monetary and dietary matters, in which Algeria seems to prefigure Black Africa's future twenty years or so hence, Miss Tillion has included in her concept of "pauperization" the crippling effect of cultural impoverishment on men's souls. To apply her percepts to the region considered in this essay, the pygmy woman of the Ituri forest who carries her bananas in hideous tin Portuguese buckets instead of handsome, classic, plaited baskets has lost something of her essence, her selfhood; becoming less of an artist she has become more of a cipher as a human being; when it comes to combating encroachments on her person and her society she finds that she is spiritually enfeebled. She cannot love; she is only strong enough to hate. The same thing goes for unemployed, ragged young Africans idling on the street corners of Leopoldville and Lagos; whether they own pants or not, they are infinitely poorer in soul than when they had the forests of Africa—booby-trapped though they were—to play and hunt in. Hunger is a terrifying experience, but a man is not truly poor until he no longer knows what is happening to him, or how to defend himself—when he feels that he is no longer a *he*.

For this chapter we invented a mythical "index of specific population," by which we intended only to propose that when every father in a society knows with near-absolute certainty that his children will be poorer in substance and opportunity than he is, then that society should be termed "overpopulated." But naturally each pauper society's pauperdom will consist of individual elements. For example, Sir John Russell tells us that the level of the Indian dietary has been falling steadily for forty years or more. Bernard Kalb of *The New York Times* reports a similar decline for Indonesia. In the case of these societies the principal contributor to the "index" must be out-and-out want of food. In Africa, with much less of an imbedded historical culture than those of ancient Asia, malnutrition is also a monstrous reality—but other kinds of deficiency must command nearly as much of our attention.

The last of the process-names we shall cite to denote what is happening to Africa is borrowed from orthodox economists who talk of the "hump" which modernizing and industrializing societies must struggle to surmount. On the near side of the "hump" capital formation (and social integration) are extremely difficult of achievement, and when an unwanted force like rapid growth of population enters the picture their difficulty and urgency are multiplied many times. Once over the "hump," where we Americans find ourselves, in the company of a piddling minority of mankind, capital formation and the other tasks of a self-generating economy become far easier, and at the same time less urgent. In the 1950's and 1960's Africa is not approaching the "hump"; she is receding from it. (The statistics to which we have devoted so much attention are but a reflection of a minor interest which "over-the-hump" societies in America and Europe have taken in Africa in the last thirty years.) But Africa is being held back from approaching the "hump" by obstacles which are built into her contemporary sociopolitical system—or so, we may be sure, it will seem to the Africans themselves. Hence it is only a matter of time until she considers replacing this unsatisfactory system with another one which promises to come across and climb the "hump." The system now on exhibit in China will make a bid, for one; but we must postpone our look at this possibility to a much later chapter.

We may conclude if we wish that Black Africa has been defrauded by the Cosmos.

She has no "black belts," deep in rich dirt and succulent grasses. She is blessed with a superfluity of unique organisms, such as those which produce rinderpest, East Coast fever, and trypanosomiasis. Her proportions of rain, sun, wind, and heat interweave into a climate which is sublimely heedless of human preferences and profits. The crops she grows, and the metals she yields up, the world in a pinch can do without or produce for itself. As often as not her classical social system heightens these shortcomings instead of compensating for them (for example, the traditional emphasis on the possession, rather than the breeding and butchering, of cattle). Up to now her only major asset, immense hydroelectric potentials, has roused the all-out interest of neither the governments nor the private capital of the West—the former fearing the political and the latter the economic uncertainties of African investment.

A fifth dimension may have to be called in to explain Africa's failure to discipline the Technological Revolution. That eminently knowledgeable student of Africa, Lord Hailey, has speculated on "other facts, as yet undetermined, which have conditioned what appears to be the inadequate response made by so many African peoples to [the] 'challenge of environment.'" Presumably at least part of this "inadequate response" coincides with what other experts on Africa have observed as a widespread lack of "entrepreneurial initiative" and "decisions to invest." These cryptic states of mind—so we are taught by modern theorists—are the real motors behind a successful capitalistic accommodation to the Technological Revolution. They evolve, not in the objective world of the market place, but in the minds of individuals, where they are synthesized from a host of religious and philosophical predispositions of which we are never more than dimly conscious; thus, as Mrs. Joan Robinson has written, "economic analysis requires to be supplemented by a kind of comparative anthropology."

But it would seem to be highly improper for Americans to make any assumption of a qualitative difference between the Africans and ourselves on the basis of "as yet undetermined" factors such as these. Only by means of the most diligent exercise of our imaginations can we even conceive of the contingency, third-rateness, and obstinacy of the resources of Africa, from which these endemically malnourished human beings are striving to patch together a modern way of life. Year after year our own country brings forth gigantic surpluses in half a dozen major food products, surpluses which we cannot even seem to find a way to donate or consume. Throughout the Southwest, and elsewhere, whole mountain ranges laden in rich ores and thoroughly surveyed lie fallow, waiting for the price per unit of the metal to surpass the high cost per unit of American miners' labor. Even with raw materials like iron ore, the highest grade deposits of which have been exhausted by the unexampled prodigalities of the past generation, an elegant and specialized technology is hard at work devising ways profitably to process second-, third-, and fourth-grade reserves. No analogy at all exists between what we and the Africans were given to work with, and therefore no analogy can be drawn between our historical responses.

But surely it would be a mistake to end this chapter on a note of theft, wretchedness, and doom, because if American brain power is to go to work to rectify Cosmic injustice it will only be after American professional pride has been piqued and—even more to the point—American affections have been stirred. I would, therefore, like here to introduce a small cast of characters mainly from my own experience of Africa, some of whom we will meet again in the pages to come, in the hope that even superficial vignettes like these can put some flesh on ugly index numbers and visions of apocalypse.

There is the barefoot boy who had just walked in from the bush, staring up open-mouthed at the girders and scaffoldings of a half-finished office building: "How do you *do* that?" he asked me. There is the haughty, good-looking water colorist at an intersection in Leopoldville, grinning while he tells a family of American tourists that his painting is the only authentic art of the Congo. There is the mine boy who received a gold-lacquered helmet for saving the life of a white apprentice in the cave-in accident where he lost his own left arm. There is the youthful Nigerian student-architect half-drunk in a bar, calumniating the hypocrisy of the West and hailing its decline. There is the ramrod-stiff old Zulu chieftain, unwilling to contaminate his manhood and his Christianity with hatred of the Afrikaner. There is the little Watusi girl clapping her hands during her first automobile ride. There is the novice reporter, whose colleagues tease him by calling him a Xhosa; he reminds them sternly that in the new times it no longer matters what he is, but he wishes they would get it straight just for the record— he is a Zulu. There is the African politician who weeps self-pityingly into his pillow at night because he cannot find a way to help, or even feed, his people; somehow he has turned into a con-man in spite of himself, and he despises himself.

Apart from my own experience, there was Pedro, leader of the Cimaroñes, descendants of slaves that escaped from the Spanish along the coast of Panama, who befriended and aided Sir Francis Drake on his great Caribbean war raids. In 1573 Chief Pedro led the English sailor up a high ridge to a house in the trees, and gave him his first look at the billowing Pacific: the Chief "took (the) Captain by the hand and prayed him to follow him, if he was desirous to see at once the two seas, which he had so longed for." It is still the custom in Black Africa for male comrades to walk along hand-in-hand (one sees it in parts of Asia and Russia as well), a simplicity of expression which in the West has long since sunk under the weight of nerves and inhibitions.

Four hundred years later there was the magnificent Emperor of Ethiopia, honoring a lifelong fidelity to the principle of collective security by contributing to the United Nations force in Korea a battalion which compiled a combat record unique in the annals of war. General S. L. A. Marshall informs us that these men, 95 per cent illiterate and handling modern military gadgets for the first time, capped their spectacular fighting achievements with even more spectacular proofs of personal honor and loyalty. He writes: "Of all national groups fighting in Korea, the Ethiopians alone could boast that they never lost a prisoner or left a dead comrade on the battlefield. Every wounded man, every shattered body, had been returned to the friendly fold."

So long as she can produce men like these everything has not been stolen from Africa. But how stupid, how infuriating, how intolerable that men like these should not have their fair chance, in a world overteeming with the instrumentalities of power and wealth—

and, for that matter, of destruction. Yet so far no one in a position to help has come forward, and therefore our Africa is dying. She does not have to die; we could help her to live; but we have been too slothful and frivolous to try. We reckon that a society possesses more than one life, like a cat. We forget that—unlike a cat—when a society finally gives up one of its lives it reappears as another breed of creature. It is fear and pity of the next Africa—that will supplant *our* Africa when ours has at last liquefied into frightfulness—that pricks the consciences of those who love the African and the American peoples.

2. The Union of South Africa – 1

Even people who know very little about Africa have heard of the strange country in the southern part of the continent, where a stubbornly rooted offshoot of the peoples of Europe is furiously entrenching itself against the new era in history. The Union of South Africa is the last of its kind, a constitutional freak, the only polity left which is based on readings from ancient scriptures. But it is an error to treat this relic of another age with tolerance—or, rather, tolerance is wasted upon it—because the walls of this curious anachronism have never been thicker and its powers of evil never more malignant.

South Africa is a largish country, about one-seventh the size of the United States, whose population of 14 millions is ruled by a peculiar group that totals less than 2 millions: the Afrikaners, descended of Dutch farmer-settlers who mostly entered the Cape in the eighteenth century. The average Afrikaner does not view himself as a curiosity and his country as a freak. When pressed, he may be willing to concede that the circumstances in which he finds himself are "unique" and "complex," but to him the laws and social practices which have drawn the fire of the rest of the world are normal responses to the facts of life. They are the only responses that occur to him; they are categorical imperatives, and no standards exist against which they can be validly judged; indeed, they are conditions of survival.

Because the Afrikaner community long ago forged and fortified all its basic decisions of value—and has convinced itself that life itself depends on the tenacity with which it upholds these values—the Afrikaner interprets the recent movements north of him in Africa very differently from the rest of us. He has no mental room to maneuver in, and so history is not a progress but a siege. For the Afrikaner, nothing that happens outside the boundaries of South Africa can alter the survival needs of Afrikanerdom within South Africa. New freedom flashing across the northern tier of African states; the universal modernization of African society, most conspicuously in his own country, do not pose problems of policy for which he must seek answers. These are only two more hostile forces joining dozens of other hostile forces which have menaced Afrikanerdom since the day it was founded—and which are to be repelled with uncompromising resolution. (Because racial issues overshadow everything else in the Union, Afrikaner philosophers sometimes like to plead that their country is a "microcosm" of the world outside. This is a radical misnomer. The world contains many races, but insofar as they are living for the future they are endeavoring to live together, if possible, in a state of moral reconcilation. In South Africa the whole aim is an impregnable compartmentation of the races. South Africa is run the way the United States would be run if only Daughters of the Confederacy had the suffrage.)

It is only humane to commiserate any country that is saddled with a truculent and unbending minority scornful of the march of time—and which complicates all the give and take of normal civic intercourse by cultivating a private language and a private history. But at least in other countries a common-sense majority stands ready to tease ostrichlike minorities out of their jejune and unrealistic humors; domestic competitive wear and tear can do wonders in cracking hard shells. But nothing of this applies to South Africa, because the political anatomy of this odd country has delivered his compatriots wholly into the Afrikaner's hands. No other group in the society can dispute his absolute domination. So long as the laws are obeyed, the police and the army feared, so long as opposition halts anywhere short of revolution, the Afrikaner is dictator of South Africa. In this country the ostrich is King of Beasts.

The history of Afrikanerdom is important because as nothing else can it illuminates the motivations of the Afrikaner personality. Of course, this is a history that has undergone vigorous artificial resuscitation, for fairly recently the Afrikaner decided that he wanted to be "awakened" as a historic nationality, as the Croatians and other European quasi-nationalities strove to "awake" in the nineteenth century. Therefore, it is more of a story than a study, a story of a persecution mania, but one which must be taken seriously when it comes to conversing with these people who believe so many things that no one else believes.

It starts at Table Bay, the wonderful natural harbor not quite at the southernmost point of Africa, overlooked by the brooding slopes of Table Mountain. In 1652 the Dutch East India Company planted the first permanent station here, as a stopover and revictualing point on its route to the Indies. For 143 years the Company maintained this post, and gradually around its fort and gardens a small colony collected, composed of retired sailors and soldiers who had received land on their discharges, other settlers, and a remarkable party of 300 French Huguenots, a tiny band of the 400,000 refugees from the Revocation of the Edict of Nantes who had found their way to this end of the earth.

While the Company ruled the colony it was a colony by courtesy only; a "colonization" it certainly was not, for it was settled on the meagerest of scales. When the British came into permanent possession of the area in 1814, and conducted a census, they found that the European population amounted only to about 27,000 men, women, and children—farmers and stockraisers who were working their lands with the help of slaves shipped in from Asia. In the century and a half of its proprietorship, the Company had systematically discouraged any form of enterprise—including large-scale immigration—which might have tended to a slackening of its bureaucratic authoritarianism. So persecuted were the Dutch farmers by regulations, work levies, arbitrary imposts, and other petty despotisms that those among them who were able embarked on climbs out of the bay area onto the silent prairies of the Karroo even before 1700—promenades of "rambling peasants," one of the early Dutch governors called them scornfully—to be free of the rough hand of the Company.

Great Britain terminated the rule of the Company in South Africa by occupying the Cape in September, 1795, as one of the smaller moves in her international strategy of the Wars of the French Revolution. And in August, 1814, with Napoleon's career drawing to a close, the British gained confirmation of this seizure by purchasing the permanent cession of the colony, along with British Guiana, for 6 million pounds. British settlers were encouraged to emigrate to the Cape; and accompanying the first settlers landed British missionaries, armed with advanced ideas about the equality of the races of man, and British administrators, armed with such newfangled statutes as the Slave Emancipation Act of 1833.

The Afrikaners held their new British compatriots, evangels, and progressive legislation in equal abhorrence, and at last, in the four years from 1836 to 1840, about one-fourth of the Afrikaner population, perhaps 7,000 individuals, emigrated out of their vicinity into the region of the High Veld, deep in the interior, where later they constituted their twin republics of the Orange Free State and the Transvaal. This movement came to be called the Great Trek. For the first time, a sizable segment of Afrikanerdom had proclaimed its independence of all external authority, British and Dutch alike. From now on to the end of their society they vowed to accept only their own commandments. Moreover, in passing out of the Cape area into south-central Africa, they encountered in significant numbers the race which thenceforward would contest their dominion over southern Africa. The Great Trek was not the first occasion of Afrikaner meeting Bantu; that historical moment had occurred sometime in the 1770's, when the Bantu, sifting down from Central Africa and shoving aside the primitive Bushmen and Hottentots, had appeared suddenly east and north of the Great Fish River, which they then crossed sporadically to claw and burn the frontier Afrikaner homesteads. For fifty years Afrikaner raiders had ridden out to punish these offending tribesmen in their own villages. But during the course of the Great Trek the Afrikaner tried conclusions with the only formidable military society that the Bantu ever produced—the Zulu. And along Blood River, on December 16, 1838, the Day of the Covenant which is South Africa's greatest annual holiday, a small Afrikaner force under Andries Pretorius, divided into a squadron of calvary and a company forted up behind wagons, broke the charges of the Zulu warriors under King Dingaan, half-brother and successor to Chaka. Brilliant tactics plus muskets won the day for the farmers; for their part, the Bantu lost with their arms that which they must recover with their loins.

At this point it seems appropriate to insert a few reflections on this received version of Afrikaner history.

In the first place, if it is important at all, the date 1652 signifies only that a few Dutchmen had settled in the Cape 100 years before the Bantu drifted into South Africa; this is the basis of the Afrikaner claim that South Africa is "white man's" country instead of "black man's." But for the 143 years that the Cape was under the management of the Dutch East India Company, the settlement cannot fairly be termed a "colony," let alone a "nation." It was part of the Company's deliberate policy that Europeans were not to colonize vigorously or rapidly; therefore, the Europeans barely kept up with, or fell behind, the Africans breeding out of sight in the unknown north. When the two races did collide, on the fringes of the High Veld, the Bantu were defeated, but not obliterated. They did not begin to die out, but on the contrary continued their *Völkerwanderrung* into southern Africa and once there commenced rapidly to take root and reproduce themselves. The Afrikaners were falling further and further behind every year, until the opening of the Transvaal mines in the 1870's instigated a flood of European newcomers and the massive infusion of European technology; now, for the first time, a "white nation" was a meaningful and practicable matter.

From time to time the Afrikaner of today likes to chaff the American visitor about the way we handled our own indigenous populations; we virtually killed them off. This is a brutal half-jest, though not unjust, but so long as the point has been raised let us draw a lesson from it. Here seems to be a rule of history: when you colonize, colonize big and colonize quick. If you are unwilling to colonize on this scale, it is soon too late to weep over the outcome. Perhaps the racial fertility of the American Indian was decisively inferior to that of the European from the start, but surely it is important that in North America the European not only placed a premium on large families—so does the Afrikaner—but welcomed into the bargain a gigantic mass immigration which was adding to the population, at the turn of the century, at an annual rate in excess of 1 million persons. Whatever the difficulties of digesting this kind of an inflow into a society, its very existence eliminates any question of racial competition. But this has always been too venturesome a policy for the Afrikaner; he does not wish to share his state with anyone, white or black. The Union Government—like the Australian—has strangled immigration from just those regions of Europe from which mass emigration is feasible and desirable, as well as from "nations of color," justifying this mean, ungenerous policy by playing variations on all the old themes of prejudice. (But, as we say, the time for regret has slipped away. The medical advances of the last 100 years have gobbled up the open spaces of the world; no more of them exist and—save for a wholesale holocaust—none can be created. The racial proportions of nearly all regions of the world are fixed, and the passage of time will mainly bring only an inflation of the present ratios and an aggravation of the tensions involved. But perhaps it is helpful to reflect that if the Afrikaner had been as bold and farsighted a pioneer as he likes to think he was, the white South African of today would not be outnumbered four to one in his own country.)

The point that needs to be made here is that Afrikanerdom is not now, and never was, a "nation." It is a tribe, whose sole principle of unity all along has been the securing of the proper conditions in which to work its will on the African. And during the whole history of the community it has resisted every temptation to assess itself at more or less than this. The Great Trek was not the tempering of martyrs that Afrikaner myth makes it out to be. It is merely the last, if the largest, chapter of the escape drama of the tribe into the solitudes, a drama that had commenced 150 years earlier with small groups of Afrikaners fashioning their tribal tyranny in the face of the opposition of their own ruling classes. And by the time the British occupied the Cape the Afrikaner tyranny had come more and more to depend on a single, immovable pin: in the words of an Afrikaner pronunciamento of 1795, the African's "bondage from generation to generation." Hence the relatively libertarian British irked the Afrikaner even more profoundly than had the despots of the Dutch East India Company. The "severe losses which we have been forced to sustain by the emancipation of our slaves, and the vexatious laws which have been enacted respecting them" furnished the gravamen of the charges with which the leaders of the community rallied the Great Trek. Nothing more positive, more exalted than African enslavement has ever vivified Afrikaner patriotism; without African enslavement the Afrikaner has never contemplated his existence, nor without it could Afrikanerdom survive in recognizable form. In the 1830's, as individuals, the Afrikaners wanted no part of grander, pioneering visions; they yearned only to proceed unhindered into the bush, there to raise farmhouses out of sight of the smoke of their neighbors' chimneys and to pass their time in impervious clumps of family, theology, and slaves. It was not so much the imperfectly comprehended new tendencies in European civilization from which the trekker fled as from Time itself—with all its ticks and rumbles.

It remains to be said that the culmination of the principle of enslavement—the ultimate enchainment of the Bantu—was the work not of Afrikaner ranch farmers but of the exploiters of the diamonds and gold of the Transvaal that were discovered in the 1860's. In the generation following the opening of the mines the European population of South Africa more than tripled; the sum of her imports and exports rose by a factor greater than ten. The country was transformed, and in proportion to its modernization rose the demand for cheap and docile labor. Today more than 6 million Africans work on the farms, in the cities, and in the industries of South Africa—and without dependable access to this pool of labor none of the profit-making enterprises of the country could continue to operate or to compete in the market places of the world. The mine boy who picks ores out of the reefs of the Witswatersrand— or, perhaps we should say, his miserable wages and his powerlessness to improve himself—is as indispensable to the prosperity of modern South Africa as the gold itself. Today, as yesterday, the Afrikaner must maintain African enslavement in order to maintain himself.

For details of the further history of Afrikanerdom the reader should consult a standard text like Arthur Keppel-Jones's *South Africa: A Short History*. Soon after the trekkers, traveling north and east, had entered the High Veld, a region then relatively insu-

lated from the ambitions of European empires, they established
the two republics of the Orange Free State and the Transvaal, whose
autonomy the British guaranteed in 1852 in the so-called Sand River
Convention. This was another case of a guarantee which it was
easier to sign than to respect. The Republics were not peaceful,
supine little principalities. No sooner were they organized than
they began to cast around for projects—looking in the specific
direction of Bechuanaland, their settlement of which the British
were determined to forestall in their own Government's interests.
Within the Republics, the Afrikaners pursued their old racial policies in a way that excited the powerful evangelical blocs of Victorian English to fervent protest. Nor did they seem to meet the
minimum standards of stability; the Afrikaner legislators conducted
themselves on the principle of the Bohemian Diet, agreeing only to
refuse taxes. When the soils of the Transvaal began to disgorge their
precious burdens of jewels and metals, the thousands of prospectors
and fortune hunters who streamed from all over Europe into the
country were even less satisfied than overseas philanthropists with
the "art of red tape qualified by corruption," as one critic characterized Kruger's government.

It all seemed to add up to yet another call on the imperial vocation,
and in 1877 the British tried to annex the Transvaal for the first
time, acquiring for their trouble a public debt of 215,000 pounds,
a treasury containing twelve shillings, and about 40,000 new subjects madder than Irishmen. But the Afrikaners resisted, and after
a minor military reverse in 1881 on the hill of Majuba had convinced a prudent Imperial government that this time the thin red
line had been stretched too far, the Republics for a season virtually
regained their independence. But by this time the African oyster
had been opened up too far for prudence to assert itself; and on
the spot was a breed of man with the money and the derring-do
to entrap even the most cautious Empire into commitments from
which it could not disengage itself. By way of the Bechuanaland
corridor, which imperialists and missionaries had jointly contrived
to keep clear of Afrikaners, Cecil Rhodes and his associates were
pressing north into the present site of the Rhodesias, surrounding
the Afrikaner Republics on three sides with British protectorates
and settlements. In the Transvaal itself, the mining men refused

to accept the verdict of Majuba and viewed the governments of the Afrikaners, now headed by Kruger, with ill concealed and ever-growing exasperation. Then they overreached themselves; the Jameson Raid of Christmastime, 1895, designed to trigger a *coup d'état* in Pretoria, was a total fiasco. Kruger defeated the volunteer revolutionaries handily, managing in the process to persuade himself that the British Empire was now weakening in South Africa and that this was the time to elaborate his own designs of empire, meant to embrace the British Cape and Natal and more besides. War was inevitable; and after rejection of his famous and absurd Ultimatum Kruger invaded the Cape on October 12, 1899.

Let us review now the catalogue of Afrikaner grievance. First, without consulting the inhabitants the English brusquely pre-empted a colony which had been Dutch for 150 years. Second, defying the word of God they displayed from the beginning an incomprehensible favoritism for the African, which jeopardized the Afrikaner's prosperity and his personal security. Third, so unbearable was this British regime that brave farmers sacrificed everything that is dear to men to pioneer a raw and hazardous frontierland. Fourth, the British solemnly pledged themselves to respect the independence of these pioneers, and they perfidiously broke this pledge—not once but twice. Finally, they shamed themselves by falling on the defenseless little Republics like a wolf on the fold. To be sure, the Afrikaners fought more like lions than lambs: for three years a total of perhaps 87,000 Afrikaner irregulars (at no time were more than 50,000 in the field simultaneously) battled to a standstill a British army which ultimately totaled 450,000 officers and men, of whom 250,000 were regulars. But the result was foregone. The wolf must win. Afrikanerdom was laid low.

There was a terrible epilogue that was more tragic, and more real, than most of the other elements of this drama. As a consequence of the military policies of the English and Boer generals, large sections of the South African countryside had been devastated. To provide for the women and children who had thereby lost their homes the British built "concentration camps" behind the lines, but the number of Afrikaner noncombatants to be accommodated within these camps they disastrously underestimated. Sanitary facilities were overwhelmed; epidemics raged through the installations; the death rate mounted to appalling proportions, averaging more than an annual 50 per cent in the children's sections. If Afrikaner history had lacked an infant martyrology up to that time now it had one. "A barrier of dead children's bodies will rise up between the British and Boer races in South Africa," Lloyd George prophesied when he heard the first reports from the camps. With this bereavement the Afrikaner now stood more alone than ever.

Unfortunately for the history of Africa, the conclusive alienation and isolation of Afrikanerdom coincided with the passing of the British Empire into its novel and splendid third period, the voluntary submission of imperial sovereignty to the collective sovereignty of the Commonwealth. The three principal forces combining into this amazing reconstruction which has seen Great Britain through the bitter tests of this century—the reforming influences of Shaftesbury, Florence Nightingale, *et al.;* the Victorian credo of an inevitable economic progress which renders political coercion superfluous; and an extremely subtle science of public administration, which in the East at any rate enabled a single British official to superintend the affairs of millions of Indians—all these movements were blended by imperial visionaries like Disraeli, Rosebery, Joseph Chamberlain, and the Marquis of Ripon into a lustrous dream of a free association of self-governing states standing shoulder to shoulder, sharing without discrimination the fruits of a Crown and Constitution that had secured a greater measure of individual liberty and prosperity than any other historical instrument of government. That this association must be voluntary—freely accepted or rejected by its constituent parts—was of course the first principle of its success. Ironically, this mature and optimistic statecraft was given its first major trial run in the Treaty of Vereeniging which ended the Boer War in 1902 and in the South Africa Act of 1909, which enacted the constitution of the Union. In the generosity of these documents the British attempted a spiritual conversion before they had secured acknowledgement of a military conquest; they tried to disencumber the emotions of the Afrikaner, to take the sting out of his defeat and free him for partnership. They misjudged him sadly, for the Afrikaner has always cared far more passionately for the black-and-white hereditary enemies whose images he enclosed in his heart than for any vistas—no matter how inspiring—of Commonwealth association.

Not that the concept of an English-speaking and Afrikaner partnership in southern Africa, ramifying into the international partnership of the Commonwealth, failed to make any impression at all on Afrikanerdom; Field Marshal Smuts was admired throughout the world, and especially so in London, just because he dedicated himself to this ideal through the whole course of his career. But the history of the Union since its proclamation in 1910 is the long record of the disintegration and absorption of the Afrikaner group who favored the cultivation of a united white South Africa, buttressed by the Commonwealth association, under the unremitting attacks of the Afrikaner group who favored the cultivation of tribal hostilities. Today the former have all but disappeared; the latter rule the state. But at no time was there a question of a suppression of Afrikanerdom per se. All the prime ministers of the Union, except for Dr. Verwoerd, the present one, who was born in Holland, have been Afrikaners; the first two, Botha and Smuts, were soldier-heroes of the Boer War. Overwhelmingly strong in the rural districts where the national elections are decided, since 1910 the Afrikaners have only had to remain united in order to rule. Only if Afrikanerdom splits—if a substantial number of Afrikaners join the English-speakers to form a moderate coalition group—can there be any dilution of the pure tribal domination.

As we say, in the past generation Afrikaner extremists have steadily outflanked and engulfed Afrikaner moderates; the split in Afrikanerdom has disappeared; the monolithic unity of the tribe which was briefly—and perhaps superficially—threatened by Smuts and his kind has been restored; the tribalists have triumphed and dug themselves into a position of power from which they cannot be dislodged. Botha and Smuts, who ran the government from 1910 to 1924, were succeeded by J. B. M. Hertzog—to their right. By 1933 Hertzog himself had come to resemble a moderate; Smuts merged with him to create the United Party. Meanwhile, further on the right the Afrikaner extremists were reassembling; in the following year Dr. D. F. Malan proclaimed the precursor of the now all-powerful Nationalist Party. Other realignments occupied the prewar years, accommodating always to Afrikaner sentiments

which were flowing steadily to the right. During World War II
itself, the South African participation in which was angrily resented
by the majority of Afrikaners, the refurbishing and hypostatizing
of hoary tribal legends reached a climacteric of make-believe. The
great dreams of Cecil Rhodes shriveled. At last, in 1948, Dr. Malan
assumed the office of prime minister by virtue of a slender parliamentary control—but a control that was to be decisively amplified
and reinforced in the elections of the years to come.

It must be pointed out that the feature of South Africa society
which provokes and disturbs foreigners the most, the race issue,
has never been the crux of any election campaign in South Africa.
Neither of the present pair of national parties, the United or the
Nationalist, nor any of their initial phases, has ever advocated an
even reasonably enlightened racial policy. The best of South African
governments—the coalition of Afrikaner moderates and English-
speakers—was hopelessly baffled by the economic convenience of
this huge, cheap labor force, coupled to the inconvenience of elevat-
ing this labor force onto a level of social and political equality, into
a kind of moral and mental paralysis. Between the United and
Nationalist parties the issues are, first, that of the Commonwealth
connection (which the Nationalists propose to sever) and, second,
"moderate" apartheid as opposed to Afrikaner apartheid (a distinction which no one understands and which enlists the passions of no
one, Africans included).

Between the three recent Nationalist regimes of Malan, Strijdom,
and Verwoerd we need to notice here only distinctions arising from
that relentless rightward shift in Afrikaner feelings that we have
already mentioned. Dr. Verwoerd is more unambiguously committed
to the principle of racial *enslavement* than were either of his predecessors. That is to say, Strijdom and Malan did not have to spell
out what they felt was perfectly implicit and obvious. Concurrently,
Verwoerd has felt it to be necessary to inject larger doses of hypocrisy into his public pronouncements than either of his predecessors
ever did, and this has led to some interesting effects which we will
take up in detail in the next chapter. But, for instance, Verwoerd's
"separate development" idea takes no account of the economic
dependence of South Africa on the African's labor, and therefore
blithely ignores the very root of the national life—but the fact that

his government pays lip service to a fatuous metaphysic rather than a workable policy gives Verwoerd a free and arbitrary hand over that national life (a lesson one imagines he learned from Adolf Hitler). The "separate development" notion is also revolutionary in the South African context, because it envisages the African's status as that of a reservation animal instead of that of the labor slave to which the Old Testament condemned him. Therefore, Afrikaners cannot be as sure of Verwoerd's orthodoxy as they were of his mentors'. Not that we can derive any comfort from this. As Professor P. V. Pistorius, himself an Afrikaner, wrote to the *Rand Daily Mail* in August, 1958: "There is not only no change in the trend toward extremism; there is not even a lessening of the rate of acceleration. Dr. Verwoerd (however impossible it may seem now) will in his turn be rejected for an even more extreme leader. . . ."

The usurpation—legal or illegal—of the national government by a rugged tribe within the white minority which is engaged in ever more flavorsome and irrational persecutions of 80 per cent of the population has induced a spicy atmosphere of foreboding in South Africa which must be altogether unique. Indeed, in a larger country, more economically and politically sophisticated, these tensions would doubtless have led to a mighty explosion before now. As it is, they express themselves in the form of interminable moonings.

With one exception, racial guilt feelings and anxieties comprise the sole subject of discourse in South Africa—at cocktail parties, around swimming pools, in the universities and lecture halls, at every gathering large or small, formal or informal. What new ingenuities of apartheid have been devised by the government? How much further will they go? When will they step over the line, driving the African berserk, so that he will thrust aside considerations of self-interest and hurl himself at the European no matter at what cost to himself? How near *is* this Day of Slaughter?

It is only when South Africans have exhausted themselves on this topic—which does not happen as often as one might think, considering that they hash it over every day of their lives—that they pass on to the minor theme of the bond with England, to which the

English-speakers cling with the desperation of the drowning but which represents to the Afrikaners the last shred of shame to be discarded as soon as they can afford it.

Consider a daily newspaper in South Africa. Here is a typical day's front page of the English-language *Rand Daily Mail* (February 2, 1959). As the lead, under an across-the-page head, a "baton charge" of sixty armed police on a meeting of 3,000 African women outside a location near Pretoria: babies were dropped, revolvers fired, seven people arrested (including the speaker), but only seventeen injured, none fatally. Other stories on the page: the emergency in Southern Rhodesia, with which that government had coped by arresting wholesale the leadership of the Southern Rhodesian African National Congress. A new Prisons Bill, making it a criminal offense to publish information on prisons or prisoners, or to take photographs of them. Another chapter in the saga of the "blonde spy," a nine-days' scandal among the English-speakers that broke when it was discovered that the government had bribed a girl student at the University of Witswatersrand to report on "subversive" discussions among her fellow students. The report of a statement by a Nationalist M.P. from Southwest Africa: "South Africa must not become a stranger in Africa." A statement from the head of the United Party, to the effect that his group had not "revised its Native policy": this was to cure the doubts of wavering contributors that the Uniteds had gone "soft on kaffirs." A terse account of the strike at the Kariba Dam construction: "the process of weeding out the agitators and malcontents among the workers was going on." Election-day riots in Somalia.

This was the front page of one of the largest papers in Africa. It all adds up, of course, to obsession—and it is fair to assume that obsession invariably masks fear. And there is plenty of fear—or, at least, profound worry—that can be observed in South Africa. For example, in the prosperous suburbs of Johannesburg, the most American of African cities, floodlights snap on after dark to illuminate the great lawns, hired watchmen (*African* watchmen) patrol the gardens throughout the night, downstairs windows are heavily barred. But on the surface South Africa is such a bustling and modern place that it is sometimes hard to see the hideous slums and the sickness of the back country—and the gnawing anxieties of the people—through the fine new glass-and-girder buildings. To such extent as they can South Africans hustle their fears into the closets of their minds and hide them with chatter. In all their never-ending discussions of Race, they only rarely venture beyond a certain point of discretion: the African Revolution—the Day of Blood—is an untouchable like Death. It is one of those uses of the imagination that middle-class society everywhere, even in America, does its best to inhibit. But of course the realities of life in South Africa are too obtrusive for total concealment behind even the best manners, and a vibrant murmur of apprehension runs through South African society like the rumble of a distant earthquake— annoying everyone, boring everyone, distracting everyone from the joyous and creative chores of living.

Different groups within the white population respond to this nagging apprehension in different ways.

First, there is in the country an exceptional group numbering perhaps 5,000, almost without exception English-speakers, who openly and candidly prophesy the coming of the Day of Blood when every white throat in South Africa will be cut from ear to ear. The diminutive Liberal Party speaks for the majority of this sect; it contains men like Alan Paton in its ranks, but it has lost its last representative in parliament. But there are at least several hundred South Africans for whom even the Liberal Party does not take a sufficiently apocalyptic line. These individuals, none of whom is particularly important at the present time, despise their fellow whites and everything they see in South Africa; they will enlist in the first promising conspiracy that comes their way—if they have not already done so. But to return to more typical spokesmen of the "liberals," listen to Father Huddleston: "Over 200 million blacks are certainly not going to accept leadership from the heirs of Paul Kruger. White South Africa will be fortunate if, fifty years from now, it is still a tolerated minority group." Or the historian Keppel-Jones: "The white electorate is increasingly 'illiberal.' I have often argued that this can end only in the destruction of the white regime altogether." Or Professor Pistorius again: "The plain fact . . . is that we are criminals against humanity, and our petty squabbles about flags and republics and language-rights and the 'divine calling' of a particular group or section constitute high treason against South

Africa and the world, for which we will be punished by history." For these "liberals," the choice between Nationalist Party and United Party is no choice at all; the Uniteds are not so depraved as the Nationalists, but their aims—insofar as they are not aimless—remain basically the same. Only from within the "liberal" group, they feel, can emerge the radical revision of South African politics which is all that can save the whites from total extinction.

Save for these few thousands in the wilderness, the great bulk of the rest of the one and a half million English-speakers sympathize with the United Party, which lost its control of the government in 1948 and its best known leader in the death of Smuts. This party is oppressed by a conflict of loyalties which it cannot evade or resolve. Its members are sufficiently English, and rational, to see that the Afrikaner policy of racial enslavement is a cancer which must sooner or later consume South Africa. Nor can they buck—even in their own minds—the whole responsibility for this policy onto the Afrikaner's broad shoulders, because it is the English-speakers who dominate the business and the economy of South Africa—and their critics do not hesitate to tell them that they could put things to rights if only they would exert themselves.

But they cannot bring themselves to do so. They are caught in a fatal crossfire between their wealth and position on one flank and the malevolence of the Afrikaners on the other. They have never been able—the United Party never has been able—to promote a really liberal African program. On the contrary, when the Afrikaners came to power in 1948 they erected their version of apartheid on the earlier version of apartheid which had been laid down by the United Party governments. The trouble is, neither the rich business-men who are the powers of the United Party, nor their representative politicians, have ever figured out how to concoct a plan whereby the African's social and civil status can be materially improved without thoroughly disrupting the economic structure of South Africa. (When they get to this point, it is not surprising that they give up.) The English-speakers know better than anyone else that the Afrikaners have gone too far; but over on the opposite side the "liberals" open up prospects of social and economic reconstruction which dizzy the average, sensual English-speaker.

Even if the English-speakers wanted to, how could they bring moderating influences—let alone restraining influences—to bear on the Afrikaner community under the present electoral setup? It is perfectly conceivable that the unanimous, organized protest of the whole English-speaking population would fail to make a dent on the Afrikaner racial offensive, which is picking up momentum every hour—and English-speaker unanimity is far to seek. What remains to him then—and to the United Party—is an itching sense of shame and a blundering, stalemated instinct which has lost the contours of an opinion or even of a hope: Put It Off, Go Slow, dream about a miracle of Afrikaner enlightenment, hedge the bets by keeping in good repair the lines to overseas finance. In public the English-speaker punctuates his life with sighs, but in private he is pretty content to let the Afrikaner drive this political machine so compromised by tremors and twinges. Perhaps the South African Englishman is the only Englishman on record who genuinely prefers political impotence to power.

The third fraction of the white population of South Africa is of course the Afrikaner himself. What is he afraid of? First and foremost, of the loss of unity. Not every Afrikaner child is born into the world inside a capsule of bitterness and bigotry; indeed, a few young Afrikaners have donated superb services to the Liberal Party and other reforming groups, at far greater personal sacrifice than is required of English-speaking do-gooders. But the herd instinct is generally decisive; mavericks are ejected from the synagogue with obscene brutality, and there are in consequence not many of them.

But if the Afrikaner is afraid of losing the multiplier effect which his solidarity confers on his political power, we can cite a number of things as well that he is *not* afraid of. For example, he is not afraid of being called a hypocrite. Government documents, which treat of "separate communities" and "harmonious multicommunity development," exhibit a certain official hypocrisy for the benefit of foreigners, but the ordinary Afrikaner is supported and comforted by the sanctions of the Prophets and Noah's curse on the children of Ham. He tells himself that *he is right*, because God has said so. He does not fear self-doubt, for he has expended a good deal of hard mental labor on formulating an exhaustive racial creed and he does not intend to waste time by calling it into question. Incredibly self-isolated, he knows and cares little about the judgment of the world outside Afrikanerdom. Those noisemakers in New York, London, and Moscow signify less than nothing. The English-speakers he regards with a scoffing, on the whole comradely lenity; he senses that they are a trifle overwilling to reap the material benefits of apartheid whilst unloading the onus of the system onto his robuster self. He even likes to fancy that the English-speakers one day will understand that he is doing only what must be done; on that day the English-speakers will teach their children Afrikaans, vote Nationalist, and aid in other ways in fulfilling God's purpose in South Africa. "Nothing is more desirable than that the European sections of the population should understand each other and cooperate with each other," Dr. Malan has told the tribe, then going on to add characteristically, "but they can only cooperate if they think alike on the country's great questions and if they stand together."

And the Afrikaner does not fear the home-grown variety of African, which gives him an inestimable advantage over the English-speakers, who most emphatically do fear him. Naturally, when an African gets uppity he must be whipped. When he gets entirely out of hand he must be shot. All this goes as a matter of course, but the Afrikaner insists that the whole business of race conflict and repression has been puffed up out of all proportion by nice-Nelly or self-interested radicals. "Any antipathy which may exist between Bantu and European is far outweighed by innumerable daily examples of mutual trust and regard," the Ministry of Native Affairs assures us.

Despite these evidences of stolidity of temperament, the Afrikaner is not quite the silent, self-reliant strong man who props up his country and the nerves of his English-speaking compatriots with the same phlegm. If he does not fear his own Africans—or, we should say, if that fear lies so deep in his consciousness that it rarely shows itself—he most certainly does fear the 100-odd millions of Africans of the north who have recently launched themselves into the seas of international ideology, independence, and interference. He fears any force which could potentially divert this unholy contagion into South Africa. Communism and America mean the same to the Afrikaner, because in different ways they both tend to stir up his Africans—and that has always been the only thing he worries about. Moreover, he vaguely understands that Communism and America are in a sense the masters of modern history: if they wish to they can overwhelm him, and take from him the power to live as an Afrikaner. Indeed, they seem to be on the verge of doing just this; for some incomprehensible reason southern Africa has become a prize in the Great Game between the bully states of the Northern Hemisphere, and by meddling with the kaffirs the ignorant bastards are wagering with Afrikaner heads. "Small, weak, and alone"; it is the voice of the Union's Minister of Economic Affairs exhorting the *Volk* on the Day of the Covenant, 1958, "the Afrikaner people again stand on the banks of Blood River facing defeat and extinction. As in 1838, we are surrounded by enemies determined to destroy us, and within the next ten or twenty years our fate will have been decided."

To look forward a bit, is there anything we can say in summation at this point about the Union of South Africa? It is the richest and healthiest country in Africa—but its government is founded upon profoundly misguided premises, and the device of its writ is "Thorough," enforced with a logical inhumanity reminiscent of the storybook communities of Plato and Thomas More. And its white citizens are no different from the rest of us—except that they lack the proper proportions of sense, feeling, and will power. But what now?

Surely the moving literature that has sprung in the last generation or two from the afflictions of South Africa can provide us a clue or two to a valid American approach. This is a literature which devotes itself particularly to studies of moral erosion, a phenomenon by no means limited to southern Africa. Here is a plain, rural, self-proud people who have been fortunate enough to find themselves in a land of limitless grandeur, but who have permitted that same strange and lovely land to conquer them by means of a unique spiritual problem. It seems that it is never oversized environments, but always undersized men, who make the tragedies of humanity. Time and again we read of individual Afrikaners struggling to wriggle out of the quicksands that are enclasping their hearts, to overcome—perhaps only for a moment—the taboos of the tribe. But time and again the tribe proves too strong: the little town on the veld, the isolated farm, the family clan, the narrow and obsessive mentality, the dearth of alternative ways of life—all these combine to win out over love and fellow feeling. Only on rare occasions does an exceptional spirit break loose to soar off into personal freedom. Mostly they choke up and fail, however hard they try—and one or two more individuals, and another generation, shuffle off into the morass where Afrikanerdom seeks its annihilation.

Here in America we can supply anyone who is interested with a surplus of little South Africans; because they are schools of human nature we could hardly afford to do without them for the sake of our own edification. They are societies which pervert themselves into cabals; clubs for the love of clubdom, whose weightiest article of membership is the exclusion or overpowering of other human beings. We find these societies everywhere, on golf links, in office cliques, churches, fraternities, lodges, and "power elites." They do not loom so large with us, thank God, as to fix the character of the Republic, but insofar as they do take part in the civic mutuality they envenom it. Hence they force the rest of us to the necessity of judging and combating them, in order to stop their slow poisoning of the national morale from which we as well as they derive our daily sustenance.

In short, we have no choice but to judge South Africa, as individuals and Americans, in the same way that we judge other nasty things. And it is a difficult judgment. A freak grown too large constitutes a public menace; that we agree on. But the view that the world as a whole is in some operational sense a "public" we have not yet generally agreed on. Yet today the Afrikaner community, puny though it seems to be, is scraping on the exposed nerve ends of a continent in the process of making up its mind about its whole future. Southern Africa is the wrong place, and the mid-twentieth century the wrong epoch, for a diehard racist regime that aspires only to be passed over by politics and time. And the Afrikaners will not come halfway to meet politics and time; they cannot be panicked or persuaded out of their religion or their emotions. They will yield only to superior force.

3. The Union of South Africa – 2

We have discussed a few of the attitudes of that minority of South African people which is white. What is the structure of the population as a whole?

The laws and social practices of the Union recognize four main fractions of a total population of 14,500,000 (1958 estimates). Two-thirds of the total number, or about 9,500,000 persons, are Bantu Africans. Functionally, the African group is divided into three further subgroups, approximately equal in size. About one-third of the Union's Africans live on "Native Reserves," protected areas like the Indian reservations of America where the "natives" are presumably safe from white interference so long as they abide by the rules of their "tribe" and its white supervisors; the Reserves occupy about 12 per cent of the total land area of the state. Another third of the African population work on farms owned by Europeans, chiefly Afrikaners. The last, and most important, third are interlocked far more intimately with European civilization, in the towns, mines, and factories of South Africa. As we noticed in the previous chapter, the decisive numerical superiority of the African over all other races in South Africa combined is only part of the story. It is his labor, its abundance and its cheapness, which is the mainspring of the extraordinary growth and prosperity of the South African economy in this century. It is not surprising that the perfect regula-

tion and management of this immense labor force constitute the
chief, unvarying aim of South African laws.

Next to the Africans we can consider a group of about a half-
million descendants of Indian, Malay, and other Asian "coolies,"
who were imported into the southeastern province of Natal in the
middle 1800's to work on sugar plantations. In the past fifty years
these ex-Asians have penetrated into the other provinces of the
Union, where they live as peddlers or tailors or proprietors of tiny
shops on the margins of the large African settlements, acting as
a kind of surrogate middle class for the Africans, who have none
of their own. Recently the Afrikaners decided to segregate the
Asians in special "group areas" along with the Africans, and the
implementation of this policy—combined with severe restrictions on
other aspects of their economic life—has brought great misery to
the Asian community. After all, middlemen cannot exclusively
buy from or sell to other middlemen; the Asian's post at the inter-
stices of the South African economy has been abolished, his crafts
cut off from his customers, and his whole scheme of life canceled
out. From time to time the Afrikaner government offers to pay the
cost of the Asians' ticket back to India, but both the leaders of the
community and the Government of India have consistently scouted
these propositions as violations of principle and an unwanted addition to the population of the homeland.

Concentrated in the south, in Cape Province, are the Cape
Coloreds—or Coloreds—a group of about 1,500,000 descended from
early miscegenations between the European settlers and Bushmen,
Hottentots, and Asian laborers. They are inclined to be handsome
and superbly talented individuals, with a dialect of their own and
a unique musical culture similar to that of the Haitians or Trini-
dadians. Despite this, they are a minority pitifully without roots
or power, caught in a vise between a white master group which
rejects them and the Africans whom their own pride compels them
to despise and reject.

The Coloreds are not significant per se, but they did serve as
the unwitting storm center of the Union's Great Debate, the constitutional crisis of 1951–1956, when the Afrikaner revealed the
full extent of his determination to conform the South Afrikan
government to his private theology. Under certain literacy and

property qualifications, the Coloreds of Cape Province had possessed the franchise for more than thirty years when the Afrikaner came to power; this was a privilege granted them by the English-speakers who preponderate in the Cape. Naturally the Afrikaner always regarded the arrangement as an intolerable anomaly, and commenced a struggle to eradicate it from the moment he settled into office, despite what had been thought to be iron-bound guarantees in the constitution protecting each constituent province's right to regulate its own electoral system.

At no time did the Coloreds qualify or vote in sufficient numbers to decide an election in the Cape; the English-speakers fought through the crisis not for a political reality but a principle—nearly the last time they were to do so. If the constitution could be arbitrarily abrogated or evaded in respect of the Coloreds' right of suffrage, then a precedent would be set whereby the remainder, and more objectionable parts, of the Afrikaner program could be more easily and speedily enacted: the proclamation of the Republic, the replacement of English by Afrikaans, bureaucratic supervision of the great corporations, and so forth. Originally the provisions for provincial autonomy in the South Africa Act of 1909 had been introduced in the spirit of imperial generosity to conciliate and brace up Afrikanerdom; now the English-speakers found that they needed them to defend their own society against the Afrikaner.

The legal question involved the competence of the South African Parliament to override the "entrenched clauses" of a constitution which was itself the font of the South African Parliament's authority; the "entrenched clauses," of course, were articles providing for provincial autonomy in certain specified areas. Ultimately it was generally agreed that the Parliament was competent to alter the constitution; with the assumption by the former imperial dominions of full independence in the 1930's their parliaments inherited the full sovereignty of the Westminster Parliament, which is absolute. But what then complicated the discussion in South Africa was the fact that over the years the most prominent leaders of Afrikanerdom had on many occasions publicly promised never to assail the "entrenched clauses," and this pledge had become—to the minds of the English-speakers at least—as important a postulate of the South African community as the formal documents of Union.

The Afrikaners broke this pledge in 1951, when they introduced a bill to remove the Coloreds from the Cape common electoral roll. But it took them five years to steamroller this bill into the statute books, and before they accomplished it they consternated the country by brutal displays of political ruthlessness, such as packing the Appeal Court and the Senate. Apparently the days ahead hold worse things in store for the Coloreds than the loss of the franchise, for Verwoerd's government has recently announced that it is proceeding to look around for an "ethnic home" to move them to. But the so-called "constitutional crisis" set precedents—the abasement of the constitution, the complete initiation of the Afrikaner into the arts of political domineering, the resignation of the English-speaker—which have drastically altered the whole tone of the prospects for life and society in South Africa. Having learned the route to the well of arbitrary power, the Afrikaner has returned with increasing frequency and rudeness. The law has been tortured into a mask which neither possesses nor requires the power to deceive; and no battlefield any longer exists on which the English-speakers are prepared to make a stand.

Of course, the fourth part of the South African population is comprised of white men of European descent, of whom there are slightly more than 3 millions in the Union, gathered into the older cities of the Cape and Natal, the booming Transvaal metropolis of Johannesburg, or sprinkled over the farms and towns of the four provinces. Sixty per cent of this population is Afrikaner, and the Afrikaners employ this white majority and a voting system weighted in favor of rural areas to dominate the national parliament, where the Nationalist Party usually manages to mobilize twice as many votes as its combined opposition. But the typical Afrikaner is a farmer and rancher; the cities, industries, wealth, and culture of South Africa are still to a large degree the preserve of the English-speaker. Although this disparity is said to be waning, in 1959 no more than 15 per cent of the national economy was estimated to be in the control of Afrikaners; and an Afrikaner government official is authority for the statement that between the years 1948 and 1955 not one important new commercial enterprise anywhere in South Africa was founded by an Afrikaner.

But we have not even begun to appreciate the racial meticulousness which is the mark of all things Afrikaner. Officially, though not for purposes of administration, the Afrikaner breaks down the Bantu into four additional "ethnic groups," the Nguni and Sotho, the smaller groups of Shangaan and Venda. The Nguni are then further subclassed into Zulus, Swazis, Xhosas, Fingos, Tembus, Pondos, and Ndebeles; the Sotho into Southern, Western, and Northern Sotho. Within the group of one-and-a-half million Coloreds, the Afrikaner discriminates the small number of Moslem "Cape Malays." And the Asians fall into Hindu and Moslem rankings, and into speakers of Gujerati, Urdu, Tamil, Hinai, Telegu, and so on. Even the most fanatic Afrikaner cannot find "ethnic homes" for each of these "nationalities," but that does not quite mean that they are categories without a difference. It is always easier to trample over a score of pebbles than two or three boulders, and if the Afrikaner can prove that the concept of "African" is a purely fictitious one, that the social reality of Africa is Xhosa, Tembu, Western Sotho, and so forth—savage tribes that would be at each others' throats were it not for the firm, white hand—the Afrikaner can justify to foreigners his self-generated metamorphosis from sheepherder to despot. He can hope to discourage potential critics from fathoming such a bewildering hodgepodge of races, and perhaps they will be content to leave the Union's government to him, as the only solid pillar on the scene.

But the deprecation of "African" is a futile business, for as if history would not have achieved the same thing in time the white man himself has deliberately assumed the task of teaching the African that he is an "African" in the only way that political semantics can be taught: the African has been shown that only as an "African" can he ever hope to enter into the mysteries of progress and liberty. Needless to say this was no lesson of charity, but an unwelcome by-product of the way that white society relates to the African. In the mine compounds, servants' quarters, kraals, everywhere the African labors for European profit, uniformity of treatment is the rule because uniformity of treatment increases that profit. Proletarians are what is wanted, not Xhosas or Zulus. If Africans want to survive they are forced to proletarianize themselves, and hence it is no surprise that everywhere in South Africa the lingering matrices of the "tribes" are dissolving far more rap-

idly than the government could reconstitute them—even if it were
serious in its program to do so. Africans become "Africans" when
their enemies look at and treat them as "Africans"; a race may always be more, but it never can afford to be less, than what its oppressors take it for.

In the past decade or so there have appeared many excellent
studies of apartheid in action, for it has enticed the sympathies of
reformers the world round, but one still runs into Americans who
think of it as a kind of Jim Crow on a Paul Bunyan scale—similar
in kind, if not in dimension, to the social system of the American
South. This is a profound misapprehension. Whatever its original
nature, apartheid is no longer simply a system of institutionalized
prejudice; it is now a heaven-defying experiment in human biology.
In the Jim Crow world escape was always a possibility, and there
were other mitigations of severity. There is no escape from
apartheid, and whenever one appears it is instantaneously eradicated;
it is Jim Crow without an underground railway or a "mammy"
lore or the capacious cities of the North. It is today far more than
naked economic exploitation; it comes down to an effort to modify
genes and chromosomes in order to manufacture 10 million zombies
who will cease to clutter up South African society with argumenta-
tions and aspirations. The Afrikaners intend to find out just how far
Noah meant to go with that old curse.

Like other self-contained social systems apartheid possesses two
faces, of law and of custom. Of judicial apartheid the foundation
is the Pass Laws. Theoretically everyone in South Africa is listed
on a "population register." Pigment of skin or "habitual association"
is ordinarily enough to determine a man's place on this register, but
a recent spate of weird legislation sets out to "define" with equal
precision the racial affiliation of the offspring of an African mother
and white father, white mother and African father, Asian father and
African mother, and so on.

The African is not permitted to walk the public streets without
his pass, and on this document is not only the record of his race
but also his specific, official authorization to be where he is. A
properly certified pass is indispensable to every move that the
African makes throughout his adult life; and by means of the passes

the government can of course manipulate the African population at its whim like a puppet. Understandably, nothing is more resented by the Africans than this pass system, and offenses against it are the main reason so many Africans go to jail.

Sexual intercourse and marriage between Europeans and members of other races is forbidden; as we mentioned, the illicit fruits of such unions are subject to special legislation. When the government discovers such unions they are broken up—even when the couples have lived happily together for twenty years or more.

According to the law the different races that live in South Africa live apart—whether this corresponds to reality in any concrete instance does not matter. When Africans and Asians work in the cities, which millions of them do, they are not permitted to reside there, but must commute back and forth to fenced-off "locations" situated at inconvenient distances, eight to fifteen miles from their places of employment. The only exception to this rule is the domestic servant, who may reside in quarters in the back yard if his white master applies for and receives the proper dispensation. In a few regions of the country Africans had succeeded in establishing significant numbers of freehold titles before the Nationalists took power in 1948: one such freehold area was the section of Johannesburg known as Sophiatown, now being bulldozed down by the Government. In all other such regions as well, these freeholds are being confiscated, and their former occupants transported to the locations or the Reserves. The main point here is that whether in the back yard, in the locations, or kenneled on Afrikaner farms, the legal home of every African in South Africa is on one of the Reserves, which, to repeat, comprise altogether some 12 per cent of the country's land area, and that very much the inferior eighth. No matter how long an African has dwelled in the white 88 per cent—no matter that he has never visited or even seen his legal home —so long as he is in the white man's country he is living on the daily sufferance of the authorities. At their whim he can be banished to a Reserve, without judicial procedure or right of appeal.

The police can enter without a warrant any private or public place where Africans are at any time. Beatings can be administered with or without a magistrate's direction. (And beatings are administered; recently, in Capetown, a quartet of female office workers complained that they were distracted from their typing by the screams of Africans being flogged in a neighboring police headquarters.) Without going to any trouble, the police can procure a suspension of the writ of habeas corpus in the case of an African for a period up to three months. If a suspected African culprit cannot be found by the police, the community of which he is a legal resident can be fined and in other ways collectively penalized.

It goes without saying that public facilities in South Africa are strictly segregated. But local authorities may also arbitrarily deny any facility ordinarily allotted to the African, such as a railway platform or a streetcar, whenever they wish. They can disperse any assembly or meeting of Africans—without pretext and using whatever methods they like—whenever they wish.

The African is legally swindled out of his share of the prosperity he has created as a producer of industrial goods and services. His salary and hours are set at conferences between the government and the heads of the great corporations. He is prohibited from rising above the menial level in his work; he is forbidden the professions entirely. He is forbidden to strike, or even publicly to discuss a strike. He cannot bargain directly with his employer, but must submit to the intermediation of a government official. He cannot apply to the courts for redress in most matters except through a governmental representative. His education is vigilantly supervised by the government.

Social intercourse between the races, including private dinner parties and church attendance, may be interrupted by the authorities at any time. On the farms, the African has been made the victim of a separate class of legislation which has as its object the vain attempt to put Afrikaner farming in the black ink. (Like the Junker of East Prussia, the Afrikaner passionately loves his farm but he just doesn't seem to be able to make it go. But they both know everything there is to know about keeping serfs.) On the Reserves, the government daily exposes the farce of its own "separate development" policy by deposing recalcitrant chiefs, transferring the vestiges of the others' authority to the Minister of Native Affairs, and in all economic matters sacrificing the interests of the Reserves to those of the European areas.

And apartheid wears armor. The laws enacting the conditions of life described here have been enhanced by other statutes which empower the government to seek out and destroy any organizing or attempt at organizing an effective protest. The notorious Suppression of Communism Act of 1950 defines Communism in a language amounting to a definition of dissent; so sweeping and vague is the authority which it bestows on the government that even many regular Nationalists opposed the bill when it was brought in. It specifies punishments for any individual who "aims at bringing about any political, industrial, social, or economic change within the Union by the promotion of disturbances or disorder" or who encourages "feelings of hostility between the European and non-European races of the Union." The Act to Amend the Suppression of Communism Act, passed the following year, further tightened the screws; a Communist is defined as anyone whom the authorities decide is a Communist, on the basis of their nonappealable interpretation of his activities, in or out of the Union.

In 1953 the government brought in a Public Safety Act and a Criminal Laws Amendment Act by means of which the Governor-General (whose powers will soon devolve on the President, when the South African Republic is proclaimed) can declare a state of emergency to prevail in any section, or all sections, of the Union; the government then can place the country under martial law, and govern by decree. Heavy penalties, including fines, imprisonments, and floggings, are to be inflicted on any man who supports a campaign of disobedience against this or any other law, or who solicits or accepts help in such a campaign.

Sad to relate, we must digress slightly at this point to notice that the United Party—the organ of the big corporate interests and most of the English-speakers—supported these latter laws when they were passed through the Parliament; they enfolded themselves in their own winding sheet. Their private rationalization, retailed to tourists and critics, is that no national party can maintain itself in South Africa which takes a "liberal" stand on issues like these, which for the majority of Europeans involve questions of physical security. Therefore, as they think they cannot stand for the truth and win, they try standing for the lie—and lose anyway; here is the primrose path down which traipse self-infatuated, "hard-headed" Men of the World of every country and time.

But let us now look at the twist which the apartheid system has imparted to the future history of the Union. In effect, the African has been left no option but to resort to gun and knife. This is an even sourer conclusion when one considers that South Africa is the only "white settler" country in Africa where so extreme a polarization could have been avoided. South Africa is a country with a split personality economically: the agricultural sector is comparatively poor and backward; the middle class is confined to Europeans; but the industrial sector is extremely advanced for Africa, and like all industrial sectors rests on a frail superstructure of intricately dovetailed parts. Hence, a massive working class could *peacefully* improve itself politically by employing the weapons of economic shock—trade unions, consumer boycotts, and the rest of it. The oligarchy could be brought to heel without spilling a drop of their blood; this is of course the method whereby the "boom and bust" capitalism of our fathers' time was housebroken into the "democratic capitalism" of our day in America itself. Conceivably a campaign to win full civil rights for the Africans of the Union could be reared on a program of scrupulous nonviolence. Indeed, this is the first age in which such a program could succeed; in earlier eras the oligarchies destroyed as great a proportion of the protesting masses as was necessary to subdue them, without having to worry about disrupting their primitive economies by the loss of life or the ephemeral disorder. In contrast to this, South Africa on the surface would seem to be exceptionally vulnerable to peaceful, nonviolent campaigns of economic pressure—and it is, in fact, to just this kind of program that the oldest and wisest African leaders have endeavored to commit their people. But it is all a waste of time and effort in Afrikanerdom. The Afrikaners are not going to submit to any kind of pressure —potential or actual. It will be Bronze Age slaughter or nothing.

The abstract position in law of a serf group may be one of unbearable subjection, while the hatefulness of this rigor is tempered by the exigencies of habitual association and cooperation in the society at large. Legally the European peasant of the Middle Ages was probably just as much at the mercy of his baron as the African is of the Afrikaner, but we may assume that the typical nobleman was open to the teachings of his humanitarian religion and calculations of self-interest; so long as his peasants cocked no snook at his theoretical prerogatives—which they rarely did—he was willing to behave with a rough-and-ready sort of decency. Not so the South African nobleman—the Afrikaner. To begin with, the Afrikaner is unbelievably blind to his self-interest; he actually appears to believe that nothing but his own pertinacity is needed for the perpetuation of the social system of South Africa into the farthest reaches of the future. And to myopia we must add his curdled and truculent compulsion to hammer every last nail in the logical structure of apartheid right down to the head. It is probably not worth while to try to trace back this compulsion to Teutonic blood or fundamentalist religion, but there is a psychological urge visibly at work in South Africa—one whose appetite is growing more and more insatiable—for the humiliation of the African as well as his enslavement. The ordinary Afrikaner contributes his bit to the government's apartheid laws with revolting zeal; and on the face-to-face level he is in a position to magnify many times the dreadfulness of the laws. Over and over again I have seen Afrikaners go out of their way to remind Africans that they are not only bondsmen but also beasts.

To cite only a few examples of this social, as distinct from legal, squeeze, the African in South Africa cannot earn enough money to live decently or self-respectfully—or, indeed, according to the best statistics, to live at all. On the farms, he is usually paid less than 3 dollars a month, and allowed for food only the least marketable, and least nourishing, leftovers. On the Reserves, the food that is grown on the spot has had in recent years to be supplemented by miserably inadequate imports, so crowded are their populations and senile their soils. But it is the plight of the urbanized African which we should take special pains to understand, for the urbanized African in South Africa is a kind of case history of the urbanized African all over the continent.

In 1954 the South Africa Institute of Race Relations (a private institution, needless to say) established that the average unskilled African worker received about 33 dollars a month. Food, rent, taxes, transportation for a family of five would take, the Institute calculated, about 69 dollars a month. There was a "short-fall" here of 36 dollars a month, the margin by which the average African family ceased to exist.

How, then, does it appear that they continued to exist? By making up the "short-fall," in one or both of two ways. First, the African educated himself to an infinite resource in winnowing and fabricating scraps and garbage, tin cans and ancient blankets, into shelter and garments for himself and his family. It is rather too much to expect that he avoid a hideous squalor of surroundings and a shabbiness of person which pierce his pride as much as it would the pride of any American, which supercomplicates the difficulties of social intercourse between the African and—say—an American visitor, and which exacerbates the debt of rage which one day the white race will have to discharge. What else can he do? Second, the short-fall can be pared down to the bare survival point by economizing on the largest single item in his expenses—namely, his food. Naturally, his diet now falls below the proper nutritional level; he has achieved a fiscal jugglery only by throwing his life expectancy into the account: the average black South African lives to thirty-seven; the average white South African lives to seventy; 50 per cent of Africans born in South Africa die before they reach the fine age of sixteen. But the budget balances.

No substantial steps of any kind have ever been taken to halt the homicidal career of the "short-fall" in South Africa. Even well meaning European employers—the majority of the English-speakers—often hesitate to irritate their fellow whites, or Afrikaner officialdom, by paying their African employees a living wage. Perhaps South Africa is the only country in Africa with a chronic labor shortage, but the classical principles of supply and demand—by the operation of which the European peasant struck off his feudal shackles after the Black Death had made his labor precious—receive no more respect in South Africa than any other principle of civilization. Indeed, the South African government has up to now responded to the situation in the spirit of Swift; recently it abandoned in great part a long-established school-feeding scheme which had been making small inroads into the hungers of African children. (According to an official explanation, African children are not as active as European children, and therefore require less milk.) Meanwhile, the African toils on toward death, earning by the sweat of his back the right to pilfer rags out of gutters and to watch his children wither up into stick figures. (As in the last decade his cost of living has risen at a faster rate than his income, he may also observe—if he likes—the walls of the pit that encloses him growing higher and more unscalable with every passing day.)

The white population of South Africa has done its best to make it clear to the African that, if it were zoologically feasible, he would be metamorphosed into a tireless insect, without voice or soul. This is, anyway, the ideal to which they are approximating. If the African works in town, he is housed in a "location" a dozen or so miles out of it, insulated from white society by a "green belt" of woodland or meadow, fatigued by incredibly strenuous commuting schedules on Toonerville trolleys which soak up five or six hours of his waking day. If he is a domestic servant he can live in proximity to his job, but he must obtain the permission of his employer to entertain friends, a girl, wife, or family in his shack near the garbage can. In the hives where miners are barracked, he is kept womanless. (The eloquent indignation of the Afrikaner who now finds that he has a homosexuality problem on his hands is wonderful to hear.) If the African forgets his pass, he is detained and beaten, usually publicly. When he wants to change jobs, he must procure his employer's consent. If he is a servant in town, he cannot purchase beer without taking the long ride out to the location. Here, on the location, he is continually harassed by the police, who invade his home, maul his friends, disperse festivals and prayer meetings, insult and club his neighbors as much as they please. When he does come to the attention of the authorities, he is made the subject of certain painful attentions in police headquarters. (This possibility is nearer to a probability: in 1956 more than 1 million Africans were arrested, more than one of every ten Africans in the Union; of these 650,000 were prosecuted, mainly for pass offenses. But last year the pass system was extended to include women, and these records will soon be far outdone.) If after his beating the African is sent on to prison, the government rents his labor out to an Afrikaner farmer. If they banish him to a Reserve, he simply contributes one more belly to rumble with the bellies of the home folk.

The dreariness and frustration of the African's life, particularly on the locations, is indescribable; the shallow reservoir in English of groans and sibilants, a measure of our luck and our complacency, is at a loss for expressions. If it is any satisfaction to anyone, it seems to be true that human protoplasm retains, for so long as it squirms at all, some of its inherent capacity for bouncing back, some of its greed for joy; even in Dachau, we are informed, men played chess and studied the stars. But in South Africa the flame is flickering feebly or is, which is more probable, undergoing a process of transmutation to bloodthirst. The natural sportiveness of the African is near to extinction. Many of the finest and most vital young urbanized Africans desert their wives and children in their early twenties as a matter of course. It is not that they do not love their families enough to want to work to support them—this is the Afrikaner view—but that they *cannot*. Therefore they elect to let them die out of sight if not of mind; and to devote what small energies they have to keeping on the move, ready to hide at a whisper, maintaining one or two rudimentary political connections, in a few instances preparing for the great flight out of South Africa.

Swamped by hopeless bitterness, a moiety of the African population lives by preying on the rest. Gangs, like the famous Msomi gang of Johannesburg, terrorize entire quarters of the "locations," mugging, robbing, raping; the African police tolerate the situation until it spills over into the white areas. Johannesburg's homicide rate surpasses that of New York or London; in 1958 better than ten murders a week were averaged, the victims predominately African. Petty crimes like purse-snatching are a much-bejoked feature of life in Johannesburg for white and black alike, despite one of the largest police forces per capita in the world.

Still, from time to time from somewhere emerges an African personality who achieves a real hegemony over the minds of his countrymen and constitutes a potential leader of the African community. From the moment this man is spotted and sized up he becomes the object of a never-relaxing governmental surveillance. Sooner or later they deal with him. If this African happens to possess a mentionable lineage—to be a chief, for example—the government deposes him and banishes him from his tribal home. Or they arrest him under the Suppression of Communism Act; then they drag out the preliminaries of his trial for years, during which period he must obsequiously abide by dozens of onerous probationary regulations. (In the world-famous "Treason Trial" ninety-one men and women —white and black—have been waiting around for trial since December, 1956. At this writing, summer, 1959, the indictment has not yet been settled; but, in most cases, the finances and careers of the defendants certainly have been.) If the government concludes that these and other legal measures against the African eminent are not sufficiently benumbing, they turn the job over to thugs, who swoop down on public meetings and set upon the unlucky leader—old man though he may be—beating and kicking him while he lies unconscious under the speaker's table. All the above-described tactics are not only available to the government, but they can be and have been practiced by it. Each of these experiences has at one time or other fallen to the lot of Chief Albert Luthuli, president of the African National Congress. (To anticipate a bit, it is curious that Chief Luthuli is perhaps the only African politician anywhere in the world who preaches a "soft" policy on Afrikaners. It requires little imagination to conceive of the treatment that will be meted out to militant Africanists, when they begin to throw their weight around in South Africa.)

When a young African intellectual—of which there are very many —cannot endure it any longer he deserts his family, starts drinking too much and lazing around in cellars, pieces together a wretched living by free-lancing essays to the few markets open to him, and— finally—applies for permission to emigrate, either to England or to one of the northern-tier states like Ghana or Nigeria. He promises never to return to his homeland; nevertheless, his application is denied. Or perhaps a foreign philanthropic institution, like the Carnegie Corporation, or a famous university like Oxford proffers him a scholarship in a field of study like public health or agricultural science, something desperately needed by his people. The application for permission to leave the country, or to accept the appointment, is denied. Or perhaps a man, by dint of epic exertions, has made himself into a lawyer; the official from the Group Areas commission comes along and tells him that he must move 400 miles away from his clientele. Or perhaps a score of Africans, sponsored by friendly, liberal Europeans, have created and staged a musical comedy like the much-publicized *King Kong* of the spring of 1959. Inevitably the mechanics and the executive decisions of the show are taken over by the white sponsors; the African is left to compose the music, sing, dance, and obey the white director. (And then there are the "people of Pretoria," who purchased space in the newspaper to thank publicly the manager of the local theater for refusing to profane that Mecca of Afrikanerdom by housing the show—in a movie house owned by an American corporation!) Or perhaps our intellectual will simply give up and go to work in the mines; here, for the year or two he can take it, he will pass twice a day under lintels on which near-illiterate Afrikaner miner apprentices have scribbled caricatures of monkeys and epithets like "Africa Dogs." And so on and so on and so on.

Nothing is forgotten; no loophole is too small; the Afrikaner has time on his hands when it comes to devising means of tormenting Africans. There are no cushions for storms or quakes; there is no balm of occasional smiles or kindness; there is no valve for relief of pressures—or even signals to give forth warning of pressures. Even the worst regimes of the past were limited by elementary technique to elementary tyranny. But Afrikanerdom is a modern state. It is a sacrilege, an atavism, a psychosis—an ineffable imbecility into the bargain. But there it is.

I should like to close these chapters on South Africa with brief sketches of the purposes and influences of three prominent men in modern South African politics.

The present Prime Minister of the Union of South Africa is a florid, white-haired, strident-voiced man in his late fifties, Hendrik Frensch Verwoerd. (In years to come we Americans are going to hear a lot from this gentleman, and it is doubtful that we shall like what we hear.) Born in Holland, brought to the Union by his family as an infant, Verwoerd possesses neither the intelligence nor the spellbinding oratory that distinguished his old master, Dr. Malan. He compensates for these deficiencies with an indefatigability in scheming which repels even his closer associates. He is a cleverer man than his immediate predecessor, Strijdom, but he lacks Strijdom's automatic instinct for the Afrikaner's soul. This too he makes up for—with a fanaticism that transcends the gruff bigotries of classical Afrikanerdom, a personal fanaticism that has evolved apartheid into a dream to be died for rather than simply a tradition to be sustained. In brief, there is a discernible progression from Malan to Verwoerd which is the working out of a demonic species of historic logic, of which the ordinary Afrikaner is only vaguely conscious and of which he is vaguely apprehensive, but which is a trap from which he cannot free himself. Evil is weaving and fouling its own nest.

As Minister of Native Affairs in the previous government Verwoerd articulated the ideals of apartheid which he is now in a position to translate *in toto* into statute. In the previous chapter we glanced over the fact that he seems to contemplate a total disentanglement of the white population from the African: whether he genuinely holds this to be an achievable target hardly matters, for the whole notion is right out of cloud-cuckoo-land, but it nevertheless serves as the doctrine of his national policy and is used therefore to justify any expedient of repression that seems desirable. Verwoerd calls his version of apartheid the "new vision," and he is now engaged in shoveling it through his tame parliament.

The "new vision" is the logical-illogical fulfillment of the apartheid notion of "separate development." Its conception of the South Africa of the future goes thusly: Europeans with their superior culture live in the "white areas" (88 per cent of the country). Asians with their quaint culture, and perhaps Coloreds, live in *their* areas (no more than a fraction of a per cent of the country). Nine-and-one-half million Africans with their primitive culture live on the Reserves, which in deference to modern trends must change their names to "Bantustans" (12 per cent of the Union's land area).

At this point the common-sensical or attentive reader may have a few questions. For example, what about the millions of African laborers who operate the South African industrial and agricultural plant? (Eighty-seven per cent of mine laborers are Africans, for instance; and the general ratio of African industrial workers to white is increasing every day.) Verwoerd replies that Africans may continue to cross from "Bantustan" into the white areas when there is work for them, but as these white areas are not their homes they naturally will not expect to possess civil or social rights there. On the other hand, if they do not like life in the white areas, they can return to Bantustan. Perhaps it is inconvenient for a man who has run an elevator for twenty years to relearn "tribal" culture, perhaps it is unfortunate that the inhabitants of the Bantustan are already on the brink of starvation, perhaps it is inconsistent of the government to raise poll taxes and take other steps to drive Reserve youths into the man-hungry industries of the Rand, but—when this is all said and done—the sooner that black men understand that their prospects in life are as black as their skins the better off they will be.

Does the government intend to permit the Bantustans to develop self-governing institutions, so that at least the African can enjoy town meetings whilst he is emaciating? Verwoerd has explicitly pledged himself to this, but his actions will not encourage skeptics. Throughout his whole career he has been the first of intimidators and deposers of African chiefs on the Reserves, both as minister and as head of the government. Considering his emotional slant, and the fact that the eight Bantustans are scattered hit or miss over the Union, the chances of a meaningful restoration of tribal life would seem to be chimerical indeed.

What of the obverse side of the coin? Will a multiclass white society come into existence, with white laborers doing the drudgeries that the "foreign" Africans now do? Not likely. As yet Verwoerd has not addressed himself to this precise matter—it contains a few implications that he will expound to his constituents at his peril—but certainly he, and previous Afrikaner prime ministers, have seen to it that those white men who might be willing to scrub floors or cut sugar cane, the refugees from Europe's wars and overjammed cities, are not welcome in South Africa. But what is the use of discussing the thing beyond this point, where it all goes blurry? At the first hint from Verwoerd that he expected his compatriots to do their own work he would disappear without a bubble, sunk in an oceanic clamor of English and Afrikaans alike. He has no intention that such a fate should overtake him; he will confine the "new vision" to the arena he knows best and where he reigns supreme—ravings and pamphleteerings. This is the "new vision" of Prime Minister Verwoerd, a political hypocrisy of such mountainous dimensions that it cannot be packaged even by a mad racist philosopher, designed to promote the "happiness, stability, and security" of South Africa by bleeding 80 per cent of her people into bestiality.

Gold mining has a unique position in South Africa's economy. It is historically responsible for Johannesburg, for the influx of the Europeans who made a modern state in southern Africa a practicable affair, for the transformation of the High Veld into Africa's richest plain. Today it is still responsible for more than 50 per cent of South Africa's foreign exchange earnings, and these funds returned to South Africa's circulation comprise the market for the internal manufactures which the government is endeavoring to stimulate. Nor have the mines suffered from the recent slump in the Union's business activity, nor from that collateral phenomenon, the excessive rise in costs compared with profits. Nor have they shared in the general agricultural depression, which is reflected in yields that are among the lowest in the civilized world in corn, wheat, potatoes, and other ordinary farm products. After ninety years, it is the heavy gold piece at the bottom of his national wallet that still gives the South African his confidence in a sunny tomorrow. When an American goes to a bar in South Africa, and reveals his nationality, he is invariably asked, "When is the United States going to raise the price of gold?"

At the apex of the gold-mining industry of South Africa stands a gigantic holding company, the Anglo-American Corporation, and at the head of the Anglo-American stands Mr. Harry Oppenheimer, son of the founder, Sir Ernest Oppenheimer, who at the time of his death a few years ago was one of the world's richest men. Harry Oppenheimer is a busy, intelligent man in his forties, continually on the move from one airport to another, surrounded by the attentive entourage of bright young male secretaries and public-relations counsels who compose the natural barrier between the world's great and the world. He is interested in his business and apparently good at it; his corporation not only dominates the gold-mining industry of South Africa but also controls the diamond trust of De Beers and many other smaller outfits in the Rhodesias and East Africa. Harry Oppenheimer is also a well educated and liberal-minded man. What hope is there that an individual of this disposition, vested with this enormous wealth and power, may throw a block at the crazy schemes of Dr. Verwoerd?

We regret to say, None. In the last chapter we tried to show the nature of the bargain which the English-speakers (politically represented by the United Party) have made with the Afrikaners. It was to be property in exchange for passivity. The English-speakers were to continue to dominate the country economically, the Afrikaners politically. The English-speakers made the deal in good faith, but they have since discovered that it is quite impossible for them to

live under it like men. A few years ago, for example, it was possible
for Harry Oppenheimer to win himself a reputation as a fighting
liberal during the "constitutional crisis." As a member of parliament
for the United Party, he spoke strongly for, and contributed lavishly
to, the fight for the "entrenched clauses." Following the death of
Sir Ernest, he gave up his seat, but he continues to forward monies
to the party. But how long ago seem these fighting days now. There
has been no effective attempt to raise the real wages or living conditions of the men who work the mines. When, a few years ago, the
new gold fields of the Orange Free State were opened Sir Ernest
proposed to erect at his own expense a family village for the workers,
where they could live like human beings instead of sexless drones.
The government quashed the proposal as a violation of its "group
areas" dogma; Sir Ernest meekly complied. Moral: Power that is
unusable is no power at all. And this powerlessness has been implicit
in the situation for years; the United Party and men like Harry
Oppenheimer do not know what they want out of life; they are
thoroughly stymied entities. It was a United Party government that
broke the African miners' strike of August, 1946—with sublime dis-
regard for the life and limb, not to mention the grievances, of the
men. It was the United Party that, out of power as it was, supported
the legislation that outlaws strikes by Africans, dissent and political
actions by Africans, and authorizes the government to conduct
ideological inquisitions in every corner of the land.

Even if, by virtue of a dazzling change of heart, the English-
speaking millionaires were converted to crusading, what could they
do? The power of money is a conventional power; a fortune remains
a fortune, property remains property, for only so long as the
political power agrees to respect it; a millionaire in a concentration
camp is no better off than a truck driver. And how secure is any
millionaire, or anyone else, in a country ruled by the likes of Hendrik
Verwoerd, who spends far more of his time keening over old
grudges and new reveries than in studying the standard operating
proprieties of international finance? The English-speakers are locked
into their side of their South African bargain, and compromised by
it to the core of their moral beings; but the Afrikaners can blow
their side of the same bargain away with a puff. Listen to this dictum
of the current Minister of Economic Affairs for the Union: "In

economic matters the State will have to act according to the principle that the welfare and happiness of the Volkunity come before
that of the individual and that economic riches and economic power
are not ends in themselves but means in the service of the Volk. . . .
The liberalistic principle of laissez-faire will have to be thrown overboard entirely. . . . All key industry, including the mining industry,
must be placed under State control . . . a State bank will have to
be founded in order to ensure that banking has a purely domestic
character and that the money and credit matters of the State are
controlled in the interests of the Volk."

In addition to the shudders that a statement like this one evokes
there is another shadow, presently no larger than a man's fist, which
is limiting the effectiveness of Mr. Oppenheimer's liberalism even
more than his moral confusion. The subject is one which is generally
tabooed or ridiculed inside the Union, but it is there all right: and
it is anti-Semitism.

It does not seem conceivable, or endurable, that the Jew should be
condemned to another maltreatment in our lifetime, but certain
colors are coalescing into patterns, and as the political wildness of the
Union increasingly undermines its economic structure the old hunt
for scapegoats—a sport in which the Afrikaners are practised craftsmen—is bound to be revived. Verwoerd's own career does not inspire
confidence. He won his first spurs as a national figure in 1936, when
as head of the department of sociology at Stellenbosch University he
protested against the government's decision to permit a small group
of German Jewish refugees to enter the Union. Shortly thereafter he
became the first editor of the Johannesburg daily *Die Transvaler,*
ownership of which he still shares with a number of his cabinet colleagues; it is this journal's fancy that Harry Oppenheimer is the
guiding genius of the United Party, and whenever the Party seems
to be getting above itself the paper likes to remonstrate with "Hoggenheimer" for his sins.

The Jew is an exceptionally well placed citizen—not to say valuable one—in South Africa. Along with Rhodes, a bold handful of
Jewish visionaries contributed far more to the modern eminence of
South Africa than all the Afrikaners combined. But that is yesterday's ice cream; today it is the Afrikaner who holds the whip, and
it is a reckless South African of any race or religion who forgets

how much Afrikaners relish the wielding of whips. Up to now there has been little to report that is concrete so far as anti-Semitism goes: official garble about the "happiness of the Volkunity"; official commendation of the ideological ties between Germany and Afrikanerdom; the special encouragement of German immigration; an important newspaper, owned by the head of the government and his ministers, which makes a habit of suggestive epithets; mysterious reproaches emanating from official quarters concerning the "ambiguous loyalties" of "so-called South Africans" who maintain "one-sided attachments" abroad. Is this odiousness with a memory? Perhaps one should conclude that Harry Oppenheimer has the best of reasons—or, to put it more honestly, *almost* the best of reasons—to keep his eyes glued firmly on his own affairs.

Against the failures and enfeeblements of the European as a backdrop, there is occurring in southern Africa a play of majestic grandeur, the modernization and politicization of millions upon millions of Bantu Africans. Every year sees a larger migration to the booming cities. In all economic weathers, fair and foul alike, Africans find their way in increasing numbers into newspaper city rooms, subclerkships, into the lifts and corridors of gleaming new edifices, into the console chambers of public utilities and marshaling yards, into debates and paper wars about democracy, capitalism, and the Conquest of Space. Their eyes and their inquiries are penetrating into every secret; the Africans are turning the switches and handling the controls of modern civilization; at first with trepidation but then with insouciance they memorize the tricks that create the glamour; one by one they tie the knots—the tens of millions of knots—by which one day the Enslaver shall become the Enslaved. Bantustan is the japery of an Afrikaner demagogue, Johannesburg is a stanza in the history of the universe.

That fraction of the African population of South Africa—approximately one-third—which has come to dwell and labor in the cities is the acre plowed by the African politician. On the Reserves and the farms the government, but even more effectually the Afrikaner community, has been able to keep the African in a state of helpless amorphousness. But the urban dwellers have supported for two generations a political organization which never fails to surprise the foreign bystander with the mildness and modesty of its outlook, qualities that issue from the character of its leadership as well as from the paucity of its resources.

Four African lawyers who happened to be Christian founded the African National Congress in 1912. At that time, of course, the South African government was still paternally guided by the Imperial Parliament in London; therefore, an appeal to the consciences of the coalition of English-speakers and moderate Afrikaners who ran the country on the spot, but which was ultimately responsible to an "enlightened" upper class in England, seemed to promise the best chance of success. The principle of operation was publicity: vividly present the African's plight to these Europeans—the theory ran— make them feel in their bones the misery of the African, and their best instincts will take over and right the perennial wrongs. Such a campaign of publicity has continued to be the main principle of Congress operations, but the audience which was meant to profit by it has sadly deteriorated. The Imperial Parliament has vanished with the Kingdom of Hanover; the English-speakers in South Africa have quite lost their Victorian religion without having lost the taste for creature comforts. And the publicity which the Congress has in mind is thrown away on the Afrikaner; he already knows everything about the plight of the African, for he created it.

Today the president-general of the African National Congress is an extremely captivating and nobleminded man, Chief Albert Luthuli, the only African who is a true national figure in the country. The Chief is an individual of subtle nuance of personality; he is one of those rare beings who commands a spiritual alchemy which changes "peace" and "brotherhood" into concepts that seem to be as exciting as "war" and "servitude." Now in his seventies, stricken with heart disease, the Chief is writing the epilogue of a lifetime spent in trying to rouse the European to "see the reasonableness of our case." Long ago, when the northern "Africa for the Africans" leaders were still in their cradles, before they had become presidents and prime ministers, the Chief was already a leader of his people. He has failed to lead them to a land of milk and honey, but this is a failure he has never conceded; and at the same time he has never modified the modesty and the finality of his political aims: "Full participation [of the African] in the government and control of their future." He is undoubtedly the only African politician on the continent who would deny himself the pleasure of devouring the Afrikaner alive, for he is a Christian and a noble who lives up to all his faiths at once. But naturally he neither expects nor receives any gratitude from the Afrikaners: they have deposed him (however, his people and the new "chief" connive at flouting this deposition), arrested him, persecuted him, insulted him, and beaten him.

In his lifetime the Chief's position as spokesman for the Congress, and for the urban Africans of South Africa, will never be challenged, but the Chief himself is the first to admit that the working leadership of the movement, the secretariat in Johannesburg, has been forced by the outrageous bellicosity of Afrikanerdom to veer far to the left of the traditional Congress stand—the stand to which the Chief is personally committed. Men can be chewed up just so much, and the Chief has little enough to show for thirty years of waiting around for European "reasonableness" to assert itself. If the Congress means to capture the loyalties of younger Africans, which of course it must do if it intends to remain effective, it must meet on new ground the new poles of African events, the diehardism in South Africa and the new freedom in northern Africa.

But inevitable innovations in programing have not reduced the Chief to a figurehead. He is too wise to begrudge the younger generation its right to chart a new path; and in his heart he suspects, I would guess, that as a younger man, facing the apartheid of the mid-century, he too would bend his convictions. So he has not simply retired from the fray, but has used his prestige to construct for himself something like the constitutional position of the British Queen: he reminds and warns the officials and young warhawks of his party of the realities of life, when their zeal seems to be overpowering their good sense. Specifically, he tells his subordinates that the Congress is not yet powerful enough for a big move. Organization on the Reserves and the farms hardly exists at all, and even in the cities party discipline is rudimentary. (When a chord in the African's soul is plucked in just the right way, he is capable of a stubbornness and solidarity that are sensational. Such a phenomenon could be seen operating at the time of the Johannesburg bus boycott of 1957; but this boycott was not a nation-wide thing, and it was more a spontaneous outburst than a Congress offensive.) Whether it is to be party or conspiracy, the Congress has far to go before it has honed itself into a true political instrument.

When the Chief tires of reminding his collaborators that they must make themselves into a political party before they can hope to achieve the aims of a political club he turns to his second theme; and that is, that when and if blood begins to flow in South Africa most of it will spill from black bodies, not white ones. The European is outnumbered four to one in South Africa; this is a sizable gap, but not sizable enough so that the Africans can deal with their enemies by drowning them in spit, as Gandhi once threatened to drown the English in India. Behind the Afrikaner's seemingly suicidal policy of leaving the African no alternative but violence there is a counter-vailing Afrikaner readiness, even eagerness, to commit violence on the African, to wind up the whole tortuous business to a climax. The Afrikaner youth is armed and drilled from the time he enters adolescence, and trained in local militias. The Afrikaner government possesses jet planes and tanks and phosphorus bombs and the other impedimenta of modern war. And the Afrikaner is sick of the African, sick of his own vitals-eating sickness; he is sick of the shroud of melancholy and guilt which the thousands of Africans of his day to day experience are wrapping around his soul; he is sick of accusing rags and protruding ribs, sick of the unconquerable pre-sumption of men who ought not to think of themselves as men.

But in falling a victim to this fearful and feckless belligerence the Afrikaner is summoning up out of the depths of African personality a complementary yearning for the consummation of violence; do-or-dieism increasingly will be the byword of young Africans. A his-torical horror is being compounded right before the old Chief's eyes, and I suspect that the disastrous courses of the past decade have finally throttled all his hopes and optimism that it can be avoided. But Chief Luthuli will go to his death preaching against a racial war of extermination. And to the end he will conceive it to be his mini-mum duty to his people to warn them of the high blood price of freedom.

What does the future hold in store for South Africa?

Up to now the question of an African uprising has hardly been raised—certainly no organizational work has been done. Indeed, the

government reckons that its own habitual violence is the true receipt
for aborting any such temptations to violence as might occur to the
Africans. And the African National Congress has so far been spending its time in confabs and more or less clumsily staged and conventional gestures to provoke a nonexistent South African chivalry.
Only two great strikes have been mounted, in 1946 and 1950; both
were ruthlessly suppressed. The Congress has mobilized mass marches
of protest against the Suppression of Communism Act and one or
two other laws. It has adopted charters, sponsored mass meetings,
circulated petitions, and watched while thousands of its sympathizers
were marched off to jail. Perhaps its most successful effort to date
was the bus boycott of the spring of 1957, when thousands of
African city workers chose to walk the ten miles into Johannesburg
twice a day rather than pay a fare hike on their only means of transportation. After weeks of this the fares were reduced to the former
level; to this extent the boycott triumphed, but since this victory the
cost of living in Johannesburg has risen sharply and the minor gain
which the boycott achieved has dropped out of sight again in the
"short-fall." With the sole, qualified exception of this boycott,
however, it is impossible to point to any deed of Congress that has
made a mark on the government. The Afrikaners have not moved a
fraction of an inch; nor do they intend to; nor do they intend to
trouble themselves even to the extent of appearing as if they were
moving. On the contrary, they have reinforced the iron in their constitution; they have rallied behind Verwoerd; they have girded
themselves for new chastisements of the African.

Nevertheless, South Africa's industry is still the chink in her
armor. And if peaceable means of exploiting this chink—genuine
trade unionism, for example—cannot in the circumstances succeed,
there is only one more thing to try: namely, sabotage. The contemporary young African in the Union who is filled with the love of
life and the desire to strike a blow for his cause can only flee his
country or conspire against it. As not many Africans are in a position
to flee, it must be conspiracy for most. Conspiracy possesses a self-
contained metabolism; starving men can survive indefinitely on conspiracy, if they cannot get ham and eggs. Conspiracy provides its
own truth and virtue; the anguish of millions reverberates unheard,
so long as the movement goes forward. The conspirator can devote

himself to tactics and management, to practical action, instead of wearing himself out on mass marches and mass boycotts. All these things, plus the shapelessness and inexperience of the African population, and the formidable means of reprisal at the disposal of the government, predetermine the channel of the new African's political activity. He must turn to narrow and vicious conspiracy, striking to rip apart the fragile industrial nexus of South Africa.

Without attempting anything so ambitious as a prophecy or time-table, perhaps one can hazard a guess or two about oncoming events.

A new generation of African leaders—who will remain anonymous so long as they can—will repudiate the principles of Chief Luthuli; they will embark on a new course of first hardening themselves to the potential massacre of millions of their fellow Africans. Theoretically, this is well founded callousness. After all, the government does not hesitate in persecuting innocent Africans every day of the week. If African politicians come to regard the whole African population as a potential hostage, then their projects are doomed before they start. In any case, revolutionaries who risk their own lives in the Cause are not notably chary of others'.

Professional revolutionaries must be imported from abroad. The existing Congress leadership—the lawyers, intellectuals, editorial writers—overmuch resemble the Viennese and North Italian ideologues of 1848, who whistled their followers out of their cellars and clubs just in time to get them cornered by the government executioner. At all events, there is no reason to improvise without the know-how of subversion, for there are plenty of friends in the outside world who will be happy to supply it—and also aid in the form of bombs, underground railways, technical guidance, liaisons, indoctrinations, United Nations advocacy, and whatnot.

Once in charge of the business, the professional will totally alter the tone of the movement; one hopes that by this time Chief Luthuli will have gone to his judgment. Here in South Africa is a white population submerged from morning to night in a sea of black faces: the logic of conspiracy compels a program of random assassination. The African police, on whom the government leans to keep order in the locations, must be infiltrated and its value destroyed. The transportation system, one of the Union's most vulnerable points, must be disrupted: pull tracks, cut wires, short-circuit cables. The mines are the Union's savings account: blow up pitheads, break machines, force slowdowns, terrorize the half-million or so Rhodesian and Portuguese Africans who are brought in to work them.

How effective can we expect a conspiracy of this nature to be in South Africa? From the beginning, of course, the government's countermeasures will be superdesperate. Probably the African in South Africa cannot defeat the European in the field, eat him up wholesale. But what he certainly can do is to wreck the country's economy—and that should be enough to send the English-speakers, who will have lost their last reason for living in Afrikanerdom, back to England, where they will sleep easier if not so warmly. Behind, on the Veld, they must leave their troublesome countryman the Afrikaner, who has nowhere to go and who—if he must—can scratch a living out of the land like a Hottentot. Between the Afrikaner and the African, now facing each other alone over mounds of gore, it must be war to the death. To whom will victory fall? Let us remember that there are 2 million Afrikaners in South Africa; there are nearly 10 million Africans, and north of the Limpopo there are hundreds of millions more. The wise man may predict that there will be no living men at all in South Africa by the year 2000, but he must agree that if there are men there they will be black.

No one, at least no one on our side of the Iron Curtain, desires this cataclysm to come to pass. Fine men like Chief Luthuli, Alan Paton, Father Huddleston, and the Afrikaner scholar P. V. Pistorius have labored for years trying to avert it; but they have achieved nothing, absolutely nothing. For our part, we have no faith in cataclysms; we have experienced a few too many of them in the first half of this century, and we have yet to learn how to heal the wounds that they inflict. But cataclysms are not warded off by conserving the diplomatic and ideological niceties. We have got to go to work, first setting off squibs under our imaginations in order to learn the proper spirit for our work. What is it like to live under the "negation of God erected into a system of government," to borrow Gladstone's phrase. What it is like to see your children writhe and curl in the fires of unappeasable hunger, to raise them in steaming stink-shacks decorated with broken bottles and goat dung; to feel the pulse and strength and mirth ebbing out of them before they have seen anything of the great world, or even to *be;* to lick the whip of the smirking *baas* while your heart is crying for some portion of the buoyancy of life? How would any one of us like to have nothing at all?

No nation in the world whose national self-interest will profit from an equitable settlement in South Africa has the power to enforce such a settlement except the United States of America. Curiously, the African understands this, even if most Americans do not.

On returning one day from an interview with officials of the Anglo-American Corporation in Johannesburg, I started a conversation with the chauffeur of the car the company had generously lent me. But this man kept interspersing his remarks with that terrible South African term of "respect," *baas.* I told him to quit it; Americans don't want to be called *baas.*

Just as I said this the driver pulled his vehicle over to the side of the road and turned round to look me in the face. "An American!" said he. "An American—I didn't know that. Well, if you really are an American, then tell me when you are coming over here to help us?"

It had been too long a time since I had heard the word "American" used like this, like a sort of invocation of the Great Spirit; Lincoln and Franklin Roosevelt used it this way, and so did this African man. He knew almost nothing of our country, but he did know of the radiant glories of our dream which has so changed the world—though not yet his world. To this man, and to hundreds of millions of men like him around the world, America shall forever be the great and gentle Paladin of the North, feeder of children and liberator of fathers. What more does anyone ask of life?

4. Southwest Africa; the High Commission Territories

West of South Africa lies the huge, unfortunate territory of Southwest Africa, aptly described in official South Africa circulars as "for many purposes, now practically a fifth province of the Union." In recent years Southwest Africa, one of the poorest lands on earth, has been the occasion of nearly as much of the criticism descending on Afrikaner heads as apartheid itself. And since the United Nations inherited the mandate system of the old League of Nations, under which Southwest Africa had been administered since the dismemberment of the old German Empire, the status and society of the territory are not outside the legitimate concern of the international community.

The country is wretched but large, as big as France and Germany combined, divided into a long, slender strip of nearly rainless coastal desert, the Namib, one of the oddest of the world's terrains—and, inland, a generally flat sector of the Great Central Plateau, which gradually rises up to highlands 6,000 and 8,000 feet in height in the southwest. Water is nearly everywhere in drastically short supply. Rainfall is inadequate, and the agricultural economy must depend upon scattered wells. As a result, with the exception of a small region around the capital, Windhoek, the range is used only for the pasturing of cattle and the karakul lambs which are the distinctive money crop of the territory.

For administrative purposes the country is transected. Europeans live almost exclusively in the so-called "Police Zone," roughly the southern two-thirds of the province. In the northern "Tribal Areas" —Ovamboland, Okovangoland, and the Kaokoveld—Africans live in an extremely modified state of tribal independence, supervised by government residents. However, here in the Tribal Areas is not the only provision for tribal society, as seventeen Native Reserves exist within the Police Zone in addition to the land which had been definitely alienated to Europeans. The country is lightly populated: 66,000 Europeans, almost all in the Police Zone; about 452,000 Africans, only half of whom live in the Police Zone.

So far in its history an early German affiliation has been the decisive influence on Southwest Africa. The story begins in the 1880's, when the British government grew temporarily hesitant about extending its sphere of responsibility farther into the wastes of southern Africa. At this point a few German fishermen and settlers who had parked themselves here and there in Southwest Africa petitioned their government for protection against raiding African tribesmen. Prince Bismarck—nearing the end of his chancellorship— inquired two or three times of the British government whether they cared to express an interest in the area, and when he received only negative responses abandoned for the time being the anticolonialism which had been one of the keystones of his policy and dispatched a sketchy colonial administration to the region.

From the first, the German regime characterized itself by a furious brutality far surpassing the Belgians' contemporary colonization of the Congo. The bulk of the indigenous inhabitants of the enormous semidesert were primitive nomads, Bushmen and Hottentots, whom the Germans treated as so many vermin. Their villages were set upon and destroyed; the population—men, women, and children—was decimated; individual Bushmen on the veld were shot for sport, from the hip. Eventually the majority of surviving Bushmen were driven into the Kalahari Desert of Bechuanaland, where they still live under their ancient ways protected by the British. Those Bushmen and Hottentots who remained in Southwest Africa are a continuing source of anxiety to the philanthropists of the world; they are constantly harassed—if not actually enslaved—by the Afrikaner government, which recently has suggested that it may soon corral them and confine them to a Reserve, where they would be unable to survive at all by their time-worn arts of stalking and hunting.

Having disposed of the aborigines, the Germans turned their attention to the Bantu in the more promising sections of the territory, rounding up a portion of the tribes for employment as forced labor on the far-flung cattle ranches that typify the country and herding the rest into the northern areas. One or two of the most warlike of the Bantu peoples rebelled at this treatment, and these soon felt the full weight of the *furor Teutonicus*. The most famous of the German campaigns against the Bantu was that led by General von Trotha against the Hereros in 1904, at the conclusion of which only 15,000 persons survived of a tribe originally numbering about 80,000; this remnant was parceled around the country as slave labor. (The modern plight of the Hereros has been much publicized by the Reverend Michael Scott, an English clergyman, who has only succeeded in making himself the most unpopular figure in southern Africa.)

Lingering overtones of the German conquest and occupation have continued to taint the atmosphere of Southwest Africa to the present day. German remains one of the official languages of the territory. One of the main streets in Windhoek, the capital, is the Goeringstrasse, named for the first German "governor" of the territory, father of the air ace and Reichsmarschall. In honor of the heroic German soldiers who died in the Herero Rebellion a monument stands in the center of the town, over an inscription in German. In honor of latter-day German heroes, those who fought in the First World War (against the Union of South Africa, incidentally), the Legislative Assembly recently passed a pension act according to which 270 ex-German Army veterans will receive from the territorial expenditures about $120,000 a year. From the beginning the Union, to which the territory was mandated after the First World War and the Versailles Treaty, did all they could to conciliate the 6,000-odd Germans who remained in the land. In 1924 a "general naturalization" act granted all but a few of these settlers full citizenship in the Union of South Africa. For their part, the Germans have reciprocated by hardening into a reliable core of support of the Afrikaner administration, and by repeatedly petitioning the Union government to terminate the mandate and trustee status of the territory by a formal annexation. Only in the 1930's, when the lure of Nazidom unsettled these otherwise unexceptionable loyalties, did a few acid notes in Southwest Africa interrupt the concert of brotherhood. But the issue of World War II put a stop to the call of the *Blut*, and— in any case—Afrikaners were not likely permanently to resent acts —like the victualing of German submarines off the Southwest African coast—which were committed against the government of General Smuts and his Anglophiliac friends.

In small groups and families Afrikaner farmers had wandered over the borders of Southwest Africa from the east since the 1880's, and it is this fragmentary frontierization which supports the modern South African claim that, once the territory had been deemed a prize of war, its natural place was within the embrace of the Union of South Africa. This view of things was not acquiesced in by the Allies at Versailles who designed the mandate system, but they did cooperate to the extent of mandating the territory to the Union under special terms whereby that government could administer it as an integral part of itself. Under this sanction the Union ruled South-west Africa in the 1920's and 1930's pretty much as it pleased, with-out any remarkable international repercussions, until World War II dissolved the League of Nations and left certain of its functions like the mandate system suspended in air. In 1946 the League formally ended its own existence and handed over its "assets" to the United Nations, but there was an improvised—even arbitrary—quality to this procedure that constituted a crack into which the Union wedged a contention that it had fulfilled its obligations and was now free uni-laterally to dispose of Southwest Africa.

Inside the Union, the mood of the Afrikaner community had long since begun to coarsen; General Smuts had refused twice, in 1946 and 1947, to submit the territory to the jurisdiction of the Trustee-ship Council, the heir presumptive of the mandate responsibilities of the League, but he did honor his general debts to his Allies by continuing to submit the regular reports of conditions inside the country which had always been part of the mandate system. Of course, even this small concession proved to be intolerable to Dr. Malan. Since 1949 the Union has not recognized the right of the international community to any special concern whatever in Southwest Africa. Reports have not been filed; commissioners have not been permitted to investigate; and a series of legislative acts has passed through the Union Parliament which has drawn the territory into closer and closer connection with the larger country. Formal annexation is now but a matter of time, fulfilling the oft-repeated plank in the Nationalist Party platform that "Southwest Africa has become one territory and one people with that of the Union."

(Strictly speaking, the only legal right which the United Nations probably possesses in respect to Southwest Africa is the right to receive these regular reports. If the United Nations does not credit the truthfulness of these reports, or is dissatisfied with the social conditions they describe, there is little or nothing the organization can do about it except to form commissions and issue resolutions. But it is just these potential resolutions of exposure and complaint, drawn up by an organization dominated by "nations of color," which the Afrikaner finds a far more unnerving prospect than the faintly illegal position in which his government has placed itself by refusing to submit reports in the first place. The Afrikaner does not object to being outlawed, but he does not wish to be lectured by colored men.)

In the Union itself the long association with the Imperial Parliament, and the leaven of a considerable English-speaking minority, have up to now tempered somewhat the full, practical applications of Afrikaner race ideas. No such restraints exist in Southwest Africa. And as a result everyone who knows the country agrees that the administration is one of the most savage in the modern world. Still it is repression with a purpose, for although there are few poorer areas on the earth's surface, there is a prosperity available to a limited number of Europeans through diamond mining, coastal fishing, and karakul ranching—the profits from all of which enterprises are proportional to the docility and cheapness of African labor. As in South Africa, except here even more brazenly, a total apartheid and an all-powerful police combine to make the taming of this labor the whole object of the legal system. Apartheid ensures that no wrongheaded humanitarian ideas will impede the economically necessary manipulation of this labor by the pass system and the police. And the alienation of African land, the shifting and confiscation of their

Reserves, the breaking of pledges and enactment of despotic new labor codes keep the population-at-large in a state of disorganized helplessness. Since 1948, when high world prices began to bring real money into the province, the bars of the African's cage have been set in place one by one, and now an out and out serfdom of the most vicious kind has been thoroughly documented.

During the past decade Michael Scott has appointed himself the spokesman for the African of Southwest Africa—along with participating in other, less impressive crusades such as picketing nuclear depots in Britain and getting himself sent off to prison. He has for years attempted to persuade the United Nations that it has a unique, formal, legitimate claim of authority in Southwest Africa which it does not possess for other victims of tyranny, and that here therefore is a God-given opportunity to strike a blow in the Good Cause—that is, to bring relief to the Africans in the territory—and also to make a start toward working out methods of judgment and justice on which the ultimate world community can base its development. If the authority of the world community—whose only modern expression is the United Nations—means nothing in a former mandate which is brutalized by the relatively insignificant power of the Union, what can the world community hope to do about so much grander and more dangerous issues in larger spheres?

The troubles Mr. Scott has encountered in trying to convey these views to the United Nations constitute a sad commentary on that organization. To begin with, though the United Nations itself and the International Court of Justice recognize that the former has some rights in Southwest Africa, the Union of South Africa does not. And nothing is further from the realm of possibility than that the United Nations will attempt to force the Union to accept its jurisdiction. And then there is the matter of credentials, which smothers the agenda of the Trusteeship Council to an extent it never did the analogous, much more professionally conducted agencies of the old League. Mr. Scott functions by means of petitions of chiefs and other aggrieved individuals in Southwest Africa which he sends or smuggles out of the country and then relays to the Secretary-General, who in turn submits them for the consideration of a special Committee on Southwest Africa, established by the General Assembly in November, 1953, to conduct hearings "until such time as an agreement is reached between the United Nations and the Union of South Africa."

But who is to say that the petitioners are authentic spokesmen of their peoples, or that the grievances they specify are anything but half-baked gripes? This is, indeed, exactly how the Union representative at the U.N. characterizes them. The Union has clearly declared that according to the only law it recognizes the petitioners have committed crimes when they address a foreign agency; the United Nations has violated its charter commitment when it meddles in the affairs of a member state; that any tribunal has compromised its dignity when it permits a notorious troublemaker and ex-Communist like Mr. Scott to appear before it; and that the causes and individuals he represents are supposititious or fraudulent. And this is a method of attack which reduces the cumbersome procedures of the United Nations to fits of blind staggers. Unfounded, or at least unverifiable, petitions are a dime a dozen in New York, and there is not time enough in all eternity to sort them out. In March, 1956, the Trusteeship Council was informed that 35,000 petitions had been received in the few previous months from the French Cameroons alone; just to translate, print, and distribute them would have cost more than $1 million. Sir Alan Burns, a former British representative on the Trusteeship Council, tells the story of an earlier petition from the same territory that concerned the Fon of Bikom, an aged chief who criminally maintained—so the complaint specified—a household containing more than 100 wives. After a few months emissaries of the United Nations reached the venerable Fon to investigate the scandal, and he received them by telling them to mind their own business. The Union of South Africa responds in the same words to the Trusteeship Council and the Fourth Committee when Michael Scott has completed his yearly testimony on affairs inside Southwest Africa.

For many reasons, the capacity of the United Nations to promote effectively the welfare of the people of non-self-governing territories is smaller than that of the old League. The organization is hamstrung by membership blocs and procedural blocks which leave it free to police the narcotic and white slave traffics but very little else. More fundamentally, the good faith of the majority of the members of the organization can certainly be questioned, and this could not be said of the membership of the League until the 1930's. Except spasmodically in the delegations of a few smaller countries, there is no will anywhere to regard the United Nations as an embryo from which a World Confederation will evolve to assume the responsibilities of war and peace. Considering the delinquency of the Great Powers in this respect, this is too much to ask—but is it too much to ask that the daily routine of the organization cease to be paralyzed by incredible, mind-numbing doses of official cynicism; interminable speeches caroming around the walls, clichés rattling the window-panes, lies and smiles exchanging beyond enumeration—all of this with an eye to the marginal effect of this noise back home in the local newspapers or party headquarters? Ironically, generally the most sincere, if hidebound, representatives at the United Nations are those of the Great Powers, though they must combat their personal despair at this dead-ending of their careers; for the rest, the pleasures of New York must make up for the perils of remoteness from the home town power plays. Michael Scott—and plaintiffs like him—could be Angels Gabriel expressing the views of the All-Highest on the Hereros, and they would be wasting their time in New York.

Nevertheless, though the United Nations may be but a feeble and mediocre reed, the claims in Southwest Africa to which it is the legatee were purchased on many battlefields with the lifeblood of millions of Allied soldiers. The Germans and Afrikaners who are now lording it over the territory are no friends of the spirit in which these young men died—and, indeed, their sanctimonious references to the pioneering hardships by which they say they earned this lordship are ludicrous. The rights of the United Nations are almost negligible —no more than the right to receive regular reports from the administering power and, if necessary, to chide the administering power. But small as this right is, the Afrikaner has ridden it down. He anticipates, in the Union and in his "fifth province," that the debility of the world community and the indifference of the American Republic will preserve for him the time he needs to poison the politics of Africa and gamble with the destiny of the West.

* * *

In the Union itself and in Southwest Africa the Afrikaner is trampling on the racial sensibilities of nine-tenths of the world and the solidarity of the Western coalition. When he casts covetous eyes at the High Commission territories of Bechuanaland, Basutoland, and Swaziland he is directly affronting the peace of Africa. And because two of these lands, Swaziland and Basutoland, are entirely surrounded by the Union, and the third, Bechuanaland, constitutes the greater part of the Union's northern frontier, this covetousness is not necessarily academic. The Afrikaner regards the High Commission lands as geographical anomalies—which they are. He also regards them as political anomalies—an unfavorable comment on his own political capacities made by Great Britain, his erstwhile Commonwealth partner. He is determined to see their status altered. As with Southwest Africa, he aims at their ultimate incorporation within a Greater Union.

The High Commission countries are Africa at its least developed, and socially have remained almost entirely in the tribal stage. Of the three, Bechuanaland is by far the largest in area, a vast domain of arid plain and scrub, extending over some 275,000 square miles, often employed as a symbol of "empty Africa," inhabited by some 300,000 Africans clustered in relatively good-sized, but widely scattered villages. Basutoland and Swaziland are smaller, far more densely populated highlands; the former has a population of about 600,000; the latter about 200,000. Only a few thousand Europeans, working in missions, hospitals, and stations, live in the territories. These are cattle raising and sheep raising economies, supplemented by back yard agriculture. But Bechuanaland boasts a minor mining industry, and Swaziland both mining and lumbering industries.

The British established an administration of Bechuanaland and Basutoland for the first time in the 1880's, for the dual purpose of keeping open the northward corridor between German Southwest Africa on the west and the Dutch Republics on the East and to check the further expansion of Afrikaner race ideas into Central Africa. In contrast, at the turn of the century Swaziland had been ruled for ten years or so by Kruger's government; the British assumed its "protection" as one of the terms of the treaty that ended the Boer War; and in 1907 its government was transferred to the "High Commission" which was already running the other two.

The three territories are all poor and primitive, without large centers or industries, neither requiring from nor yielding up any large-scale revenues to the responsible authority. From the first, the

British have here gone along with their policy of "indirect rule," under which the High Commissioner, acting through Resident Commissioners, interferes as rarely as possible with the tribal chiefs' independent jurisdictions. In other parts of British Africa, progressive Africans began long ago to chafe under this tolerant system, which tends to perpetuate political medievalisms long after the needs and aspirations of the mass of people for modernization have rendered them irksome and obsolete. But it is probable that the world will have to listen to few petitions on this score from the inhabitants of the High Commission territories; for the alternative to the easy tempos of the High Commissioner is the goosestep of the Union's Minister of Native Affairs.

In one of the articles of the Act of 1909 which created the Union of South Africa, the vague prospect was held out of a day when the High Commission would be terminated and its responsibilities united with the government of the Union, and from this time forward the Afrikaner has never ceased to agitate about the matter and to urge that these enclaves of Victorian imperialism in such intimate proximity to himself be given over to him. But as the mood of Afrikanerdom has soured from the relatively reasonable age of Botha and Smuts, the temperature of this agitation has risen correspondingly. There is now a strong feeling of personal resentment that these arbitrary limits have been set to the *Lebensraum* of Afrikanerdom and that High Commission "liberalism" is impeding the rounding out of apartheid in southern Africa.

Officially, the Union Government regards the three tribal protectorates as "geographically, ethnographically, and economically parts of South Africa and only temporarily excluded from the Union as a result largely of accidental historical and political considerations." The Afrikaner proves this point by demonstrating the economic dependence of the territories on the Union. Perhaps 100,000 workers work in the Union from the territories, joining the army of other hundreds of thousands from Portuguese Africa and the Rhodesias. By permitting these men to send on their earnings to their families at home, and by allowing the territorial administrations a share of the take from the South African Customs Union, the Afrikaner feels that he is supporting the High Commissioner— and, therefore, should have the right to annex the territories. Moreover, the Afrikaner declares that the present setup is old-fashioned and inefficient. Dr. Malan used to reproach the High Commissioner with being "soft on Communism" in the territories, and also with permitting "floods of illegal Indian immigrants" to seep into the Union by way of Swaziland. The fraternal and common-sense thing for the British to do, the Afrikaner declares, is to clear out and permit the Union to turn the three territories into three more Bantustans, adding them to the eight Bantustans now in preparation within the Union itself. Then, by means of passes, taxes, and the other stops on the Afrikaner organ, these 1 million Africans can also contribute their full share to the prosperity and glory of the Volk.

It is unnecessary to describe the reaction of the African chiefs and tribesmen in the territories to this proposition. Many, many times they have begged the British and the world to leave their international status as it is. In 1927 a British officer reported back to London that even an attempt to ascertain the sentiment of the inhabitants toward a change of this kind would result in mass upheaval. The territories would, of course, be absolutely helpless in the face of Afrikaner "reconstruction." Indeed, about one-half of Swaziland is already alienated from the African, as a result of private deals made by Swazi chiefs of the last century. About one-half of Bechuanaland is listed as Crown land, which could be alienated with a flick of a pen when and if the Queen's sovereignty is replaced by that of a President of the South African Republic. The Africans know their peril, but up to now they have only been able to secure a promise from the British that no alteration in status will take place without a "consultation" of the inhabitants of the territories. However, their strongest safeguard is not this promise but the present mood of the British people, who do not like the Afrikaner and do not trust him.

But the English have their problems, too. First, the considerable English-speaking population in South Africa *is* a valued component of the Commonwealth, linked by bonds of social and financial interest to the homeland. Until the moment that the Afrikaners take the final, conclusive step out of the Commonwealth they can—as they are in fact doing—use the welfare of this group as a bribe wherewith to purchase various kinds of deals from the London government. It would be unfair to underrate the temptations of this bribe.

Second, if it so chooses the Union government can make the administration of the protectorates very costly, if not altogether impracticable. For example, it can interrupt communications, impound credits, forbid the annual migrations of laborers. Already the High Commissioner has shown that on small issues he is willing to compromise with the Afrikaner. When one of the chiefs of Bechuanaland, Seretse Khama, married an Englishwoman while studying in London in September, 1949, he was suspended from his tribal functions after representations from the governments of Southern Rhodesia and South Africa. There were, in addition, other elements in this case. The original complainant was Seretse's uncle Tshekedi, who had been ruling undisturbed for some twenty-three years as regent and apparently wished to continue to do so indefinitely. But there is no question that the deposition was mainly in response to the hysterical objections emanating from the neighboring white settler countries. (It was an unfortunate precedent for the early, formative years of a Commonwealth the overwhelming majority of whose membership is nonwhite. Probably if a similar case ever arises again the Colonial Office will take a different line.)

Third, the existing "indirect rule" administration, infinitely preferable as it is to Bantustan, cannot be prolonged forever. The territorial populations are booming, and the cost of the rehabilitation and development projects needed to fit more of the sun-baked immensities of Bechuanaland for human settlement is quite beyond the resources of the High Commissioner. The great migration of young Bechuanas to the industries of South Africa, amounting almost to an annual depopulation, is a measure of the failure of their own lands to support them. The existing structures of village, chief, and tribal powwow cannot exploit the large but stubborn potentialities of the territory. But these old ways are breaking down anyway, under the weight of their incompetence to face all the other problems of Africa in the modern world; the Seretse incident was only one case of this. The British are caught in a very troublesome crossfire: between their own advanced Commonwealth ideal, the belligerence of the Afrikaner, and the profound decay of the old Africa. They are doing their best in the situation: in September

1959 a constitution was granted Basutoland by Queen Elizabeth II, which provides for early elections on a basis amounting to universal suffrage.

If the Colonial Office had the money to do it, it would really go to work on the economies of the High Commission territories in an effort to make them centers of genuine self-government and industrial progress in southern Africa. This, of course, the Afrikaner would object to even more strenuously than he objects to their present lackadaisical condition. But the British government no longer commands funds of this dimension for colonial development, and therefore must rest content with fulfilling its negative function of limiting the spread of apartheid. This they can and will do on their own, without requiring American moral support; the British are still capable of defending their own against the Afrikaner. But they certainly could make good use of some American money.

5. The Federation of the Rhodesias and Nyasaland

In no place in Africa is the white man's failure so deplorable, so hard for the outsider to pardon, as in the Federation of the Rhodesias and Nyasaland.

The auguries were unprecedentedly propitious. After World War II the world was at last weary of the Race Question, and all the Superbias and Nemeses associated with the Race Question. It was ready to think of itself in a fresh light, as a newly breeched master of marvelous new physical and metaphysical powers. If there must be contention between men, at least let it rage around the Yalta Agreements, or something of that nature, not the energy-draining, boring, mind-freezing clichés of yellow, black, red, and white. In England itself, both parties—Conservative and Labour—agreed on the desirability of a mooring place in Central Africa to whose strength and tranquillity the aimless, muddy politics of the continent should attach themselves. Let the gold miners' and bond speculators' empire vanish into the past, to be replaced by something which was part modern and part a resurrection of great, but long disused ideals of the old "West." Bantu and European were to be forgiven their unlikenesses, and a "partnership"—that concept that has meant so much to philosophers but so little to history—was to be practically fabricated by the most skillful and experienced legal draftsmen in the world. It was all to be a showcase of magisterial British political arts and highmindedness. And the whole of this massive dreaming and machinery—the whole opportunity to create in the Rhodesias something which had never existed before under the sun—it all came to nothing, because on the spot in Africa were some 200,000-odd colonial Europeans, like so many teredos ready to sink the ship before she was fairly launched.

Perhaps it will be good for us to look for a moment at the ideas of the men who actually created the Empire. In going through state papers of the nineteenth century a man is often surprised at the "progressive" tones to which our great-grandfathers were accustomed; the misadventures of the twentieth century have dispirited a good part of our generation, and made skeptics of another good part, but our great-grandfathers were as often as not *enlightened*— in the best and most naïve sense of that word. They were so much weaker when it came to moving mountains than we are; but at least the landscape they lived in was familiar to them, and they knew which mountains ought to be moved and which left alone. (We sometimes forget that it was from the Royal Commission reports and the Blue Books of the early factory inspectors that Karl Marx obtained most of the data he used in *Capital;* in other words, Marx was not the only man in Europe trying to understand and to humanize the New Era.)

Of course, the Empire was largely an extemporization, and it was not until January, 1883, in a famous speech at Adelaide, when the Earl of Rosebery prophesied a "commonwealth" of equal, self-governing comrade nations, that a form of permanent association for all these far-flung and heterogeneous dominions—which in our day has become *the* form—became dimly visible deep down in the pools of possibility and time. But long before this great moment the best men in England had conducted themselves by a code of virtues and aspirations (and exalted enthusiasms) which has been almost totally neglected in contemporary discussions of imperialism —and, it is only fair to say, pretty well junked in practice in the two or three generations before the Second World War. For example, in 1812 we find Warren Hastings advising a friend who is going off to India in these terms: "Among the natives of India, there are men of as strong intellect, as sound integrity, and as honourable feelings as any of this Kingdom . . . by your example make it the fashion among our countrymen to treat them with courtesy and as participators in the same equal rights with themselves." Six years later one of Hastings' successors as governor-general explains with a touch of vanity why he believes in his job: "We have bestowed blessings upon millions. . . . Nothing can be more delightful than the reports I receive of the sensibility manifested by the inhabitants to this change in their circumstances. . . . Multitudes of people have . . . come from the hills and fastnesses in which they had sought refuge for years and have reoccupied their ancient deserted villages. The ploughshare is again in every quarter turning up a soil which had for many seasons never been stirred, except by the hoofs of predatory cavalry."

This is all very well, but at the same time what were the actual bases of the laws? We are astonished to find that they were equally "liberal." By the terms of the Charter Act of 1833, for example, there was to be no discrimination of employment under the East India Company by "reason only of religion, place of birth, descent, colour, or any of them." In the same year, a Parliamentary Committee resolved that: "It is recognized as an indisputable principle, that the interests of the Native Subjects are to be consulted in preference to those of Europeans, whenever the two come in competition." Two generations later, even after the Mutiny had poisoned race feelings in India and the Empire was set on its long decline from which the Commonwealth has rescued it, Lord Ripon as viceroy could issue a statute like the so-called Ilbert Bill of 1883, which removed "every judicial disqualification which is based merely on race distinctions," and which in some cases gave Indian judges the right to try Europeans. It was a bird of ill-omen when Englishmen residents in India protested so violently against this measure that the Imperial Government withdrew and revised it, but when Ripon completed his tour of duty and left for home thousands upon thousands of the Queen's Indian subjects cheered and wept him down to his ship. (I have taken these points from the history of the Raj in India to illustrate this aspect of the imperial idea because for various reasons Africa never got her rightful share of "enlighten-

ment." Nevertheless, the best was still very good. We can remember
the heartbreaking query of an old African chief when he was first
told that the British were returning the Transvaal to the Afrikaners
after Majuba: "When I was a child, the Matabele came, they swept
over us like the wind and we bowed before them like the long
white grass on the plains. They left us and we stood upright again.
The Boers came and we bowed ourselves under them in like manner. The British came and we rose upright, our hearts lived within
us and we said: Now we are the children of the Great Lady. And
now that is past and we must lie flat again under the wind—who
knows what are the ways of God?")

We have taken this trouble to review some of the principles of
the men who made the Empire precisely because it was men like
these who *did* make the Empire—not the bragging and whining
softies-toughies who have settled down in the Rhodesias and elsewhere and refuse to curb their selfishnesses and greeds. Admittedly,
even in the best of days these high imperial moralities must have
been more honored in the breach than the observance. There is
dross in every one of us; and doubtless the highflying Victorian
confidence in railroads, say, seems pretty specious today. But
without some high tone to act as a partial weed killer there is soon
no way of telling human society from a kind of peculiarly treacher-
ous and nauseating jungle. Actually, what are the white settlers
in Africa suffering, and what reasonable thing do they want, that
the world is expected to sympathize with them? They want to
keep what they have and—if possible—grab more. Probably each
one of us can say the same about himself—but we hardly regard
this as one of humanity's more admirable traits, and certainly no
justification for systematic plundering.

The European-at-large first became aware of the Lake Nyasa and
upper Zambezi regions in the 1850's and 1860's with the magnificent
antislavery expeditions of David Livingstone—a man remarkable his
life long for his extraordinary affection for Africans, and for that
matter for the ardor with which Africans returned this affection.
But the real father of the Rhodesias, Cecil Rhodes, came along a
generation later, thrusting up from South Africa on the first step
in his campaign to give the continent a British spine from Capetown

to Cairo. In a personal coup, in the 1880's Rhodes contrived to finesse President Kruger out of Bechuanaland and the famed "missionaries' road" area, and in 1885 he managed to persuade the Imperial Government explicitly to extend its sphere of responsibility into these regions. Four years later, in October, 1889, Rhodes secured a royal charter for his British South Africa Company, by the terms of which he was granted large but indefinite authorization to explore, negotiate treaties, and develop lands on behalf of Her Majesty's Government in the site of the modern Rhodesias.

Then, in 1890, a band of 200 picked men—the "Pioneers"—passed up the "missionaries' road," across the front of tens of thousands of Matabele warriors in a precarious state of pacification, onto the pleasant, rolling plains where now is situated Salisbury, the modern capital of the Federation. While the Pioneers were staking out this practical claim, Rhodes had his agents collecting treaties and cessions from the local chieftains, which enabled him legally—or so he said—to endow each Pioneer upon his arrival with fifteen gold claims and a farm of 3,000 acres. So was planted the seed of Southern Rhodesia, which has so flourished in sixty years that it is now—next to South Africa—the most populous and prosperous "white man's" country in Africa.

When the Pioneers entered Central Africa in 1890 Black Africa was still dark and black. There was no settled, indigenous civilization there; to Europeans the region appeared like a vacuum qualified by chaos; in the name of common sense and humanitarianism both, any measure which the European adopted to subdue or develop the land seemed to be justified by necessity. Specifically, in the Rhodesias the European stumbled upon the fragments of a complex breakup of the Zulu nation which followed on its defeat by the Afrikaners and ejection from South Africa, but fragments which retained the warriorlike habits of the Zulus in their prime: the Matabele, Barotses, and two or three others who lived by preying on passive tribes like the Mashona. In Nyasaland the British ran into another tribe, the Yao, which lived by raiding their neighbors and selling them as slaves to the Arabs and Portuguese. The cruelty of some of these tribesmen, and of the King of the Matabele in particular, was a prodigy—or so it struck the contemporary Englishman. Thus, it seemed only right to introduce the "torch of culture

and progress" to these benighted and unplowed kingdoms, these
"abode[s] of barbarism and cruelty," and in this way, as Lord
Lugard was fond of putting it, to repay the Romans for introducing
the English to civilization in Celtic times. In Africa it took only
a few years to write off the Roman debt. After a number of negotiations at cross-purposes—similar to those by which the white man
"purchased" the Great Plains from the Sioux—during which the
principal chiefs grew increasingly puzzled and restless, the Matabele
rose up and took to the warpath. They were smashed in 1893; the
next year Lobengula, their last king, died in the bush. Southern
Rhodesia was definitively white man's country.

The invariable first impression garnered by new immigrants to
white man's country is of the insuperable abyss that divides the
Europe from which they have come from the indigenous culture
of their new home. There was an unlikeness in kind between the
Bantu African of the turn of the century and even the lowest dregs
of the London slums which could be overlooked (or absorbed) by
only the most powerful, disengaged spirits, and which seemed to
beg for assurance that a social and cultural merger between the two
was permanently and unassailably inconceivable. In the case of the
Rhodesias this assurance was easy to justify. The Matabele were
parasites and pillagers, who procured their slaves with the greatest
savagery from all the tribes of their vicinity. They had entered
southern Africa itself only a century or so previously; only a half-
century ago they had rebounded against the wall of Afrikanerdom
and come to settle in the Rhodesias proper. They had put down no
roots, erected no permanent villages, instituted no self-generating
or self-regulating society. Their last king, Lobengula, was a man
of redoubtable and legendary bloodthirst, whose favorite recreation
was the prolonged torment of prisoners-of-war. What was there
African on this lofty plateau which it was desirable—or even possible
—to conserve?

No more than in South Africa did the possibility exist of ex-
terminating the Bantu en masse. What had to be done was to transform the Bantu, Matabele as well as Mashona, into "herdsmen and
agriculturalists," under the enlightened supervision of a British
administration which specially developed the concept—for this place
and the rest of British Africa—of the "Dual Mandate." According

to this ruling idea the administration by a superior civilization of an inferior one is justified and repaid by an exchange of political commodities: The British contributed order and the knowledge how to market whatever salable items the territory could produce; the African contributed his title to his lands (whatever that was) plus his willingness to enter into the Western economic nexus. Therefore, the Dual Mandate was a dual agreement in the same sense that an almshouse is a dual agreement. The stated purpose of the almshouse is the shelter and nurture of the poor; the daily schedule and menu are set by the warden.

The only exception we can take to this arrangement—if we deem it worth while at all to judge our forebears—is an intangible one, an exception to (or questioning of) the boisterous self-confidence that was implicit in it. Our grandfathers did not palsy themselves with self-doubt. They never reflected that a Martian tourist might be unable to spot the moral distinctions between the Thirty Years' War, the life of a London chimney sweep in the 1840's, and the gruesome kraal of King Lobengula. The indisputable reality was, that in the 1890's the Bantu had been defeated and demoralized by a superior arms technology, and this had left a vacuum into which—without bothering about it any further—something had to move. Naturally, it was the superior European society: the European governors and magistrates who sent reports to, and received instructions from, Europe; European commercial routines which were intertwined with these European political interests; and, so soon as a sufficient number of white settlers had moved into the colony that talk of self-government began to be heard, European concepts of political liberalism extending to the European section of the population.

This was not an educational process for the African but an estranging one, for the further the colony developed the further it developed along European lines and the further away from the African bystanders on the sidelines. When the Matabele promised to give up raiding and to live on Reservations, they had no way of appealing from dishonest surveyors who imposed on the well meaning government by assigning to the Africans the worst land of the territory; and, in a generation, when this inequity became a pressing matter, it was too late to rectify it without challenging the property rights of half the European residents. Moreover, when the Matabele signed their copy of the Dual Mandate contract by permitting themselves to lose the crucial battles of their war, they were not told that in ten or twenty years hence the chief part of this bargain would be interpreted by their white neighbors as being a readiness to labor for the prosperity of white Rhodesia. Perforce the Matabele, and the other African tribes, retreated to the miserable Reservations which had been set aside for them, but they soon learned that this was not all that was wanted. A new tone, a new querulousness entered the picture to the effect that the African was still not doing his full part. One of the most active, if not the most spiritual, of imperial statesmen, Lord Milner, expressed the new look in 1901: "I have never shared the objections, which are so strongly felt at home, to a well-regulated system of state compulsion, whereby natives of a certain age, fit for labour and not otherwise engaged in it, should be compelled to do a certain number of months' work every year, under proper securities of good treatment and for adequate remuneration. . . . The black man is naturally inclined, much more than the white, to do nothing at all." Where now was the Great Lady who let men hold their heads high? Where was the principle that "natives' " welfare must in all cases predominate over every other consideration?

The Federation that was put together in 1953, after many years of planning and discussion, joined together three very different territories.

Southern Rhodesia was the oak from the original pioneering in 1890 of Rhodes's selected acorns. By 1923, when the British Crown annexed it from the Company and Southern Rhodesia became a self-governing colony, it had a European population of about 34,000, which supported itself by mining, ranching, and tobacco farming. By 1953 this number had zoomed to 155,000 as a result of healthy natural increase plus a most energetic immigration program. (In 1960 there are about 211,000 Europeans in Southern Rhodesia; about 2,600,000 Africans.) But during the forties this substantial expansion of the population, plus lavish government expenditures and hardening markets for Southern Rhodesia's produce, had involved the country in some fairly severe financial tangles. At the time of

Federation the public debt of the ex-colony was about $370 millions, about six times the public debt of Northern Rhodesia at the time, more than twenty times that of Nyasaland. The proximity of South Africa had also been steadily nibbling on its morale—indeed, one of the principal motives of the British Government in fomenting the Federation was the hope that in this way Southern Rhodesia could be permanently swung out of South Africa's orbit. Increasingly stringent apartheid measures had become more and more a part of the colony's legal and civil system. And the Europeans had all but cornered the franchise: in the elections of 1953, 47,000 Europeans voted, 429 Africans—and this ratio did not change in the elections of 1958. Lastly, 50 per cent of the land of Southern Rhodesia has been alienated to whites, and that which remains to the African is the inferior half—low, hot, infested with tsetse fly.

Until our own generation the second member of the new Federation, Northern Rhodesia, had been a very primitive colony, administrated as a "protectorate" since its formation out of two predecessor protectorates in 1911. But in the 1920's Europeans began to dig into the hillsides of the Copper Belt, where the northwestern sector of Northern Rhodesia marches with the Katanga province of the Belgian Congo, and although she has still failed to attract substantial European colonizers aside from mine operators and their families (most of her land is paternally guarded by the protectorate administration) everything has now changed in Northern Rhodesia. She is the second largest copper-producing nation in the world. Her industry has mushroomed to more than twenty times its prewar dimensions, and this modernization—featuring in particular the power grid which the new Kariba Dam installations will lay down over the whole of the country—has transformed the economy and society of Central Africa. More than 65 per cent of the total income tax revenues of the Federation come from Northern Rhodesia, the vast bulk of this contributed by the copper companies. More than 60 per cent of the value of the Federation's exports derives from copper. The activity surrounding the new mining centers has given the territory a sort of frontier air of raw vitality, with new towns like Ndola and Kitwe flashing new buildings and new promotions on every side. From all over the area Africans come to work in the mines, where (partly because of the huge

American interests here) they may live in family units instead of the compounds of South Africa. In 1924 there were only 4,000 Europeans in Northern Rhodesia; at the time of Federation in 1953 about 40,000; in 1960 about 75,000 (against 2,200,000 Africans). Those Europeans not occupied in the mines are mainly farmers— strung out along the railroad that connects the territory to the south.

The third member of the Federation, Nyasaland, has been a British protectorate since 1891. She is smaller in area than her fellows, but the most densely populated of the three, with a population of about 2,700,000 Africans and 9,000 Europeans. She is a poor, but occasionally very lovely country of slopes and lakesides, with a humid low-lying southern basin; an agricultural country specializing in tobacco and tea and the subsistence croppings of her huge African population. (In neither Nyasaland nor Northern Rhodesia is land alienation a problem, because of their "protected" status.)

The Federation which wedded these three territories was there- fore—on paper, at least—a more balanced entity than any of them alone, a state in which 300,000 whites balance off 7,500,000 Africans; and in which one very profitable industry balances off a modest modern economy on the one hand and an extremely backward one on the other. It was the achievement of this pleasant equilibrium which was the aim of the plan of 1953. Given the disagreeable surprises that are always lurking in the African bush, for politicians and businessmen alike, the idea of steadying oneself with larger and more diversified administrations is a very tempting one, and as we can see in the north the African leaders are as tempted by this idea as Europeans. A "Central African Federation" was also the best way to seal off the Union of South Africa from any expansion- ist ideas, which—after the pre-Nationalist truce of the Smuts-Hertzog years—is now as much an aim of British policy as it was in the nine- teenth century. But, even taking these things into consideration, the decisive motive for Federation was the financial hole in which the most important of the territories—from the home government's point of view—found itself in the 1940's. No one wished to see Southern Rhodesia compelled into closer and closer association with South Africa because of sheer economic need. What was desired was the consolidation of a viable nucleus of British influence in Central Africa that could open welcoming arms to the new concept of the Commonwealth, offset Afrikaner influence, befriend the new African states, and ease similar independence arrangements in British East Africa. Northern Rhodesia had a negligible European population, but a full treasury. Southern Rhodesia had an exceptionally well established white settlement, but for more or less temporary reasons an empty treasury. And to add to this duo—canceling the weaknesses and adding to the strengths of each component, so the constitution-makers hoped—there was Nyasaland, a very backward province which regularly contributed a huge labor force to the copper mines.

But when it came to designing the Federation's legal structure, the British found that in addition to "balancing" it was necessary to make formal allowances for wide differences in social preferences and cultural level—they found, in fact, that the task was beyond even their famous ability to house blatant contradictions within the same act of legislation. At the time of Federation, Southern Rhodesia's husky white population had governed itself for thirty years. They could be asked to accept nothing less than a continuance of this self-government. There was nothing the British could do about the fact that while exercising these rights of self-government for so long the Southern Rhodesian European had been voluntarily approximating to Afrikaner apartheid ideals, which made teaming him up with overwhelmingly African states a very awkward business. He could not even be asked to accept a tripartite structure under which each province would have an equal say in the Federal government—because of course under this arrangement Southern Rhodesia someday might be outvoted by the two northern, "black" states. The only concession the European of Southern Rhodesia would make was to an arrangement whereby the responsibilities of the Northern Rhodesian and Nyasaland administrations which were specifically concerned with African society—such as education and social welfare—would remain in the jurisdiction of the Colonial Office, and thus in this sense the "protectorate" status of these territories would survive their inclusion within the Federation; to the Federal government was given authority in matters such as foreign and defense affairs. Moreover, the constitution was so designed that in the Federal Parliament Southern Rhodesia has what amounts to a free hand (the same goes, of course, for European constituencies over African ones).

Whether this was the wisest of possible constitutions for this experimental federal creation no one will ever know—for it has already signally failed to earn the loyalty of the overwhelming majority of the people whom it governs and its replacement, the upcoming revision of 1960, will be even less successful. It is a tragedy that its designers felt compelled to incorporate so many compromises into the edifice they were rearing with such great hopes just to placate the Southern Rhodesian minority, because it is of course just these compromises which have destroyed its chances of winning and helping the African. After all, the Northern Rhodesian and the Nyasalander see everywhere around them the surrender of imperial sovereignty and the rising up of free African nations, which with almost no rancor at all then take an equal place at the Commonwealth table. It is not surprising that the African in the Rhodesias would like for himself the opportunities that have come the way of the Ghanaian and Nigerian. But smack in the road is Southern Rhodesia, which became "free" a generation past, but not free for Africans. By yoking Northern Rhodesia and Nyasaland to Southern Rhodesia the British have erected what they know perfectly well cannot endure; they are flouting the wise and idealistic policies they evolved for Ghana and other states; they are pretending to be able to cut off from self-government more or less forever about 5 million Africans. The Northern Rhodesian African feels with a good deal of justice that "his" mines are paying the bills of a Federation whose anti-African policies are growing more onerous every day; the Nyasalander feels that it is "his" labor that is working the mines. They never wanted to be affiliated with Southern Rhodesia, and in 1953 their leaders protested as vociferously as they knew how—but no one heeded them, and here they are, stuck. Their only hope is to make such a hullabaloo before constitutional revision time comes round in 1960 that the British government will see the futility of the arrangement and dismember the Federation into its old parts, which can then start afresh. This is what the Africans are now doing, but as we saw in the Blantyre riots of the spring of 1959 this kind of hullabaloo can be a bloody business—and perhaps even boomerang. The best thing that can be said for the whole affair is that British drafters of the original constitution knew the risks they were running, looked at their probable failure with eyes open, could not—or would not—pressure the Southern Rhodesian white, but still went ahead and tried anyway.

It remains to say a little about the group that has the upper hand under the present Federal constitution, the Southern Rhodesian white. Whence the majority of white men who settle in Africa get the idea that here they can behave themselves in a fashion they never could get away with in their home countries—and whence they obtain their hardness of heart, and the willingness to see more and more of their lives wasted in stubbornly, crassly carrying through these affectations—these are all psychological mysteries which are still unplumbed. Lord Hailey has written of the "inadequate responses" of African peoples to Africa; it might be interesting if someone undertook a study of the white man's "inadequate responses" to Africa. In any case, "partnership" and "multiracial society" were never anything but empty phrases to the average Southern Rhodesian white, which he accepted only so long as they cost him nothing.

In Southern Rhodesia, like the Union, the African is subject to a host of discriminatory and hostile legislation like pass laws, laws against drinking any spirits but weak beer, and so forth. Granted that things are not so bad as they are in the Union, the newspapers and conversations are still overloaded with stories about the inferiority of Africans: the African man who tries to get something to eat in a "white" restaurant; first he is slapped by a waitress, then he is punched by one of the other patrons; finally the police are called and they cart him away. In August, 1959, *The New York Times* ran an account which perfectly epitomizes the hopelessness of "partnership." The first African physician in the service of the Federal government, a Dr. Samuel Parerenyatwa, was given a post in which he had, from time to time, to perform autopsies on whites; this upset the white community, and the doctor was removed from this post. He was then shifted to the position of medical-officer-in-charge of a 190-bed hospital in the Antelope Mine area of Southern Rhodesia, where there are 600 Europeans and 51,000 Africans. The hospital is for Africans, but the medical officer in charge of the hospital is also expected to take care of the few Europeans in the vicinity. However, as a white lady expressed herself, "It is going too far to expect women patients to accept a black doctor." The last news on the episode was that the Federal Minister of Health publicly announced that he would consider making new arrangements. (What is never told in such stories as this one, but what gives them their real poignance, is the fantastic hardships in the way of this man's achieving his medical degree in the first place.)

Then there was the "Borrowdale incident" of the fall of 1958. For some time the government had been concerned about 18,000-odd Africans working as domestics in the wealthy northern suburbs of Salisbury, because the only recreational facilities available to them on their days off were situated in African townships far to the south. Eventually the government decided to buy land for an African recreational area somewhere on the north side. The first landowner approached objected with full vigor and self-righteousness; naturally he contributed all his arguments to the newspapers. Then a rumor swept the prosperous village of Borrowdale that the odious improvement was to be foisted on their community. An "indignation meeting" was immediately called, at which red-faced orators delineated at great length the prospect of bands of drunken Africans from the beerhalls overrunning the quiet lawns of Borrowdale and attacking white mothers. Also, of course, property values would crumble. Then there was the certainty, sooner or later, of miscegenation. One remarkable man rose from somewhere to say that so far the discussion had been perfectly frivolous, because it was ignoring the realities of this situation on the north side where there were not even latrines available to Africans over large areas, let alone playgrounds. This man was roundly booed by the congregation, but he persisted by saying something about the African's being entitled to some "family life." Now he had gone too far. "What about Europeans?" shouted a corps of hecklers. "This is taking away our family life!" Our hero had to sit down. At the end of the meeting, as a coda, the chairman, an attendant at a local gas station, requested the few participants who had voted against the resolution attacking the recreation ground to rise, "so that we can see who they are."

This all sounds horribly familiar, and I am certainly not suggesting that we Americans are a strain of men entirely above ugly noises and attitudes such as these. But remember that Borrowdale is in Africa, not Alabama; the white man in the Federation is out-numbered twenty-four to one; Africa is the African's by virtue of this disproportion alone, and it is ridiculous to talk about "white man's country" in a place which is so manifestly "black man's." This is to discount the purely ethical factors more than I think we ought to do, but remember too that in Southern Rhodesia even the government itself does not pay lip service to the "partnership" ideal which is its basic premise, but has also come down 100 per cent on the side of Alabamaism.

The clearest instance of this was the recent Nyasaland trouble. In January, 1959, the Federal government began to receive reports (or so it says) of "secret meetings" being held in the forests of Nyasaland preparatory to a general massacre of the white settlers. They informed the Colonial Secretary in London of the conspiracy. (After everything was over the Colonial Secretary passed the news on to Parliament, but as neither he nor the Rhodesian government had ever possessed a shred of real evidence about these "secret meet-ings" he was severely mauled by his legislative peers. Ultimately he was forced to agree to appoint an investigatory commission, and they also were unable to uncover any evidence.) But by February the Africans were demonstrably stirring, though it occurred to no one to reflect that—desperate as the Africans of Nyasaland were, and are, to dissolve the tie with Southern Rhodesia—their time for unequivocally making their feelings clear was growing short. Any-way, European cars began to be stoned on the highways, mobs gathered around the airfields and interfered with take-offs and sang their party songs and slogans; casual passers-by began to insult Europeans walking in the streets of the major towns. When larger mobs formed, which attempted to liberate prisoners from the local jails, the Federal government acted. Sir Roy Welensky, Prime Min-ister of the Federation and an honest, bluff man who wants to see his Federation work but has no idea of how to do so, moved fast—far too fast. He first ordered tear gas attacks and bayonet charges on the African mobs; and when the local forces proved to be in-adequate for the job he called in six or seven regiments from South-ern Rhodesia and Tanganyika armed with jet planes, machine guns, and armored cars. He banned the Nyasaland African National Congress, though, as I say, no one ever demonstrated a clear connection between the Congress and the disorders. Singing the Congress song was forbidden. The leader of the Congress, Dr. Hastings Banda, who had recently returned to Nyasaland after a (self-imposed) exile of nearly forty years, was arrested, although he had remained inside his house during the whole affair. All in all, about 100 persons were killed in the business—all Africans.

This was the story in Nyasaland, where the Africans unquestionably were building up to mass violence. But Sir Roy moved also in the other two provinces, where there had been no open trouble at all. A white Labourite member of the British House of Commons, who had been visiting the Federation on a lecture tour, was arrested in Northern Rhodesia and deported to England. His crime had been making speeches to Africans in which he delivered himself of sentiments like, "I would like you to know that the British Labour movement would like you to look upon this as a joint struggle," "We are all in this together," and "Lift your heads high and behave as though the country belongs to you." Whether the government of the Federation possesses the right to arrest and deport a member of the Westminster Parliament who has not broken any specific statute still dwells among the unresolved controversies of the affair. But it did not pass without notice that Sir Roy and his government conducted themselves as if *Northern Rhodesia*, which is presumably still a partial protectorate where the rights of the people are still hedged about by British safeguards, were no more than a northern extension of the long self-governing Southern Rhodesia. In any case martial law was declared in Southern Rhodesia before it was in Nyasaland. Censorship was imposed over the whole Federation. At two o'clock in the morning about 250 leaders of the Southern Rhodesian African National Congress, where there had been almost no trouble at all, were routed out of bed and taken off to detention, incommunicado. When reporters inquired of Sir Roy about the occasion of these comprehensive measures he explained that they were necessary because he had (never-revealed) proof that the Congresses of all three territories had been involved in the conspiracy together (thereby belying the traditional white-settler view that the African is congenitally incapable of coordinated political action), the roots of which were to be directly traced to the pan-African All-African People's Conference held at Accra in the previous December and to Russian Communism (this last allusion for the benefit of chance American auditors).

This Nyasaland incident—fortunately no bloodier than it was but unfortunately not quite the last word on the subject—was the fulfillment of the prophecy that African leaders in the Federation had made from the beginning—that given her head, with the shield of the London Colonial Office removed, Southern Rhodesia meant to employ the Federation as a mask behind which to Afrikanerize the northern territories. Long before violence was even the issue the Africans were able to present more than enough proof of this intent. In November, 1958, for example, Sir Roy Welensky requested the London Colonial Office to put off changes in the constitution of Northern Rhodesia which would have doubled the number of Africans on the territorial Legislative Council; this was a concrete violation of the Federation principle that the political development of the two northern African territories was not to be interfered with or hindered by the Southern Rhodesian whites. Such promises as these mean nothing in Africa; it is almost impossible any more to believe anything a white settler says, and if you happen to be an African you would be a fool to. The European society and government of Southern Rhodesia are visibly hardening their racial attitudes with force. They attacked the pathetic, sophomoric political movements of Northern Rhodesia and Nyasaland as if they were the battalions of a formidable aggressor. Any brotherliness, any patience, understanding, cordiality, or readiness for self-sacrifice— such as compatriots are supposed to feel for each other, if not human beings in general—absolutely do not exist. The mildest possible comment is that of Lord Hailey, that "partnership is more an aspiration than a policy." Mr. H. M. Nkumbula, president of the Northern Rhodesian African National Congress, puts it more succinctly: "Partnership has failed." And Mr. H. B. Chipembere, a member of the Nyasaland Legislative Council, puts it still more succinctly and ominously: "Every white man is now the enemy of every African in Nyasaland." But the Africans' only nonviolent chance is to outtalk Sir Roy Welensky at the constitutional revision talks in 1960 on the alien ground of Lancaster House in London, convincing the British government to admit their mistake and to resume their former full responsibilities in Nyasaland and Northern Rhodesia. (And, of course, even if they accomplish this feat, they will not have done anything to aid the Africans of Southern Rhodesia.)

Economically, new people and new businesses and big money have brought a real glow of prosperity to the Federation, particularly around the mines of Northern Rhodesia and a fast growing secondary industry in Southern Rhodesia, which has been sufficient to warm even the African to some extent. In the years 1953 to 1957 the annual per capita income of the African in the Federation rose by about 40 per cent. (This brought him up to $35 a year; the same figure for the European reads $1,500.) But it is practically certain that this is largely an ephemeral advance, because it has been accompanied by a steep rise in the cost of living plus a notable slowdown in urban employment and general business activity since the massive decline in copper prices in 1957. (Also, the time for paying debts—rather than just incurring them—has now arrived.) Due as much as anything to the American ownership of one of the two biggest mining companies of Northern Rhodesia, the African Mineworkers' Union there is one of the best organized and most potentially powerful African organizations on the continent. But, here again, its effectiveness as a check and balance is mortgaged to the threat that constantly hangs over it of arbitrary governmental suppression. And, perhaps even more important, to the hostility of the 4,000-member European Mineworkers' Union, which strikes the mines—as it did in the fall of 1958—whenever it begins to fear that the Africans are advancing beyond the "semiskilled" category which is the basis of an informal agreement between the parties. An increasingly partial and wary European government will, as time goes on, take its cue increasingly from these white miners, so far as mine wages and conditions are concerned.

Indeed, it is this incurable, self-feeding process of hostility growth which is at the center of things in the Rhodesias—and especially Southern Rhodesia—expressing itself in a hundred ways from platitudes about the African's intractable juvenility to tightening up the pass and curfew laws. What can an American do in the face of a spiritual decay of so extreme a character that these people themselves are destroying the concept—"partnership"—which they themselves invented, and which in bleak actuality proffers them their only chance to survive in Africa? And how quickly and rabidly this decay has acted on them. Consider the case of Lord Malvern, the principal founder and first prime minister of the Federation. In 1953 Malvern warned his countrymen, "The only way Europeans can survive in Africa is to get on with Africans and make them friends. . . . The African must be given a chance, otherwise the European would have to leave Africa." And only six years later, after the 1959 riots in Nyasaland had broken out, Malvern told the House of Lords in London that all Africans are liars "until they are very much advanced," and that the "people of the Federation . . . have not the slightest intention of surrendering Nyasaland to destruction by its own people."

And what of the chance the African is supposed to be offered, as a reward for totally repudiating—in the Rhodesias more light-heartedly than anywhere else—his own shapeless and unsatisfactory traditions. He has been willing, even eager, to become, as Malinowsky wrote of him, "a new type of human being, endowed with abilities and energies, with advantages and handicaps, with problems and visions, which neither his European neighbors nor his 'blanket' brother are heirs to." What then? He organizes for himself the most powerful trade union on the continent, which is powerless even to begin to close the huge gap that exists between the African and European mineworker. In Southern Rhodesia—despite the most pressing kind of inequity—there is no prospect of land reform, and the African into the bargain is victimized by ever more humiliating forms of social apartheid. After sixty years of docilely creeping around in the labyrinth of white society the African is still told he must prove himself as a worker, but he is allowed to work only as a menial laborer (and when he is too old to work any more he is told that he has proved nothing because modern times demand managerial skills and international connections which he has not established). And how is he meant to demonstrate his political education, given the present Federal structure dominated by hardbitten white Southern Rhodesians? He fails every test—or so he is told. His leaders and politics are irresponsible; they must be arrested and outlawed, and their assemblies put to the bayonet. His trade union is irresponsible, and if ever it were let off its leading strings it would damage the economy of the country. He has not learned to read—and the government explains that African proposals of a really significant school building program would place too heavy a load on the Federal budget. When he agitates for civil rights in Southern Rhodesia he displays an ignorance of history and psychology; he ought to understand that this province has always shared the racial attitudes of South Africa, which it cannot be expected to alter. He fails and fails, because he does not understand that the "chance" Lord Malvern referred to—and the "rights" which the older generation of imperialists used to talk about—were only the chance and the rights to sweat and groan and heft a pickax.

What will happen to the Federation?

One proposal, recently put forward by the Dominion Party, a new rightist group in Southern Rhodesia, suggests that the Copper Belt be detached from Northern Rhodesia and merged into a Greater Southern Rhodesia; when this has been done the Federation can be liquidated and the rump of Northern Rhodesia and Nyasaland donated back to the Colonial Office. The simplicity of this scheme is somewhat outweighed by its turpitude; but it would be interesting to see if the British taxpayer would love his white Southern Rhodesian cousin to the extent of an annual subsidy of 30 million pounds or so.

The better known, and certainly more respectable if no wiser, policy is that advocated by the Prime Minister, Sir Roy Welensky, whose United Federal Party won a sweeping majority in the Federal Parliament in the elections of November, 1958. That is, simply bull the Federation idea through every obstacle, until sometime—somehow—it takes hold and people stop doubting it and wondering about dissolving it. D-Day for Sir Roy, is, of course, revision time in 1960. What he wants to secure on this date is British recognition of the Federation as a self-governing unit within the Commonwealth (in other words, the termination of the "protectorate" status of Nyasaland and Northern Rhodesia), and he is holding at arm's length every one of his other problems—land reform, a reasonable franchise, the new apartheid mood of Southern Rhodesia—until he has won through these constitutional talks. Sir Roy also understands that American support will be a great asset, both in 1960 and afterward, and this he is going about securing by making himself the busiest Communist-watcher in Africa. For the past two years or so, every speech of Sir Roy's has contained at least one sentence about the Communist agents who are supposed to have honeycombed all the African nationalist movements, and who will unquestionably take over Africa unless the Free World stands stanchly behind its skirmishers in the Dark Continent—naturally, the white settlers of Southern Rhodesia.

The people who will ultimately bring down the Federation are the Africans—but at the moment they are badly placed to do so. Regardless of the conspiratorial details purveyed by the Federal government in the spring of 1959, there is no unity among the four African National Congresses of the Rhodesias (Northern Rhodesia has a spare organization, the Zambia African National Congress). So far the government has not only been able to prevent them from mounting any impressive political offensive, but their own leaderships are riddled with puerile and personal disputes. This is particularly true of the Nyasaland Congress, the party of Dr. Hastings Banda. But none of this comparative political ineptitude impairs in any way Dr. Banda's—and his friends'—powers as demagogues; and it is by means of installing a permanent hatred and resentment of the Federation in the souls of the people that these men plan to gain their ultimate ends. Actually, what else can they do? As we remarked in the section on South Africa, when a government—or a community—deliberately fortifies itself against responding peacefully and conventionally to the majority of its people—and, indeed, goes out of its way to drive that majority mad—then it has only itself to blame when the inevitable blowup comes.

For what it is worth, my own guess is that, unless there is a Labour Government in London at the time of the talks, the British will decide to play along with Sir Roy and the Federationists, and give him more or less what he wants. It is improbable that the African politicians of Northern Rhodesia and Nyasaland will be able to create a stir of riots and window breakings of sufficient volume to dampen the appeal of Sir Roy's oratory. But the new constitution will, of course, be entirely unacceptable to the Africans of the two northern territories—even more so than the one they now live under. And, after all, there are many, many years ahead in the future, in some one of which the Africans will have finally become strong enough to shatter this Federation—with its *ignis fatuus* of "partnership." And they will.

6. Portuguese Africa: Mozambique and Angola

At the shoulders of the Rhodesias, furnishing them with access to the markets of the world through ports on the Atlantic and Indian Oceans, lie two of the oddities of the modern world, the great colonies of Angola and Mozambique, biggest and richest vestiges of the ancient empire of Portugal's mariner-kings. They are oddities for whom no one has a kind word to say, except the Portuguese themselves. To the student of Africa they pose a hundred mysteries: it is not easy to extract data on them from the Portuguese government, and it is not wise to trust the data which are reluctantly yielded up. The ordinary European in Africa, who hopes to keep the turbulent African politician off balance by the breath-taking rate of his modernization and industrialization, the stubborn and procrastinating "paternalism" of their administration sends into frenzies of frustration. To the modern African, of course, the colonies appear as sinkholes of iniquity.

Together, Angola and Mozambique possess a land area more than twenty times that of Portugal's. Their total population is about 10 millions; Portugal's is about 8 millions. The essence of their administrations—as distinguished from the legal formalities—is altogether different from that of any place else in Africa or in the world.

The other colonial powers in Africa have long sought the capital and the mineral resources with which to foster the economic development, if not the settlement, of their lands; they have planted and nurtured cities and industries; they have built roads, airlines, mining camps, and hospitals; they have sought to catch the eye of the world with precious produce, on the revenues from which to support the peculiar way of life of the European-in-Africa. But this is not the Portuguese way. The industrialization of Africa represents nothing but a threat to a colonial power which is herself hardly industrialized and which has maintained at home, intact to a remarkable degree, the hierarchical and tradition-crippled social structure of a bygone era. Hence she has not even surveyed, let alone exploited, the possibilities of her African provinces.

The wealth of Angola, for example, is proverbial in southern Africa (but for all anyone knows quite legendary). One prominent Belgian businessman in the Congo told me that northern Angola is covered with ranges richer in minerals than those of the Katanga; that mountains of copper, gold, cobalt, and tin lie waiting for prospectors and company developers. But the Portuguese officials walk right over them, he went on to say bitterly; they wouldn't stoop over to pick up a gold nugget if they saw it in front of their shoe. While it is true that a few Portuguese corporations which have made their peace with the government—that is to say, which are members of the "family" of the "New State" in Portugal—do operate in Portuguese Africa on terms that resemble those of the state monopolies of Elizabethan times, and are responsible for the changes which have taken place there since the war, Portugal is a poor country, and home-grown capitalists—even if they are government-befriended—are few and far between. Foreign capital, because it always involves prying eyes and soon or later a bit of carping, is not desired. Not only large-scale foreign-investment capital is rebuffed, but in the past the British government, for example, has felt compelled to protest to the Portuguese about the difficulties put in the way of establishing branch offices of—say—English tire manufacturing concerns in the cities of the coast. The Portuguese turn a deaf ear, despite their venerable treaty of alliance with England and what the rest of the world would judge to be their common interest in Africa. They do not believe that anyone besides themselves understands the proper government of Africa—and so far as they are concerned that proper government marches ahead at the dead-slow beat of the Middle Ages.

Therefore, a capital starvation reminiscent of conditions of the precapitalist age characterizes every facet of the economy and society of Portuguese Africa. The only mining enterprise of any moment, the Diamonds of Angola Company, is responsible for but 11 per cent of the value of Angola's exports. The financial health of the provinces depends, in the first instance, not on indigenous industries, but on the geographical good fortune by the mercy of which the most convenient vents for the ores of the Rhodesias and Transvaal are the port cities of Lourenço Marques and Beira in Mozambique and Lobito in Angola, reached by railways through Portuguese territory. Since the war the few significant schemes for colonizing areas of the interior with Europeans, and developing irrigation and development projects for their benefit, have either been abandoned or allowed to wither into virtual abandonment. In spite of the hundreds of years during which the Portuguese have been in occupation in Africa, their colonies are not their "own" to the extent that the Belgians and the British have made "their" Africa their own: Angola has only about 80,000 European residents (4,500,000 Africans); Mozambique 49,000 Europeans (5,500,000 Africans). Aside from the remunerative transit trade we have mentioned, they are backward and agricultural lands, raising their cash crops—coffee for Angola, cotton for Mozambique—on huge plantations run on the style of another world many centuries out of date.

But Portugal is in a different position from the other colonial powers in Africa, for she needs the money that she gets from them to balance her domestic budget. Therefore, like the old East India Company, she must make up in revenues what she cannot obtain by profits. And, as in the rest of "unfree" Africa, the source of needed monies is the African's labor. The African must work, and work where and how he is told, to keep the old machine running—and it is the function of the administration to see that it does run. It is a government by decree, the chain of command running from the Minister of Overseas Provinces in Portugal to the governors-general, and then out to local administrators—in which everyone understands one another and responds evenly enough to the requirements of stated policy, making a high-speed, responsive, modern organization unnecessary. This tacit understanding permeates to the lowest level, for the administrators—whose official salaries are hardly enough for them to live on—are also "advised" by councils composed of representatives of leading local business interests.

The point of it all is a compulsory labor institution which embraces every individual in Portuguese Africa except the Europeans and the approximately 10,000 Africans who have been "assimilated" (and to whom we shall return in a moment). The origin of this system lies back in the 1890's, when the Germans and the British began to eye the desuetude of Portuguese Africa with a certain disfavor mixed with cupidity, and Portugal had to bestir herself in order that she not lose her colonies simply by default. To defend her rights Portugal had to give the appearance of "Europeanizing" the territories, and to do this she had to round up the Africans and put them to work. First, on modern cities, roads, and so forth. Second, in the labor-hungry mines of booming South Africa; in 1909 the Portuguese signed their labor agreement with South Africa, by the terms of which they contracted to "facilitate" the hiring of Africans in Mozambique by South African recruiting agents in exchange for South Africa's routing a large percentage of her seabound traffic through Portuguese East African ports. And in trying to fulfill these domestic and foreign commitments—and to give her colonies something of an air of prosperous bustle—the Portuguese ran up against the African's reluctance to desert his family, home, land, and traditions to go to work for the white man at the white man's terms. As one of the governors-general of Mozambique put it: "The large majority of [Africans] do not work, neither for themselves nor for others, but simply live from the labor of their wives."

As the Portuguese had always justified their occupation of Africa by denominating it a "civilizing mission"—the Europeanization and Catholicization of pagan wastes—it was only necessary to define "work" as the chief feature of "civilization," and then construct a legal system in which force would do what economic incentives had failed to do. The labor code of 1899 proclaims the spirit which has guided the Portuguese administration ever since. It ordains, in part, that "all the natives of the Portuguese Overseas Provinces are subject to the moral and legal obligation of seeking through work the means which they lack for subsisting and for improving their social condition." Of course, the main point of the code is not its principles of morality, but the machinery it sets up for compelling the labor of men who do not care to sell their labor at the going price. And this was a machinery that ground along to an accompaniment of noisome scandals which disturbed the international community and ultimately forced the Portuguese to revise the code in 1928; it was now specified in new ordinances that the African could be forced to work only on projects of public welfare such as roads and harbor works. But these were provisos which the international community was not curious to examine or supervise, and so the Portuguese never really surrendered their old practices; in a few years they had once again publicly claimed the right to force Africans to work at any labor by which they earned the money to pay taxes.

For a detailed study of how Portugal manages to extort this labor from her millions of African dependents without ostentatiously violating the many international compacts against forced labor that she has signed we are much indebted to a young professor from Columbia University, Mr. Marvin Harris, who has recently returned from two years in Mozambique. As we might have expected, Professor Harris explains that the basis of the system is the statutes which make African idleness both immoral and illegal. And, he writes, "today in Mozambique all active males (Africans) between the ages of eighteen and fifty-five are presumed to be 'idle' unless they can prove the contrary." Once it has been thus established that the African must work, it is comparatively easy to determine where he works and at what wages. When required by one of the authorities to prove that he is not idle, the African must present a pass on which is written his employment record. Naturally, if there is any hiatus or discrepancy the African is carried off to the station house. Assuming that he is not a criminal African, but only an idle one, he is now theoretically confronted with three choices. He can find a European employer. He can sign up with one of the South African recruiting agencies who maintain offices in Mozambique. Or the government

will draft him into one of the conscript gangs which are construct-
ing the spacious esplanades and modern docks of the most beautiful
cities in Africa.

In reality, of course, the African has no choice at all, because it is
the government who manipulates these alternatives like so many
puppet strings, directing the African's labor into whatever channels
it desires. If local planters or other European employers happen to
be short a hand or so on the day our African is hauled up before the
administrator, their agent is sitting in the office waiting for him. If,
at another season, the government happens to be trying to fulfill its
contract with the South Africans, off he goes to the mines. Finally,
if the government wants to finish its new piers, he is marched on
down to the waterfront. As a salesman of his labor, the African is
nowhere at all. The worst that can befall him is conscription into one
of the government's work gangs, called *shibalos;* for here he works
for a compulsory term of six months at next to no pay. But the
threat of these levies is the background against which the wages and
all the other conditions of his civilian employment are set, to his
plain disadvantage.

From a purely monetary point of view, the African who goes to
the South African mines makes out best. The official bargain worked
out between the Portuguese and Union governments specifies that
the Portuguese will cooperate in finding labor in their territories in
exchange for receiving through their ports about 50 per cent of the
ocean traffic of the Johannesburg area. South Africa also pays the
Portuguese a head price per recruit, permits the Portuguese to
maintain tax collecting posts inside the Union, delivers about half
the recruit's wages to the Portuguese for payment upon repatriation,
and guarantees this repatriation. Even under these seemingly un-
propitious circumstances, the wages and living conditions in the
South African mine compounds are so much more attractive than
life in Mozambique that some areas of Portuguese Africa have been
virtually denuded of young male Africans.

According to one estimate, probably 1 million Africans have
emigrated illegally from Angola to Bechuanaland and Northern
Rhodesia in the past forty years (many of these, of course, were not
heading for the mines); this is in addition to a small number who are
officially recruited in Angola. (As an aftermath of the Leopoldville

riots of January, 1959, the Belgian police picked up unknown numbers—but many thousands—of Angolans who were illegally living in the Congo; they were then turned over to the Portuguese and there, on the border and in full sight of the Belgian authorities, were handcuffed to horizontal bars and flogged.) About 250,000 Mozambiqueans are always officially out of the country; and perhaps that many again have stolen over the border. To all this we must add a huge movement, perhaps amounting to a half-million, of tribesmen in Northern Mozambique, the Ngurus, who not long ago traveled en masse into the tribal regions of southern Nyasaland. Professor Harris estimates that the total population of able-bodied, working-age males in that part of southern Mozambique which is the main center of South African recruitment is about 600,000. He calculates that, by conservative estimates, 400,000 of this group are actually working in South Africa. The effect of this fantastic displacement on the agriculture and society of the affected area can be imagined.

In Angola and northern Mozambique, the government has set the work population controls for cash cropping coffee and cotton respectively rather than foreign recruitment. The management of the agriculture itself is in the hands of Portuguese landlords or, in certain tribal areas, of special concessionaires. The Africans own no mineral rights in Portuguese Africa and next to no individual property rights; less than one-tenth of 1 per cent of the land area of Angola is owned by Africans. Once again it is the threat of imprisonment or conscription into the *shibalos* which forces the African to obey the government's directives, in this case to plant a specified percentage of his tribal farm in the cash crop. Overseers donate the seed and make the decisions when to plant and to harvest; the government sets the purchase price, which invariably is comfortably under the world price, and contributes the necessary doses of coercion. As his contribution the African hazards his labor and perhaps his life. When a bad season destroys the crop, when the price of the cash crop falls, when the time and space allotted to the cash crop have fatally injured the prospects of the food crops on which he and his family subsist—when any or all of these things happen no one suffers but the African. Recently a number of these accidents have indeed overtaken the cotton plantings in northern Mozambique, and the misery which the government practices have inflicted there is perhaps the blackest mark to date on the record of the Portuguese administration.

So far, the Portuguese have come up against almost no opposition from the Africans to their tyrannous proceedings. The first reason for this is that they are swift and unhesitating in the application of force. Portuguese Africa is one of the last places on earth where physical beating is an acknowledged part of normal administrative procedure. Theoretically, only a government official can beat an African on the complaint of his employer, using a strange little instrument called the *palmatorio*, which is applied to the hand. But the African is naturally anxious to avoid all contact with the police and therefore prefers to be punished by his own boss, who uses his belt, a stick, or anything else that is handy. In practice, therefore, it is not surprising to find that beating is far more widespread—nay, universal—than apologists for the Portuguese regime ever admit. In the course of a talk a Roman Catholic priest (a Dutchman) from Lobito, in Angola, admitted to me that the tedium of life in Angola was almost intolerable, and that the silliness and obtuseness of his Africans drove him nearly crazy, but that he made it a rule never to beat one of them. I said that I was surprised to hear him say that; as a priest, it would never have occurred to me to suppose that he did beat them. What did being a priest have to do with it? he asked. Two brother-priests lived with him in the Lobito mission and they both beat their Africans continually. The eldest, in fact, a Frenchman, had a favorite maxim about it: if it is necessary to beat the African into understanding the plow, it is also necessary to beat him into understanding Jesus Christ.

If backwardness and beatings and work levies and shackles fail, the Portuguese have another trump: deportation. In addition to Angola and Mozambique, the Portuguese have retained two other souvenirs of the Age of Exploration. Portuguese Guinea is a small peanut-and-coconut enclave lying on the Atlantic Ocean north of French Guinea. And in the Gulf of Guinea are the "Cocoa Islands" of São Tomé and Principe, a separate province of Portuguese Africa. The reputation of this latter possession is such that it has continually engaged the attention of the British government, and charitable and antislavery organizations, since before the turn of the century. (Also French popular novelists, who call them "les plus mystérieux îsles du monde," and populate them with ingeniously debauched white girls.) Whenever, in his closet, a Portuguese administrator in Mozambique or Angola decides that a particular African is unreconstructably unamenable to "civilization," he classes him as an "undesirable"; at once, without juridical process of any kind, this African is slated for deportation to the cocoa plantations of São Tomé. Here is a resort of which the Portuguese administrators can make use, in gloomy obscurity, whenever they please, and the islands are thus fated to become the final resting place of an increasing number of aspiring African politicians. Of the kind of life they will live there before they rest for the last time almost nothing is known. In the old days, conditions in São Tomé were so odoriferous that British cocoa firms refused to purchase their produce. Even today, Professor Harris informs us, the threat to ship her "boy" to São Tomé is a far more effective weapon in the hands of the wrathful housewife than any whip.

When, from time to time, the Portuguese try to explain or justify their occupation of Africa they sooner or later come round to the much vaunted "social equality" that distinguishes Portuguese Africa from, say, the Union of South Africa. For example, there are no "European only" signs on public facilities like restaurants, buses, or water fountains. (However, the African's freedom to ride a white man's bus does not put the fare in his pocket. In Lourenço Marques, one bus ride costs the equivalent of one-quarter of an African daily wage, and this compulsory pauperdom is quite sufficient to keep the African segregated.) There is genuine social equality of a kind, in that Portuguese men can and do live with African women without losing their jobs or social positions. It is, unfortunately, not easy to understand how it contributes to the "civilizing mission" that a Portuguese clerk sires four or five half-caste children who are (almost always) raised with their mother's people in African shanty towns. But one is astounded to discover that there actually exists a small society of featherbrained Portuguese-admirers who claim that, on the sole basis of this sexual casualness, the Portuguese can lay a claim to being the greatest of all the colonial peoples. Presumably, by not living simply as masters of inferior beings, but going about creating "*luso*-populations" which merge the best of both races, the Portuguese have found the secret to the Reconciliation of Peoples. Unfortunately, tiresome as life in Portuguese Africa unquestionably is, and virile as Portuguese males unquestionably are, 5 million African women are rather too many for 60,000 "civilizers"—and when the "*luso*-population" eventually emerges, whatever its superb qualities, it is likely to be perfectly indistinguishable from the present one.

The same easygoing prevaricating which dims the luster of "social equality" in Portuguese Africa also qualifies the liberalism of the "assimilation" process, which the Portuguese explain to the world is their way of raising up their African charges to full participation in political life. The law divides Portuguese Africans into two groups: *indigenas*, or tribal Africans; and *assimilados*, Africans who have "given up their tribal ways of life," can speak Portuguese, and work at respectable jobs. Theoretically, any African can advance to the status of *assimilado* by merely passing certain tests which satisfy his administrator of his maturity and responsibility; once in possession of this status, the African is a full Portuguese citizen, with all the civil and social rights of any other Portuguese. But in practice the whole institution is only a distraction languidly waved in the faces of the critical. To begin with, the procedures of assimilation lie entirely within the discretion of the bureaucracy; and the number of *assimilados*—4,349 in Mozambique (1950)—after 400-odd years of Portuguese rule is a clue to the seriousness with which the bureaucracy views the institution. About five years ago, the government became even less enthusiastic than formerly about the program, and really put the brakes on, chiefly by stepping up the qualifications for assimilation. For example, the administrator must now judge that the candidate speaks Portuguese "correctly," rather than just speaks it. And applications from artisan groups, like construction workers, from whom many older *assimilados* were previously drawn, are now being turned down.

What has happened to alter the government's policy is that the Portuguese authorities have been dismayed and astonished to find that—despite all their best efforts—the new Africa has managed somehow to creep here and there into Mozambique and Angola. The boom imparted by World War II to all of Central Africa, the tremendous expansion of the Rhodesias, have acted at a distance to create the infinitesimal embryo of an African middle class in the coastal cities of Portuguese Africa in the form of clerks, machine operators, bricklayers, and the like. A tiny moiety of the trembling in the north has communicated itself to Portuguese Africa; the Middle Ages seem to be ever so slightly slipping away. Given the least relaxation of vigilance, the Portuguese fear, they might wake up one morning and find unions and political parties in their back yard; mobs of protestors and petitioners might be swirling over the magnificently tiled boulevards. The institution of "assimilation," which was designed to alienate a few thousands of "upper clerk" Africans from the masses, would then turn into the educated and action-oriented nucleus of a revolutionary movement of the kind that is plaguing all of Portuguese Africa's neighbors. The word went out, and so far as the administrators' "discretion" is concerned *Maybe* has turned into *No*.

Can one predict or conclude anything about these sluggard, dreary lands?

For example, what hope is there that a reformation in its African policy will come from the government of metropolitan Portugal itself? None. As everyone knows, the old homeland has been ruled for many years by an antiquated gentry of pious, authoritarian pedants. Since the late twenties this clique has been ruled in its turn by that durable professor of political economy, Antonio de Oliveira Salazar, who in 1933 composed his own constitution for the "New State" and has governed by it since. Dr. Salazar's receptivity to new ideas can be deduced from a characteristic response to the open letter of July, 1958, to the dictator signed by the Bishop of Porto, Monsignor Ferreira Gomez, in which the prelate sharply complained of the "unmerited miseries" suffered by the Portuguese people, of the ban against strikes, and of the "great inequalities between the social classes." Salazar replied to this attack by haughtily reminding His Grace that overzealous churchmen without academic qualifications are forever forgetting that "progressivism" plays into the hands of the forces of evil. In their ignorance of political economy, he went on, some clerics in Portugal even seemed to wish to "baptize Communism." But none of these matters were a proper concern of the Church and the bishop should refrain from making suggestions on things not within his province.

Even when Salazar passes away there is no likelihood of a party
or individual in contemporary Portugal that would revise her
colonial policies. The Portuguese are an extraordinarily proud and
ingrown people, and if European history has somewhat passed them
by in the last 400 years they still possess in Angola and Mozambique
two imperial monuments to erstwhile greatness. Of both these territories they have been in occupation since the early days of the sixteenth century. Long ago they retired from competition with other
European nationalities, and so they rarely look around themselves,
but when they do they see in the Rhodesias and the Union even less
successful accommodations to the political-racial problem than their
own. Certainly they see nothing that inspires them to alter their
basic ideas. There are no African politicians in Mozambique and
Angola: no riots, no petitions, no stone throwings, no strikes, no
rapings, no sauciness. In Lourenço Marques, a man does not have to
illuminate his house at night with floodlamps, or hire guards to
patrol his gardens, as in Johannesburg. The African abides by the
curfew, or he soon wishes that he had. Why should the Portuguese
invoke a rain of disasters on their own heads with an ill-timed liberalism, and even if they decided to do so whence would come the
money to tide the territories over the difficult transition period?

The motto therefore: *Quieta non movere.* But even so they have
not been able to scrape by entirely without criticism. Anyone who
takes an interest in Africa soon learns that Portuguese Africa is one
of the worst governed areas of the world, and every once in a while
a group of specialists, or the United Nations Fourth Committee, or
some other similar interest shakes a finger at the administrators.
They reply, naturally, that Portuguese Africa is an integral part of
the motherland, and that Portugal will tolerate no interference in
her internal affairs. Indeed, the government recently added substance
to this claim by moving strongly in the direction of greater administrative integration with the homeland at the expense of provincial
autonomy. As we have remarked, the other European colonials in
southern Africa do not forcefully object to the Portuguese policy,
although they are irritated by their want of economic enterprise.
(However, in 1959 officials of the Union government were trying to collect sympathy and funds for a tiny company of Afrikaners who wandered into Angola fifty years ago and who now

wish to return to the Volkunity.) But, like the English and the French, the South African and Rhodesian whites have enough to worry about these days without hectoring the Portuguese about their stagnant backwaters. Even the Africans know, or care, little more about Portuguese Africa than the rest of us; no contact has been made with any potential leadership there, although the All-Africa People's Conference of December, 1958, did request the International Red Cross to investigate conditions in Angola and Mozambique. And, as for America, we hardly know that these territories exist. American tourists rarely visit them, and those of us who do almost never penetrate into their interiors. We are, however, for what it is worth, their largest customer next to Portugal herself.

It would be nonsense to overstate the case. Latin paternalism is not the worst form of government that exists; Portuguese Africa is not a land of unrelieved strain and malice like the Union; so long as a Portuguese African obeys his master he is not followed into his home by storm troopers who take pleasure in tormenting him. The Portuguese will be able to hold out until a general convulsion in southern Africa spills over the frontiers and enkindles their own Africans. Brutality does of course exist there—and at certain times and places, such as the prevailing wretchedness of the past few years in northern Mozambique, that brutality overwhelms the careless Portuguese good nature which usually tempers the injustice and serfdom that is the lot of the Portuguese African. But even in this instance it seems to be such a small-time, easily overlooked brutality. Angola and Mozambique are only little cloudy pools of human misery, lands of sere green-brown hills, shattered forests, rundown plantations (and hauntingly beautiful mask-cities); their total population perhaps only one-fourth the number of Chinese farmers who have been executed since 1950 by the Peking government for obstructing "agricultural reconstruction." But of course one day they must awake from dreams of Allan Quatermain and Prester John; a light from somewhere will strike into the depths of their people's souls, and they will find a voice.

7. The Belgian Congo

Having inherited a sad history of bungling and cruelty along with the jointure of King Leopold II, the Belgian government has striven for fifty years to justify its presence in the Belgian Congo by making the country a model of sober-minded, right-minded "social engineering." The aim of the administration, officially described as a "vigilant paternal supervision," has been to strike a fair balance between the exigencies of social change and the necessities of social order. Proper profits to those who risk their capital in developing the colony must be balanced against the enticing frailties of a backward society. The education, work opportunities, and political activity that are made available to the African must be balanced against his painful inexperience and inferior culture. The benefits of industrialization must be balanced against the benefits of a leisurely, all-knowing centralization. In short, the Belgians have administered their colony like something midway between a Flemish farm and a wild-bird sanctuary; their principles are probity and omniscience.

For many years the Belgians seemed to have discovered in this policy toward their enormous possession, eighty times the size of their own country, a secret which had eluded colonial powers who had many times their powers and responsibilities. The British principle of "indirect rule"—which left ordinary jurisdictions in the hands of the traditional chiefs—broke down under the pressures of westernization. The French and Portuguese systems left the African more or less naked against the depredations of unwise or dishonest bureaucrats—and their friends or patrons, the businessmen. But the Belgians seemed to have combined brilliantly the two approaches. Every visitor to the Congo remarked on the handsome, hygienic, whitewashed two- or three-room houses that lodged the African city workers; the hospitals, social welfare and maternity centers scattered over the land; the official inspectors tirelessly touring the country, watching over the Africans' interests. And this prudent trusteeship was only half of the picture. There were also the modern changes which the Belgians, a progressive and hard-working people, had wrought in the land: the spotless, spacious cities; the busy industries; the efficient transportation network of planes, boats, and railroads opening up some of the most formidable country on earth; the high-quality restaurants in the heart of the bush; the professionalism of the magistrates and the fairness of the police. To what ultimate destination this "paternal supervision" was tending—that is to say, what the Belgians had in mind for the remote future when their incessant pinpricks should finally have stirred the Congo Giant to life—the government never specified, either to inquirers or to itself. But the question hardly ever arose, so capable did the Belgians seem of handling any conceivable situation.

Nineteen fifty-nine was the year in which the Belgians were taught that, for all their good intentions and real triumphs, the Djinn was just too big for them. The twentieth century and the call of the North (from Ghana and French Africa) reached at last into Central Africa—which is practically conterminous with the Congo—and quickened her heart. A few bubbles in the sea of 13,000,000 Africans rose and popped, a signal from fathomless, uncharted depths; the Belgian administration began to find itself swimming against a dark, invisible tide of opposition; officiousness unwillingly recognized itself as repression. The Belgians could not understand that by priming the modernization of Africa they had themselves created this tide; a split parted what they had actually done in the Congo and what they believed themselves to have done, and as this split widened it became more and more difficult to merge into a unified policy what the Belgians wanted to do in the Congo and what it was practicable for them to do. The coherence of the administration crumbled and—as so often and so tragically has happened in Africa—the problem of managing Africa turned into the problem of fixing shackles on the African.

The Belgian Congo is shaped like a gigantic, concave kidney, the slopes and body of which form the chief geographical phenomenon of the country, the basin of the Congo River and its affluents. About half the land area of the colony stands in equatorial rainforest; the rest is mainly scrub and savanna, the denseness of which is dependent upon the plain's elevation above sea level. A tiny tongue of territory, like a renal duct to the giant kidney, follows the river down to the sea between the Portuguese lands of Angola and Cabinda; this projection constitutes the sole maritime connection of the oversized country.

Northward, the marshes of Equator province join the forests and swamps of former French Equatorial Africa; and, to the east of this, the savanna of the Congo runs into the savanna of the Sudan. To the south, the plateau rises into a region of richer grasslands that climb toward the hills of northern Angola and the Copper Belt, shared with Northern Rhodesia. But the most remarkable and intriguing portion of the country lies on the far eastern frontier, the spine of the Lesser Rift Valley, where volcanoes towering over lake-smooth game plains, cloud-topped mountains, and warm, clear lakes come together in one of the most wonderful arenas on earth. Only here, in the lofty heart of Africa, is the land of the Congo free of the African maladies of man and creature which bleed and weaken life at the basin's center.

One-third the size of the United States, this vast bowl is lightly populated; and after one has flown for hours over its vacancies one sooner or later wonders whether it is populated at all. About 13 million Africans are believed to live in the Congo; there are 125,000 Europeans, most of whom are administrative or military employees of the Belgian government, or engineers or managers working for the huge companies that are responsible for the colony's industry. The smallness of the population is chiefly due to the unhealthiness of the country, plus the savagery of the slave trade here in the last century, but it is a population now undergoing a rapid increase of about 3 per cent annually. Indeed, as we shall see, it might even be said that the Congo is already "overpopulated," using this term as we defined it in Chapter 1.

The name and history of the Congo will be linked forever to the partnership between two very different but characteristically Victorian personalities: the greatest of all the explorers of Africa, Sir Henry M. Stanley, and his patron, the un-Belgian ruler of the Belgians, King Leopold II.

In 1874, three years after the famous encounter with Dr. Livingstone at Ujiji, Stanley embarked on the first of three great expeditions into the Congo basin, piecing together the relations of the central African lake and river system and following the river itself down to the sea. His enthusiasm for what he observed along the way knew no bounds. Find a way to surmount the rapids and waterfalls that strangle the lower Congo and prevent its use as a highway into the interior, Stanley reported, and Central Africa would spring open like a feeding clam, revealing incredible riches. Back in Europe, Leopold of Belgium, who had made a hobby of African ambitions since before his accession in 1865, heard about Stanley's ideas and persuaded him to become his agent, and to return to West Africa in 1879 for another fact-finding and development junket under the auspices of an "association" of Brussels businessmen, behind which hid the fleshy visage of the monarch himself. This time Stanley remained in the region five years, so successfully exerting himself that in 1884 the United States was the first of the powers to recognize his settlements as an independent state, the Congo Free State, with Leopold as chief.

In 1887 Stanley returned to the Congo for the last time, crossing from Zanzibar and traveling overland. But in the meantime Leopold had been leaving no stone unturned to find a way to extract a personal fortune from his brand-new private empire. At the Conference of Berlin in 1884–1885 he won international recognition and guarantees of Stanley's coup. His royal prestige and his promise to bequeath the Congo to Belgium on his death were sufficient inducements to secure the approval and subsidy of his own government. And to obtain the massive heaps of capital necessary for the exploitation of the basin he granted tremendous concessions to interested Belgian financiers in the form of palatine authority over the mineral, land, and human resources of hundreds of millions of acres. A share of the profits from these concessions was directed into the regal purse, of course, as well as those from a personal plot of some 112,000 square miles in the center of the most promising rubber land of the basin.

But none of this planning could amount to anything, no money could be made in the Congo, until there was some practical means of entering the interior. The great river which gave the province its name provided a marvelous network of watercourses within the basin itself, but when it gets to within a few hundred miles of the coast the Congo dives into a chain of gorges cutting through a mountain range, churning into impassable rapids which had vetoed direct sea communications for thousands of years. A railway had to be built, 260 miles long, to connect the port of Matadi on the Congo estuary with the Stanley Pool, the point farthest seaward on the central, navigable reach of the river. And after eleven years of stupendous toil, and the deaths of thousands of the laborers, this track was completed in 1898.

But just as the King was ready to cash in the states of Europe began to take an unwelcome interest in this new member of the community of nations which they had so readily embraced fourteen years before. The reason for this was that during the 1890's dire rumors had begun to seep out of the torrid, water-soaked fastnesses of the Congo that shocked and appalled the world; there were reports of horrifying conditions in the camps of the railroad gangs working on the Matadi-Stanley Pool track and of the laborers on the King's rubber plantations. Wholesale dragnets for tribesmen, scourgings and shootings, epidemics, a fantastic death toll—it seemed as if the Balance of Power had turned the jungle over to a far worse regime than that of the old cannibal witch doctors and Arab slavers. Even the United States Senate fired off a protest to the Belgian government. And Europe's financial eminents objected to other aspects of Leopold's management even more than to his maltreatment of the Africans. They found out what it meant to them when Leopold, in order to bail himself out of his overambitious projects, delegated more and more of his sovereign rights in the Congo to great Belgian capitalists who had no notion at all of inviting general competition. The race for Africa was now in its overheated final stretch; Leopold had been just wily enough to anticipate most of the other nations in securing guarantees for the Congo Free State before the international community fully comprehended what it was they were giving away—but it was too much for them that this tiny Belgium which had outwitted them now forbade them even to taste the loot. The foreign offices of England and Germany began sententiously to grumble.

Pressed by his difficulties, the inextricable confusion enveloping his own fortune and the enormous debts of the Congo Free State, and the representations of the European powers Leopold at last consented to be relieved of his Congo by his Belgian ministers. In 1908 the Belgians completed their arrangements; they assumed the administrative responsibilities of the Congo, and in exchange pledged themselves to protect the personal properties of the royal family and Leopold's private deals with the concessionaires. A year later the king died, having embroiled the end of his life not only in the fetid fiascos of the Congo but also in a routine of hearty dissipation that amused Europe and in prolonged, scandalous public litigations with other members of his family which outraged his brother monarchs, including Queen Victoria, who for so long had been the admiring pupil of this Leopold's father, the "Nestor of Europe." But what did Leopold II care for all this? He died a king, and rich. And today, in the Congo itself, this prince who preferred riding through Cannes in the company of naughty actresses to all other things has been metamorphosed into a prophetic and heroic genius of statecraft, a man of preternatural vision and patriotism. This is Belgium's way of thanking the prince who made it possible for her to stride about the world like a colossus by bestowing on her dozens of kingdoms larger than herself. In the Congo, one is never far from Leopold. The colony's capital is Leopoldville; and in the center of the mighty avenue that bisects the city there stands the huge figure of the "Founder"—his heavy German face with its luxuriant square beard surveying the infinite spaces of his design. There is a Lake Leopold II and a Mount Leopold II, and every official history of the colony, or broadside to the world, commences with a paean of praise and gratitude to Leopold II, whose old plantation is now troubling his countrymen more than ever it did himself.

When in 1908 the Belgian government confirmed the privileges of the corporations which had been Leopold's Congo partners, they poured the character of the colonization into a mold which it has retained ever since. There were to be no wildcatting, no get-rich-quick promotion schemes, no spectacular bank failures and bankruptcies, no overclever interlopers. The rights of great companies like the Comité Spécial du Katanga, which operates the copper mining industry that is the basis of the colony's prosperity, have been checked and delimited over the years, but their oligopoly status has never been touched. From the start, entrepreneurship was to be rationally bureaucratized—originally by the holders of capital themselves; now, with the Ten Year Plan of 1949, by the state plus the capitalists.

But the state plus the capitalists—the men who run the Congo—are the *same* men. At home Belgium herself is run by one of the smallest, the most conservative, oligarchies that still operates in the world. Government officers, the army, the hierarchy of the Roman Church, the upper reaches of society, the Court, the financiers of Antwerp and Brussels—they are all the same people, formed into a club within whose precincts outsiders are rarely seen. The economic department of this club is a vast trust, the Société Générale de Belgique—a modern fiscal giant with the mentality of a medieval craftsman— which reigns supreme over the economic life of the little country. "The Société Générale *is* Belgium," a small shopkeeper dourly declared to me. And it is only natural that this entrenched and immensely wealthy fraternity should protect its grip on the Congo as well as on Belgium. The political oligarchy and the Société Générale —acting through its subsidiaries on the spot—boss the huge colony with a wonderful patriarchal absolutism which is right out of another age.

But large differences exist between conditions in the Lowlands and in Central Africa, and over the years these differences have added up to many shortcomings in the colonial administration. For example, although there is a real need for wild-eyed gamblers in Africa, the only risks that are taken in the Congo are taken by the oligarchy— and they tend to ponder each risk a long time. From the beginning, when Leopold II turned down a British offer to construct the Matadi-Stanley Pool railway, choosing to wait a few years until a Belgian concessionaire assumed the task, the Belgians have discouraged the entry of foreign capital into the colony. In the Congo itself, the oligarchy subjects small Belgian traders, ranchers, prospectors, and so forth, who are independent of the Société Générale, to a smothering regimen of interference and regulation, reducing them to the status of clients. As the population figures show, immigration has been generally held up. And for Belgians and others who do reside in the Congo, "settlement" is held up. (In 1956, only about 10,000 Europeans in the colony were counted as "settlers"; the rest were employees and bureaucrats and soldiers, and their kin.) When a Belgian wants to emigrate to the Congo, he must plod through a long and tortuous process of investigation in the homeland. If he is finally judged responsible enough for admission, he is told what craft he is to practice and where he is to practice it in his new home. He is given an identity card which he must keep about him at all times. Whenever he goes from province to province, or stays the night at a hotel, he can be asked to show this card; the Belgians are proud of the fact that the Congo police, who check these registers, theoretically know the whereabouts of every European in the massive colony every moment of the day. In some ways it is easier for a foreigner to move around the Congo than a Belgian citizen; all he needs is a visaed passport. But even so, from time to time a region will be "closed" to tourists, as recently the southern portion of Equator province was, on the grounds that there were no suitable accommodations for Europeans. All this bureaucratic fussiness is usually tempered by Belgian kindliness and good humor; it rarely turns tyrannical. But these time-wasting form fillings are symptomatic of a whole development philosophy about a region like the Congo which conceals within itself, buried under an outward show of efficient and helpful supervision, many grave faults. Interestingly, it is Belgians, and especially small businessmen, who are the bitterest of all the critics of the present regime.

The politics of the country are managed in the same way, and of course by the same people, as the economy. Neither colonist nor African possesses any genuine political power. The basis of the administration is decrees, which come down from the Belgian Legislature by way of the Minister for the Congo and the Crown. (However, this will soon be changed. As part of the "reform" of January, 1959, the government will hold an election in winter, 1959, to elect members of Territorial and Provincial Councils, and a single **General Council.** The franchise will be open to every male over twenty-one years of age. When they come into existence, these councils will replace the present council system, which is composed of purely advisory bodies that are virtually nominated by the administration. But whether the new councils are to be anything but advisory also has not yet been specified; there have been vague promises of real legislative responsibility, but the government is doubtless waiting to learn the composition of the new bodies before it decides on the degree of autonomy to grant them. In short, the attitude of the Belgian government toward self-government for the Congolese, black and white, has changed noticeably in twelve months, but it is dubious that it has changed far enough, or fast enough, to compel a recharacterization of the administration.)

Whatever the future of the impending political innovation, it is not the dictates of their master plan, but the pressure of events, which has forced the Belgians to try it. The master plan theory of how to colonize and develop enormous dominions in Africa has been thrown out the window by the revolution in the economy and society of Africa that has taken place since the end of the Second World War. The deliberate supercalculations of slow-moving directorates, smoking cigars around heavy tables in Antwerp board rooms, have been swamped by the tide which is pouring out of the villages of Africa in response to the stimuli of the Modern Era. Ironically, nowhere in Africa is the New Day more splendidly on parade than in the Congo; and it is the Belgian himself who is proudest of the gleaming new buildings; the meticulously tended public promenades and plazas; the ports and marshaling yards, processing plants, hotels, banks, and schools. The newness of everything is the strongest impression that the visitor brings away from the Congo—that plus an apperception of the titantic energies that are on the loose here. Even the people are new; 43 per cent of Africans in the Congo are younger than fifteen years of age. An old-world, go-slow management has lit the fuse to its own self-explosion—but it is too late to regret it now.

As elsewhere in Africa, the main ingredients of the bang are the hordes of African males who have left country, tribes, and often family to come to work in the big city. In 1938 only about 8 per cent of Congolese Africans lived in towns; the figure now is in excess of 25 per cent of a considerably larger population. Forty per cent of adult males live in towns; 45 per cent of adult African males work for wages. The effect on the cities themselves of this vast internal redistribution of population can be imagined. No more than a collection of huts on the Stanley Pool in 1900, Leopoldville in 1939 boasted 50,000 inhabitants. Now its official population is 325,000; with perhaps another 100,000 who are illegally dwelling in the "townships" who should be added to the totals. Elisabethville and Jadotville, the chief cities of the Copper Belt, which has about doubled the value of its prewar output, have shown an expansion that is even more spectacular. Other new towns, and "population concentrations," have appeared to service the cobalt mines, also in the Katanga; the coffee areas and the cotton plantations of Kivu; the tin, diamond, and uranium mining centers; and the palm oil industry of the Basin. Everywhere, even in the most insufferably torrid regions of the country, one hears the sounds of earth-movers, tractors, hammers, rivet guns, the coughs of engines. Everywhere men are tearing at the African earth. Everything is unfinished.

To return to the sketch of this process given in Chapter 1, the "urbanization" phenomenon in Africa is a tiger which carries its riders to various uncomfortable destinations at the same time. The new city dwellers form into a genuine proletariat in the Marxist sense of the word. They are a mass of laborers who have only their labor to sell but possess no controls over the economic and political conditions of the sale, and in the West we have learned over the past century that it is just these controls—developed through the cumbersome processes of political democracy—which prevent the fructification of this proletariat into the Marxist catastrophe. This life-and-death lesson has yet to be learned or applied in Africa. As a proletarian the African loses the psychological stabilizations built into the tribal system without gaining any of the stabilizations that have been cemented by time and experience into the great Western states. He soon becomes an "African" among millions of other "Africans," but no gear exists by which this new affiliation can operate constructively on the new milieu. And as a group, this new proletariat poses monstrous challenges to the administration, first and foremost of which is the necessity for providing the employment that lured its members out of the bush in the first place. The African proletarian has no savings, no reserves, no margin. If activity around the wharfs slows down, if the copper plants are shut down for a month or two, a social crisis of first-class dimensions is immediately on hand. At the minimum the African city dweller must be fed; and sooner or later something must be found for him to do.

While "urbanization" has thus created these veering, sensitive aggregations of human beings in the "townships" that encircle the cities of Africa, the backlash effect we discussed earlier is also destroying the countryside. One soon comes to feel that "urbanization" is the hateful font from which flow all the malevolent disruptions which are killing the best things of the old Africa and wrecking the promise of the new Africa. But, of course, nothing is so clear as that "urbanization" *is* the New Africa—and despite the shocking appearance on the scene of the unmanageable mass miseries which are implicit in it, one might as well try to check the surge of man into space as the growth of these cities. To control the cities of Africa, indeed, is to control Africa; but to control these cities one must keep them at work.

When a community has been swept out into the flood of a "transition" of such startling dimensions that it resembles nothing so much as a full-scale war, its success in keeping afloat depends more than anything else on the morale and good faith of its citizens.

Superficially, the Belgians have done extremely well by their African charges. Wages in the Congo compare favorably with those found anywhere on the continent. In the eastern, coffee-planting country, African fieldworkers are better dressed, their bicycles newer and finer, than those in most sharecropping regions of our South. Everywhere there are handsome hospitals, clinics, social welfare centers. The African is not prohibited from learning, using, and getting properly paid for high-grade technical skills: the skipper of a lake steamer may be an African, or the cashier of a bank. Lastly, the paternalistic administration sees to it that the African is not left the helpless prey of unscrupulous European operators. Only 9 per cent of the land of the Congo has been alienated to Europeans; and it is now almost impossible for a European (or an African, for that matter) to obtain the equivalent of a freehold title. Land, tribes, health, working conditions, and so forth—on all these fronts the

Africans' interests are guarded by a superintending bureaucracy of high caliber and integrity.

Nevertheless, the tone of the colonization is bad. Perhaps this must be true of autocratic regimes in all times and places, because superiority of status is corrosive of the morality of the bulk of our fallible race. Of course, the Belgians are nowhere near the category of Afrikaners; they are no worse than most British colonists; but even so they have been weak enough to adopt a racial attitude which has already damaged irremediably the chances of a black-and-white sharing of the future in the Congo.

To begin with, the official philosophy of the colonization is obsolescent, and in this one respect the Belgians have fallen short of the grandiose spiritual standards of the greatest British imperialists. The Belgians postulate a crucial fundamental dissimilarity that divides the European from the African. As a government booklet puts it: "Our racial mind has been conditioned and molded over the centuries; ours was an effortless evolution. Such is not the case in Africa, where the natives must be taught the meaning of progress." So far as the government goes, the doctrine of "racial mind" explains such things as why there are only two universities open to Africans in the Congo, and why only about 200 Africans attend them, and why, until recently, Africans were not permitted to study abroad at all. But it is not until the notion of "racial mind" percolates into the mentality of the ordinary colonist that it degenerates into a real community-dissolving caustic. Most Belgians view the differences between the tidy ancient towns of Flanders and Brabant and the stinks and bugs of Africa with extreme, and articulate, distaste. For them Africa is a tour of duty, during which they can earn more money than at home and live a more luxurious way of life than at home. But *home* is Belgium and Africa is a sewer, and anything which tends to fuzz the sharp edges of this image—or to interfere with the regular holiday—is contumaciously and continuously attacked.

Frequently the mood turns positively rancid. Here is a story told me by a café owner in Leopoldville. One of the councilmen of one of the African townships complained that he had been denied service at this man's café. Because the Belgians take pride in the desegregated public facilities in the Congo the owner was next day reprimanded by the authorities. The day after that the African councilman reappeared with his wife and sat down at a booth. He continued to return for lunch for two or three days, until one noontime a Belgian garage operator from next door came in with a pet monkey, seated him on a bar stool, and demanded two beers. "We don't serve beer to animals," the owner declared disingenuously. "Why not?" asked the garageman. "He's not the only monkey in the place drinking beer." (A quarter-hour or so after he finished telling me this story, this café owner described for me with enthusiasm a huge new hospital for Africans that the administration was erecting in one of the townships. Like all Belgians, he was exceedingly proud of the outward signs of Belgian enterprise. He did not realize, and he could not be made to realize—at least by me—that one single such incident as this one in his café obliterated the beneficial political effects of a dozen good works like this hospital.)

This kind of story can be retailed by the gross. As every European in the Congo has at least one servant working for him all conversation sooner or later settles down to the servant problem. Then one is treated at length to the world's emptiest and most sickening clichés. You don't dare leave your young daughter alone in the house with the African boy—no matter that he is sixty years old and has been with the family for forty of them. If he doesn't actually touch her he will peep at her, or whisper obscenities to her. You don't dare leave the baby alone with an African nurse, because African mothers pacify their children by caressing their genitals.

Then there is the boy who worked for the family for a generation but who stood by grinning when his European master was attacked, for no reason at all, by a drunken African on a riverboat. Or the man who repaid his master's wife for many favors of the past by running away on the evening of the big party. Or the chauffeur who will starve to death before he will consent to mow the lawn. Or the man whose bush relatives are forever moving in on him, preventing him from saving up his money for a bicycle. Or the African politician who, at his trial for seditious speaking, tells the magistrate that when Freedom Day comes every African will be given a Buick. Or the cook who cannot be persuaded by a charitable matron into purchasing cigarettes in packs of twenty at twenty francs, instead of one at a time for four francs apiece. Or the African technician who got back a bottle of valuable solvent that had been stolen from the laboratory by hexing the unknown thief. Or the African who lets himself get dirty and smelly after twenty years of satisfactory kitchen work. Or the pilferer of bric-a-brac and linen, who must be handed over to the police.

Two of the commonest of these moth-eaten stereotypes warrant a little digression. First, the accusation heard all over Africa that cannibalism is still an active practice in the bush. Apparently there can be no sound doubt that cannibalism remains a reality in many parts of the continent, without including in this consideration the cannibalistic features of special rituals like that of the Mau-Mau, which are based on no tribal tradition but are tacked onto the oath-taking ceremonies as another way of frightening the novices into total obedience. Of course, there is no way of knowing the dimensions of the practice of cannibalism, nor is there any way of telling what proportion is hunger cannibalism and what proportion ceremonial cannibalism. However, the point that we wish to stress here is that not only is cannibalism a fugitive feature of African society but also that it does not, of itself, put the African beyond the pale of human sympathy. In the nineteenth century a famous case tried in Great Britain concerned a lifeboatful of castaways who had, after days on the open water, slain and butchered the cabinboy. And in the great famines of 1920 and 1933 it has been documented that cannibalism was practiced over large areas of the southern part of the Soviet Union. Doubtless the unfortunates involved in these cases would plead absolute necessity. But, for what it is worth, so could the African, protein deficiency in Africa being what it is.

Second, the accusation that the ordinary African is just biding his time until he can crawl into bed with a blonde. Any blonde will do, it seems—nuns, grandmothers, pregnant housewives, eight-year-old girls. Sexual fears and jealousies are topics far beyond the competence of this essayist, but they must be mentioned because—incredible as it seems—they are the prime knitters of a tissue of inflammation which separates the white from the African everywhere in Africa; and when compromises and comradeships of other kinds have been fairly negotiated, sexual antagonism survives to poison the life of the community. The lore accompanying this antagonism has about the same description as that of which we have a superabundance in America, and therefore I may spare myself and my readers any specific illustrations. But someday it will be worth while for an anthropologist to investigate the possibility that these hideous tensions are the man-made disfigurements of a serviceable natural force. That is to say, from a long-run genetic point of view it is of course desirable to mix widely the human genetic material, and an excited curiosity about the males and females of different races and cultures may be the first stage of an instinct that promotes this mixing. Probably the races of mankind share equally in the propensity for amorous variety; certainly the white race is not backward in this respect. But then social man comes along who would rather bully than make love; the natural outlet of this sexual fascination is shut down, or relegated to stolen and guilty moments; and what could have been affection putrefies into ugly passions of hate and filth.

But whether a community ever becomes a *Community*, or remains simply a heap of individuals living in propinquity, depends directly on the ratio that holds between people who can rise above this kind of thing to the levels of idealism and compassion and those who cannot. Sniggerings and swaggerings taint the edges of every power class in the history of human society. We are weak, we are sinful beings—no teaching ever required less, or received more, demonstration than this one. But when a power class permits itself to aspire to its own ideals more and more infrequently, when sniggerings and swaggerings are imbedded into the institutions of the society, public and private, then that power class has of its own choice ruptured the psychological membranes that hold together the Community and produced, in its stead, an amorphous indifferent mass which awaits the fires of new ideals and loyalties to a new structure. That power class has simultaneously destroyed its reason for existence and its capacity to exist.

This is what has happened in the Belgian Congo—and in the rest of colonial Africa also. All the sweetness has gone out of life—and good faith and good will with it. The Belgian matron of Luluabourg or Goma has no intention of giving up intimate daily contact with the African servants who are her principal consolations for being in Africa in the first place, but she will not consent to sympathize with them, or compassionate them, although they share the air of her own home. All the weaknesses of human nature join together in these situations to amputate one whole priceless aspect of life. Into her home this matron brings the War that should take place in legislative assemblies, between men abiding by ancient rules of procedure and in fundamental agreement on the basic values of life, and in so doing she ensures that one day this same War will be fought in the streets outside her home, with guns and knives. After all, she leaves her cook and her houseboy no choice—save that of sinking into brute animality. Where can he go, what can he do, to get out of this choking atmosphere?

It is this pervasive infirmity of morale, projected into the larger sphere, which will nullify the promise of the new initiative taken by the Belgians in the first months of 1959. And, moreover, the timing was unfortunate. For some time the Belgian government had recognized that it had been lucky for about as long as it was possible to be lucky in Africa, and that pretty soon nationalist excitements were going to infect the Congo. Hence, in the fall of 1958 the King and the Prime Minister prepared a statement of Belgium's ultimate objectives in Africa: self-government was on the way, but no timetable was drawn up. However, the Leopoldville riots, which were really caused by a serious unemployment problem rather than political unrest, premeditated the publication of the new decree. When the King's proposal was made public, on January 13, 1959, that the government intended to "organize a democracy capable of exercising the prerogatives of sovereignty and of deciding its independence," it had to be scrutinized by the Africans through a film of blood.

As we have seen, the new order provides for a tier of councils, 60 per cent of the members of lowest level of which are elected by universal, adult, male suffrage. But the omission of specifications of the real powers of these councils has not gone unremarked by the Congo's Africans. In a statement issued jointly by three executives of the Abako Association shortly after their release in May, 1959, from custody in Belgium—where they had been held on charges of complicity in the January troubles, but during which custody the Belgians characteristically junketed them around Belgium to look at factories and engineering schools—the African politicians said that the King's promises are "incomplete."

They are, of course, but this statement means that the Africans

do not trust the Belgians or the winter 1959 elections, a want
of faith to be attributed both to the social attitudes of the colonists
and to systematic hedging on the part of the officialdom. For example, after the January riots the then Minister for the Congo, Mr.
Maurice Van Hemelrijck, visited the colony to inquire into things
and to explain what the King intended by the new policy. The minister found that the Congo administration had coped effectively
with the immediate problem of restoring civil order, but that the
administration was profoundly distressed—as was he himself—by
the violence of the restoratives they had felt compelled to employ.
The Belgians are a basically decent people, and if nationalism had
come to the Congo in such a virulent form that their basically
decent soldiery had to bombard mobs of unarmed women and
children, was it not already far too late to think about "organizing
a democracy"? Mr. Van Hemelrijck set out to reassure all parties.
In press interviews in Leopoldville he repeated the King's proclamation of January 13 and insisted that it meant everything it said,
no more and no less. He called in for friendly little chats the leaders
of the "respectable" African political parties; and succeeded in
persuading most of them to issue in their turn conciliatory statements to the newspapers. But when he got to Kivu province, in
the easternmost sector of the colony, he found he had to modify
these tactics of tranquilization. Here, in Bukavu, the provincial
capital, most of the Europeans had organized themselves into a
"white citizens' council" that was holding symbolic strikes and
sending off long daily protests to the King and the government
against the liberalism of the new policy. But the minister still tried
to "dissipate misunderstandings." Never for an instant did the government or the King contemplate abandoning ultimate authority
over the Congo, he told the umbrageous burghers. Belgians could
count on living forever in the colony, their lives and properties
safeguarded by the metropole.

If the minister was counting on the spaces that divide Leopoldville from Bukavu to prevent the discrepancies in his interpretation
from marring the sunniness of its impression, he was only following the oldest rule in the colonial book. Every old African hand,
and nearly every colonial officer, will tell you that the Africans are
tribesmen who hate each other worse than they hate the European,

and that the very word "African"—with all that it implies—is the devilish invention of ignorant foreign troublemakers. The Abako, which is the noisiest and best organized African political party of the Congo, is supposed by the authorities to exist only in Leopold-ville (although my train was stoned all the way from Matadi to Leopoldville by Africans yelling *"Vive l'Abako"*). Then there are other primitive African political organizations—another one in Leo-poldville, one in Elisabethville, one in Bakavu, and so on. But they are all sealed off from one another—and, according to the Belgians, from the ability to mobilize anything like a Congolese "nation"— by the limitless plains and the valleys, mountains, rivers, and lakes of the awesome hinterland. Moreover, the tribesmen who thinly inhabit this hinterland dislike and distrust their urban cousins, the doctrine goes on further to explain, and will fight for Belgian rule if it comes to a showdown with the Abako or any similar party. Indeed, in the spring of 1959 the Belgian government briefly con-sidered shifting the colony's capital from Leopold II's monument city to Luluabourg, in order to nestle more securely in the bosom of these loyal tribesmen. But after they had a chance to reflect on the realities of political and biological power—and particularly on some fiscal realities—this scheme was allowed to subside into a pigeon-hole labeled Nostalgia. For all the reasons we have discussed at length in this chapter, and so many more besides, the authority which cannot rule the cities of Africa cannot rule the countries.

It would be nearly impossible to overestimate the shock adminis-tered to the Belgians, and to the history of the Congo, by the Leopoldville riots of January, 1959. For the Belgians are not Ger-mans. For all the fatuous bellicosity of a few young lieutenants, the ordinary Belgian does not relish firing on helpless men, women, and children with machine guns, mortars, and small arms. When it was all over, his optimistic self-esteem and self-confidence had been shaken to their roots.

That big trouble was brewing the government did not anticipate. Growing numbers of unemployed, a laggard response to the Ameri-can Recession, were swelling the populations of the streets in the townships, but apparently the officials overcredited their own con-servative statistics. The Africans illegally in the city—and also unemployed—were far more numerous than the government had estimated them to be. Then, in December, the insults began; groups of idlers, hanging around in front of the miserable little shops, began to howl at passing Europeans in their cars. Little spontaneous meetings congealed at this or that intersection, lining up in improvised processions that marched down the avenues and threw stones. Nocturnal looting commenced; barricades were hurriedly thrown up on some of the entry roads to Leopoldville, and Europeans were hauled out of their cars, beaten up, and in at least two cases raped. It was during this phase of the trouble that four or five white women were reportedly assaulted and murdered, though for eight weeks after the riots had been suppressed the administration refused to admit that there had been any loss whatever of European life.

But when, on January 5, the mobs spilled over to the main market place of the town the government stepped in massively. Armories were opened up and guns, along with from thirty to fifty rounds, were issued to any European who presented himself at the door. In addition to arming themselves, the colonists formed into voluntary platoons and regiments which took over the guarding of vital spots like oil dumps and railroad yards, while the regular army and the police—with armored cars and mortar units—took on the African townships themselves. A curfew and an illegal-assembly law were decreed, and for two nights every African on the streets—individual or part of a mob—was fired upon. A paratroop unit already on the high seas, returning to Belgium, was hastily flown back to the colony.

By the middle of the month the external trouble had been put down. The African population returned to its pastimes with that plasticity of temperament which is the despair of colonials, no matter how many years they have lived in the midst of it. Although the riots had mainly limited themselves to the Leopoldville area, there were also outbreaks of violence directed against churches and schools 100 miles or more away, and Matadi, the capital's port, also had its own small-sized riot. These were all suppressed. Also, so far as anyone has ever been able to deduce from the evidence, the Abako leadership was caught just as far off base by the upheaval as the Belgian administration. Nevertheless, the top echelon of the Abako were arrested, including Joseph Kasavubu, its chief, and taken to Belgium on the charge that an illegal meeting which they attended had fomented the trouble. Two months later the accusations were withdrawn and the Abako leaders returned to Africa, after promising to conduct further political activities "in order and in legality," but in November, 1959, they announced their intention to boycott the much-hoped-for elections.

The question that remains is the cost of the affair. No one in a position to know believes the published estimate that only 47 Africans lost their lives in the crucial two days. It seems certain that 500 or more were killed; and some people put the toll as high as 3,000. This is not to count the tens of thousands of passless Africans whom the government picked up afterward and shipped back to their countries, without of course coping with the forces which had driven these men to walk to the city in the first place. (Nor did it seem a particularly canny policy to seed the presumably loyal tribes—whom the Belgians are courting—with citified individuals fresh from this harsh brush with Belgian justice.)

But with these riots we come to the vital, but quasi-philosophical, question of the Belgians' "mandate" in the Congo—and this is important to the Belgians, because if they are to rule they wish to do so with a comforting sense of rectitude and self-satisfaction. But can they now?

If the official estimates of the unemployed in Leopoldville on which the administration was basing its social policies were only one-third what they should have been—and this is a conservative view; if official estimates of the number of Africans who were killed in suppressing the outbreak were off by a factor of ten or more—there inevitably is born a serious doubt that the Belgians any longer understand or discipline the realities of life in the Congo. And this doubt is now very widespread among Belgians in the Congo. It is no good to say that whatever is the most radical African political party on the stage at a given moment is responsible for every social and economic upheaval. It is no good howling along with a few Bukavu traders and beardless corporals that these troubles should teach the government not to "baby the blacks." Most Belgians have been sharply brought up against some of the implications of non-responsive, non-self-intercommunicating political power—and they are aware of it. In this aspect the Leopoldville affray resembles the Amritsar "massacre" of April, 1919, after which a blood-gulf yawned between the Briton and the Indian, and what should have been ephemeral attitudes were cast in bronze—things which would have constituted insuperable obstacles to common understanding had it not been for the splendid accident of the skills of the Earl Mountbatten and Prime Minister Nehru later on.

So the Belgians are asking themselves of what a true "mandate" consists—what is their repayment for the wealth and satisfactions they are obtaining in the Congo? After all, it is no joke for an African to tramp halfway across the continent to seek a job in the big city. He would not make the trip unless he had to—and in this sense the government's prohibition against traveling without permission has always been frivolous. When our African arrives and there is no job, is it not part of administration's duty to provide somehow for him? If it does not, who will? Can he walk back home? But, to linger further on all this, when the government—at least partly deluded by its own data—does not provide for him, or even know where he is, and he grows hungrier, is it wrong for him to seek a means of self-expression? What means are available? Politics? Hardly, in an authoritarian society in which even the Belgian colonist does not have the vote. What can he do but come together with thousands of friends and neighbors in the same plight as himself, shout himself hoarse, break into grogshops, and overturn automobiles? Does the government, while he is doing these things, have the right to shoot him down—*and his women and children*—like verminous toads?

It will not do to claim that problems of mass unemployment, famine, epidemic, and the like are too Brobdingnagian for any government to be asked to take hold of. This is the old, smug, discredited principle of autocracy, perfectly expressed in a flatulent minute of the Marquess of Curzon in 1896: "To ask any government to prevent the occurrence of famine in a country the meterological conditions of which are what they are here [India], is to ask us to wrest the keys of the universe from the hands of the Almighty." What then, if not to prevent famine, can you reasonably ask of a colonial government? A government which rests an all-too-slender claim to legitimacy on cultural, military, or racial superi-

ority must justify itself in a thousand ways that are unnecessary
and redundant for a government that is based on popular support
and constantly refreshing itself in response to popular insistence.
What right has the European got to rule Africa, not to say mulct
Africa, unless he can do just these things—stop pestilence, provide
modernization and mass employment, found universities and research centers—that the African presumably cannot do so well for
himself? But if the problems of Africa are simply too big for the
European powers—as indeed they are for the existing colonial governments—then there is no use talking of morality or legitimacy at
all, on anyone's terms. It is all a farce; the European regime is in
reality founded on nothing but commanding force—and if there
is any "right" in the situation it is the African's right to counter
this commanding force with force of his own, even to murdering
every colonial in his bed. That is, after all, the way history usually
changes mandates.

But before we leave this I-hope-not-too-abstract consideration
of "mandate," let us see if we can frame a few ideas around which
a genuine and lasting mandate in the Congo would revolve. The
secret, of course, is to ride with the governing trends—the urbanization, modernization, industrialization—of the country, and in riding
with them to master them and blend them into a social harmony.
This may sound an impossibly large order, and perhaps it is—although the consequences of failure to fill this order are something I
wish pessimists would talk over more often than they do—but we
cannot know this until we have tried and failed, and the one thing
that is certain in Africa is that no one has tried. For example, locked
in her continent-wide river basin the Congo possesses what has been
calculated to be more than 25 per cent of the potential hydroelectric
energy of the whole world, more than enough to remake the economic map of West Africa and to go very far toward relieving the
impoverishment of the country. Since 1945, there have been numerous surveys of various parts of this system, particularly the falls and
rapids that intercept the river's course from Leopoldville, on the
Stanley Pool, to Matadi on the estuary. Along this passage engineers
have drafted a feasible project that would yield about 30 million
kilowatts, or a fifth of the total electric-power consumption of the
United States. But look at what has happened to this Inga Falls

project, the estimated cost of which is about $4 billion. In the early postwar years the Belgian government itself showed little interest in it. There was nowhere to market the power which it would produce; it would be a huge white elephant, generating fantastic quantities of juice in a region without light bulbs or other electrical appliances. But then Nkrumah started angling for money with which to build his dam; before the French were trounced out of Guinea they boasted about a dam they were going to construct there; in the Rhodesias work actually went forward on the Kariba Dam. It struck the Belgians that, with a development at Inga Falls, aluminum and other industrial metals could be processed right in the Congo, the ores coming from other parts of Africa, from the Caribbean, or from the Congo itself. They began to show a real interest in the monster project.

As they do not possess the kind of money themselves that it will take to develop the Congo River, the Belgians now turned to American capital. And they found—to their ironical bewilderment— that American capital was even more cautious than they themselves had been ten years previous. Although it is nearly, or absolutely, impossible to find one example of a power-producing facility in the modern world that has not been oversubscribed a year or two after completion, the old white elephant argument is one that is constantly on the lips of American businessmen abroad; they do not see how much more overactive modern human fertility is than modern capitalism. Therefore, moderation-in-everything is the standard first ploy used on hungry foreign applicants for our private capital. And then there is the "problem of confidence," perfectly expressed in the winter of 1958–1959 by two important visitors to the Congo of whom much was expected, a representative of the Chase Manhattan Bank (Mr. David Rockefeller) and a representative of Dillon, Read. American business is absolutely sure that the Belgian administration of the Congo is one of the best in the world, these gentlemen told their hosts at Chamber of Commerce meetings around the country, but before it will want to risk its stockholders' money in Africa it will want to have absolute surety as well in the stable political future of the continent. The poor Belgians—immersed to their necks in an increasingly unstable and declining world copper price, a zooming population, a revolutionary urban proletariat, the menacing gestures of Nkrumah and the freedom-boys of the north, the withdrawal of the French and British colonial administrations, the entrenchment of Afrikanerdom—puzzled quietly to themselves how to communicate a radiant inner self-confidence that would sweep Wall Street off its feet to the extent of $3–4 billions. With these visitors they got enough of their own medicine to give them a really salutary headache.

Meanwhile, of course, no one is building Inga. So the African waits and wilts. We have seen what kind of "democracy" he has been indoctrinated into. And now what about the variety of "capitalism" that has come to Africa? All the African has known is the buccanneer-capitalism of the slave trader and ivory hunter, the great planter, the corporation agent. Of the capitalism which we have developed in this country—the strength of which is drawn from, and modified by, biennial consultations with our citizenry— he knows nothing whatever. For him, "democratic capitalism" is the system under which white men do what they want to do, and do not do what they do not want to do. It is not as if the African is a savage who never heard of the Inga Falls project; on the contrary, I heard it spoken of all over the Congo, and only once found a man who knew nothing of it—and he was a pygmy. Mistakenly or not, the ordinary African—and particularly the citified African— feels that the project is the first indispensable step toward the Better Life. And why should he not feel that way? What else has he got to hope for? Naturally he is not able to sit down and list all the American businessman's technical objections to the monster investment. But does he actually err in concluding that the real reason that nothing is being done—the real reason the dam is not yet a-building—is that white men are not absolutely sure they will make a profit by it? Is he really wrong in believing that no one cares about what the project will mean to him, the African? In any case, the Belgians have not done what should have been done years ago. And it is inactivity of this kind, building up a tension between the pretensions and the accomplishments of a government, that attenuates and then terminates a political mandate.

I pray that the many Belgians who were so kind to me in my travels around their African colony will not set me down in their books as just one more of those ungrateful strangers that men of good will must grin and bear. I especially wish to thank the government and the government-controlled airline, Sabena, which provided me with a journalist's pass that took me gratis all over the giant country. I found, as I went, that nowhere in Africa does the African appear to be better off materially than here. The Belgians are well aware of this, which is why their comparative unpopularity with the African upsets and hurts them. In this chapter I have tried to set down a few things which may help to explain this failure.

But, then, a chapter on the Congo is the logical setting for something else that needs saying—namely, that it is inexcusable folly to go to Africa to look only at the politics. When the final trump is sounded it is the magic of Africa that shall be found to have won more helpful friends to her than all the indignation or high strategy in creation. Nothing, for instance, could be more dramatic than an ocean ship's entrance up the great river from Shark's Point, where it debouches into the Atlantic, to Matadi. In one dimension the river embraces an Image of Africa: the slow water laded with red silt, staining the ocean for many miles out of sight of land; a shuddering, mute energy, levying tribute on the continent by way of thousands of unknown watercourses thousands of miles into the interior, interring the broken belongings and the leftovers of hundreds of tribes and clans along its route; by its very hugeness and slovenliness mutinying against the Modern Day and the petty human fabricators of the Modern Day. In the evening a man can stand on the fantail of such a ship going upriver and look across the lower reaches of the Congo to the sea. The tangled wilderness of mangrove swamps, intersected by sinister bayous, frame the river and the carmine sphere of the sun; across the sky, crimson and canary-yellow banners blazon from one horizon's end to the other. Belowdecks the African crew is softly singing or sniffing the smells of equatorial nightfall, or leaning over the rails and looking at the glory of their homeland. This is the way to arrive in Africa.

Equally marvelous in its way is a visit to the "real" Africa, as the old hands call it: Kivu province, the game plains of the Albert National Park, the Mountains of the Moon (that seem to be on the point of falling on a man, when they are approached from the

West); the necklace of the Central Lakes which the Congo shares with East Africa; and their border of green-mantled volcanoes. Set in this country like the prize gem of an incomparable pendant is the loveliest country of Africa, the tiny trust land of Ruanda-Urundi—a place of hills and coffee ranches, of floral brilliance outdazzling California's, of waterfalls and silent coves in dark lakes, of the smiling and exquisitely mannered senior race, the giant Watusis, supposed to be the descendants of ancient Egyptian wanderers; of the Kagera Park and the source of the Nile. Ruanda-Urundi happens to have serious overpopulation, overgrazing, and racial-political problems, but it is the industrious pedant indeed who thinks of these things until weeks after he has left this delightful land.

Lastly, I want to pay tribute to a Belgian friend, who I hope may stand here for the best of the European contribution to Africa and without whose quality of contribution it will be impossible for any policy—white or black—to mend her. Twenty-five years ago Mr. Carl Esser came out from Belgium with a small sum of money borrowed from his family and began to carve out a ranch in Kasai province, near the Angolan border. He started on a small scale, and necessarily with a herd of the runty, stringy native African breed which at that time were the only cattle resistant to the tsetse fly and other scourges of the plateau. The labors he has faced are nothing short of Herculean. The fly has chronically infected, and still infects, 30 per cent of his stock. He has had to battle through mountains of governmental red tape. He has had to gain the cooperation of the neighboring chiefs—who do not understand why his breeding stock must be kept celibate (so far as their cows are concerned) or why his pasture land, after twenty years of manuring and experimenting with new grasses, looks so much lusher than theirs. He has had to fight the Société Générale, which operates a larger ranch in the neighborhood. He has had to exercise unsleeping vigilance against natural breaks in his fence, through which the native cattle casually stroll. All this in addition to combating the climate, the drouths, the diseases of the low veld.

Nevertheless, Esser has succeeded in building up a herd of about 5,000 head, the annual yield from which he sells in Luluabourg or to the Angolan diamond company. (Like every other cattle grower in a protein-poor continent, the marketing and shipping of his beef are the least of Esser's problems; if he wished, he could get rid of them at his front gate.) But Esser has done far more than simply turn a good profit. At his own expense, without government advice or aid of any kind, he has engaged in some of the most far-reaching and potentially valuable experiments in stockraising that have been conducted anywhere in Africa. He has established several breeds of grass which are more appetizing and nutritious than the indigenous cover of the African plain. He has imported Brahman cattle from Pakistan and crossed them with his native stock, in a long-range effort to build up a strain that can defend itself against the African environment as well as carry heavier layers of meat. He has corresponded with the managers of the King Ranch about Santa Gertrudis bulls; he thinks that if this breed were introduced skillfully into Africa it might eventually double the weight of ordinary African stock. But he has found that to purchase a Santa Gertrudis stud is beyond his private means. "The big boy might fall over from Africanitis the day he stepped off the plane," Esser says. "But if Mr. Kleberg would like to go half-and-half I would make the deal."

All this intelligent, courageous, and persevering work has resulted in the increase, within twenty years, of the average weight of his livestock by about 50 per cent. Kasai is not an especially healthy province; it is not a fortunate highland area; and therefore the implications of Essor's work, for all the similar savanna plains everywhere in Black Africa, are breath-taking. But Esser and his ranch are not a laboratory isolated in the middle of the continent. He has family responsibilities; he has shrewdly appraised the recent unsettling political events in the Congo, and he has about decided that his day is over. Of course he would prefer to remain in Africa; he loves ranching; he takes enormous pride in his pioneering work; but he has a different way of looking at the new African politics from that of most Americans—which is, it goes without saying, his God-given right—and he has no intention of remaining in business if it means that one day his ranch will be overrun and confiscated by "nationalists" and that the substantial nest egg he plans to leave his children will be lost in the mess.

He might take an American partner. As he says, when the revolution came to Indonesia the Dutch firms were expropriated, but the English and Americans were left alone. When the revolution came to Burma the Dutch and Americans were left alone, but the English were expropriated. If he had an American partner, and an American name on his letterhead, perhaps he could continue to ranch as a silent partner right into the unpredictable new era of African self-government. But up to now this is just a dream, and so at present Esser is not permitting his eldest son to come to the Congo or take any interest in the ranch. He has given his life to the ranch; he has made money by the ranch; he has accomplished work on the ranch which matches the experimental work done in similar savanna areas anywhere else in Africa—and work that is more desperately needed than anything that can be thought of; he loves the ranch, and has nothing else in the creative way to live for. But he is a Belgian and a businessman, and so his final word is, "I will wait a little longer; if nothing turns up I'll send my animals to the butcher, pack up my profits, and walk off the place."

And when and if Esser walks off his ranch there is no possibility of any kind of government—white or black—reaching out from Leopoldville and inheriting these operational functions away off in the Kasai. He will have slaughtered his animals; his studbooks will be burned or dispersed; his carefully cherished grasslands ruined by bad management; the houses, toil, and experience dissipated like so much steam in the air. Africa shall then have lost, the world shall have lost, what it can ill afford to lose.

Neither can Africa nor the world afford to lose the other positive achievements of the Belgian rule of the Congo: the highways, airlines, factories, schools, and hospitals. No one wants to lose these things: this is the finest possible testimonial to the value of what the Belgians have built in Africa. But so long as it is made impossible for the African to accept the gifts of the Belgian and to remain at the same time a full-fledged, proud, and self-respecting human being, then the African must throw them away for the sake of his own soul. The choice is not the African's.

8. The French Community in Africa

In grandeur the French Community is a breath of the great old Europe of pre-1914, but it has yet to prove that it is more than a death rattle.

It is the dire implications of a hostile future Africa very different from the Africa we see today—and culturally, or anyway technologically, much more nearly on a par with us—that have set certain men in the past century to devising ways of binding Africa to Europe by hoops of steel or necessity or, even, affection. If, for example, independent new nations of Africa were to join with the nations of Asia in a "confederation of color" the Atlantic frontier would be unhinged, and Europe would be enclosed within a geopolitical capsule, the only exit from which would lie in the direction of the New World, distinctly smaller—both in point of area and population—than the old one. Indeed, the station of South America in this alignment would be equivocal, to say the least of it, because so far as racial configuration goes South America is also a "continent of color."

Hence the apparition which has overcome a select band of frights in each of the last four or five generations, the specter of a "West" pressed back into the narrow regions of North America, a few European offshore islands like Iceland and Great Britain, and perhaps an outpost or two on the "heartland" itself like France or Denmark. Recently, in fact, the specter has grown more redoubtable than ever, because what we now deem a far more critical social variable than race—namely, the over-all capacity for responding creatively to the Technological Revolution—turns out to be establishing a territorial frontier which coincides roughly with the old-fashioned "color" frontier—so that whether you look at politics in the "old" way or the "new" the hypothetical rollback of the West arrives at about the same borders. What disturbs old and new seers alike, then, is a prospect of inherent, potent, and propulsive *differences* in the natures of populations or their environments conveying eight-tenths-plus of the human race down an evolutionary road which we of the West would not wish to take even if we could. And the foreseen end of it all is first a polarization of mankind, and then the progressive isolation and ostracism of our segment of it, with incalculable effects on our political and spiritual lives—the majority of which it is only candid to characterize as highly disagreeable. (As we shall see, though Russia does not exactly play the pivotal role in this process that her own philosophers like to claim for her, her role is certainly ambiguous. So far as economic society goes she is on our side: that is to say, she has conquered the Technological Revolution. But there are other questions at stake, which for the time being we must leave up in the air: whether Russia is part of "Europe" or of "Asia"; whether a "racial" categorization of Russia means anything at all; whether ideological distinctions like, say, "Communism" and "Free World" are the truly significant distinctions, cutting across or transcending the other ones we have been considering here.)

Now this is very fancy, one might say Edwardian, discourse, and it may be feared that if we continue along these lines we will run into the sort of "geopolitical" dogmatizing which the fathers of the Second World War taught us to mistrust. Moreover, we know that in the modern world serious power readjustments are rarely consummated without the intercession of a major war—and once in train modern wars have a way of rebounding unpredictably on victors, losers, and political theorizers alike. Nonetheless, despite these caveats, it would be foolish to deny that the general idea of polarizing social antagonisms does indeed cast a shadow over all the politico-socio-economic lucubrations of our day. The present author, for instance, can only too easily imagine the world that is diagramed by so many shrewd, up-to-date economists—the world consisting of North America and Europe living at one standard, and all the rest of humanity at another, with the two zones sundered more every day by a growing unwillingness to share on the one side and a growing disgust and jealousy on the other.

Not only can we conceive such a world model, but the prospect of it should distress us mightily. But when, in this distress, we get down to the business of deciding what we of the West *are* that we wish other men to be too, in order to forestall our potential isolation, we find ourselves in trouble—for what we are and desire in this context cannot be readily pinned down and measured like constitutional "rights" or telephones per capita of citizens. All the same—and to skip over a great many weighty fields of inquiry like "Western civilization" and what Silas Wegg called "declining and falling"—it strikes me that "Free World" is a perfectly admissible representation of what we Americans are trying to communicate to the world and to employ as a bridge over these various gaps that threaten to separate us from so much of that world. But it is a representation whose validity surely depends on our defining "free" fully, as we ourselves live the concept and mean it. That is to say, as we practice it here in America, freedom is not primarily freedom *from* slave labor camps and secret police—but a positive, energizing, enlarging freedom: to think, dream, talk, experiment, to lose onself, to live at a little leisure, to advance toward the conquest of creation-crippling miseries and of the solar system, the dozens of humdrum personal privileges planted in down-to-earth statutes like the Bill of Rights which political moralizers never refer to but which are the real ground on which the whole structure rests, and so on. In short, we live in a house of open doors that is labeled Freedom—and we hope and believe that it is possible for the other people in our world to live with us in this house, regardless of their race, economic and political history, or any other of the society-dividing pressures that beset them.

I wish to offer only two more suggestions before concluding this protracted introductory. First, no definition of "freedom" that will impassion anyone can include polities like Spain's, where religious minorities are disabled from practicing their own faith, where the general populaton is forbidden to read a healthy proportion of the West's creative and scientific literature, where a specific liberty like Freedom of the Press is regularly denounced by government and in the state schools. Sooner or later we are going to have to sacrifice a few of our treasured circumlocutions about "freedom" or we will lose entirely our notion of who we are ourselves and where we want to go. But the second suggestion can be more properly stressed in an essay on Africa. It is, simply, the well known fact that a coupling exists between a man's freedom to work, create, and ratiocinate and his freedom from crucial environmental shortages. When a man is really hungry, and has *always* been hungry and—in fact—only half alive, his brain and his spirit cannot get a grip on the delicate little threads of speculation by which we of the West are climbing toward our mysterious goal of a more perfect understanding of mind, society, and cosmos—which progress, all bundled together, is in reality the "freedom" that we speak so much about. A genuinely starving man, half mad with worrying about his starving children into the bargain, cannot profit from listening to Mozart, the Gettysburg Address, or the latest news from the moon. He is not a "free" man in any meaningful sense of the word; his spirit is a slave to his belly; and when somehow fate tests him, his reactions are compelled to be more animal—or, to return to an idea in the Foreword, more monstrous—than human. And it is when you scan the world, trying to locate a boundary line between men who are free of their bellies and men who are not, that you receive a palpable shock, for the frontier that emerges from this overlook roughly coincides with the old frontier of "color" and also the economists' frontier dividing societies which have surmounted the developmental "hump" from those which have not. Here, in short, is a polarization process motored by three quasi-independent forces—a formidable historical engine indeed. It means that freedom is more than an idea and a jurisprudence; it is also bread and meat.

My excuse for this standard defense of Technical Assistance, *et al.* —an anticipation of some of the conclusions of the last chapter—is that, trite or not, this demarcation between Free and Unfree Belly-Spirits—or rather the abolition of this demarcation—is the crux of the problem of Eurafrica, of which the French Community is at one and the same time the exemplar and the splendid promise. If

the French Community works, Charles De Gaulle and his Constitution of October 4 (1958) will merit the humble and deathless
gratitude of "free men" and of the whole world. But it can work
only if the magic in the dream engenders a correspondingly radical
reformation in daily practice. There is a bargain in the Community
that the French must observe with a scrupulosity which will be new
to them. When some 13 million French Africans voted to remain
within the Community as "autonomous republics" (fewer than
2 million voted No); when eleven of the twelve components of
French West Africa and French Equatorial Africa voted for the
French connection (as we know, French Guinea was the exception),
the Africans said in effect that they so needed and respected the
social advantages of the Community that they were willing to bury
their sterile old political grievances and to indoctrinate themselves
with a brand-new set of political principles. The Africans were
capable of explaining this with great bluntness. "We will need
French aid until the year X," said Prime Minister Youlou of the
Congo Republic, for example. But the easier path was still that favored by Guinea, that of indulging old passions at the expense of new
opportunities. In any case, French Africa demonstrated as decisively
as she could that she will give the Community a try. France herself
wants to try the Community, for her own reasons. And we of the
West *need* the Community as insistently as we need anything. Thus,
the only question before the house is whether De Gaulle, the ordinary Frenchman, and the ordinary Westerner will be willing to
foot the bill for obliterating the "empty belly" line which, so long
as it exists, condemns the dream of Community to a nonsense fan-
tasy.

"While the British Empire was built by businessmen wanting to
make money, the French Empire was built by bored officers looking
for excitement," runs the comment of a French historian. The French
Empire in Black Africa is a story that goes back to the 1500's,
when French missionaries and freebooters—joining the other European nations who were plying the slave and ivory trades of West
Africa—established forlorn little posts in various river mouths on
the African coast from the Senegal to the Gabon. In planting these
stations they were broaching a gigantic, unknown, and kaleidoscopic

universe—or rather many universes—the Sahara and the "Sudanese" plains of French West Africa, oases and marshes and illimitable dunes thinly populated by dozens of mulatto and pure Negro tribes of nomads and farmers and forest dwellers, some of whom had been quasi-incorporated into the evanescent village confederacies of Ghana, Mali, Goa, Ouagadougou, and so on; to the south, the sullen rivers and rainforests of French Equatorial Africa. Until the nineteenth century little penetration was made into this hinterland, but then—inspired by the ennui of officers like Louis Léon César Faidherbe, scholar of the Berber tongue, geographer and historian of West Africa, general and administrator (whose colonial maxim was "peace or powder")—the French nation and army began to envisage a giant empire stretching across the continent from St. Louis in Senegal to the Red Sea.

Faidherbe himself was the leader of expeditions into the interior which rounded up chiefs, reduced them to dependency on the French, and opened up the populous valleys of the Senegal and the basin of the Niger. South of this, in the 1870's, Savorgnan de Brazza cruised up the Congo and the Ogowe Rivers, fencing off the thrusts of Leopold II's Congo agents, bestowing on France millions of square miles of the jungle. And in the following two decades, impelled by a now thoroughly aroused public taste for imperialism, French units took off from these staging centers on an eastward race to the Nile, which they reached in 1898 at Fashoda, a tiny village about 500 miles south of Khartoum. Here they ran up against the counterambitions of a people even more aroused than themselves. The "Fashoda Incident"—in which a French contingent was ordered out of its camp by a British officer who claimed prior occupation—was one of those pre-World War I crises which it is difficult to take seriously nowadays, although authorities assure us that a European war was avoided by a narrow margin. However this may be, the incident was finally closed in 1904 with an agreement whereby France recognized Britain's position in Egypt and the Sudan in exchange for British recognition of the French interests in Morocco.

And by this time the French Empire in Black Africa was more or less complete, and with the exception of some of the smaller, better concealed tribes of the deep forests more or less in the harness of orderly administration. With the territories which later came to be called French West Africa and French Equatorial Africa, France found herself with a domain in the Dark Continent about 3 million square miles in extent; in which came to dwell, by 1958, about 25 million people; and which had for landscape one gigantic desert, lightly peppered with unwholesome oases; the "Sudanese" belt cut by slow-moving and malarial rivers; the Guinea forests, dark with menace; and the jungles of Gabon and the Middle Congo.

Until the outbreak of World War II the French rule in Black Africa can fairly be termed "sleepy." Without embarking on re- markable campaigns of violence or persecution, the French—follow- ing their principle of "direct" administration—managed to break up most of the paramount chieftaincies of FWA, reorganize the tribes of FEA, and subject the Africans generally to a "central" authority manned by French military and political officers. By and large the populace settled peacefully down to a way of life that was certainly stabler than any they had known, and with the exception of a troublesome famine in the early 1900's in FWA the sub- sistence farming system, which at first was hardly disrupted by the few cash cropping projects of the French, fairly well met the needs of the people. Of course, Africans were not without their standard grievances—forced labor, military conscription, and so on—when in the 1920's political parties in France herself, first the Socialists, then the Popular Front and the Communists, took the initiative of sponsoring youthful Africans in political training programs in Paris, and then keeping up contacts with these apprentices and the parties they formed upon their return to Africa. Theoretically, also, an "evolution" process in French Africa similar to the "assimilation" institution in Portuguese Africa was making provision for those Africans who were maturing toward equality and self-government, but this process hardly made a dent on the African subject peoples; in 1939 there were only 2,136 French-African citizens in FWA (plus the citizens of the Senegalese "communes," who had a special status).

We must also remember one of the curious features of the French personality, that from time to time Mme. Recamier turns, like an anti-Cinderella, into Mme. Defarge—and the "soul of Europe" appears as a twisted, mindless ogre, crawling with hatreds and bestialities which Tocqueville would have us believe go back to the evil and fissiparous reign of Louis XIV. However this may be, in the colonial sphere the part of atavistic France has been more than adequately played by the colonial army, which has been responsible for a half-dozen or so terrifying incidents in our own time: for example, the bombardment of Haiphong in 1946, and the "pacification" of Madagascar in the spring of 1947, during which more than 80,000 Malagasy were mowed down in reprisal for the murders of 200 Frenchmen. This is not to mention the excruciatingly dragged-out woes of the Algerian war. As I say, these are exceptional episodes, but the fact that they are exceptional makes them stick in the mind, and perhaps renders it even more surprising and creditable that the French Community—which of course includes Madagascar—is still considered by French-African politicians to be a practical possibility.

The effects of World War II on French Africa were paradoxical. Economically, the brief separation of the territories from their accustomed markets in metropolitan France subjected them to a deep strain. Then, too, the German victory of 1940 introduced the men of Vichy into the drama, and in their few hours they followed a very different racial and social policy from that of the prewar governments of statesmen like Blum, who was noted for his congeniality if not his attentiveness to the problems of French Africa. But at the same time, in the early 1940's, the French Africans amazed the world by refusing to take the collapse of the metropole for an opportunity to close the French out of Africa; although it was naturally the "true French," in the phrase of the Moro Naba, one of the chiefs of the Upper Volta, to whom they adhered, not the French of Pétain and Darlan.

Partly because of this loyalty, since the war the French African has been on the receiving end of a continuous procession of political rewards which have now come to their logical conclusion in his freedom to associate with France or not as he pleases: the Brazzaville Conference of 1944, when Free French leaders proposed the objectives of equality and brotherhood; the abolition of numerous forced labor and other oppressive laws under the French Constitution of 1946; the Labor Code of December, 1952, which protected his right to strike; the *"loi-cadre"* of June, 1956, which in addition to administrative reforms spelled out some of the economic obligations of the central power of the "French Union"; finally, De Gaulle's Constitution of 1958, which has placed the French-African relationship on an entirely fresh juridical basis, to be, like the Commonwealth, a voluntary association of free, fraternal states.

That the whole edifice of the French Empire did not crumple to the ground during and after the war, and instead has taken on this new lease of liberal life, is due in part to the Leftish forces in postwar France herself (conspicuously—though not for acceptably liberal reasons—the large and powerful French Communist Party), but due even more perhaps to the articulate idealism and skills of a handful of highly Gallicized French-African leaders, who have proved themselves capable of deploying the dogmatic anti-imperialism of the far Left and the "grandeur"-mystique of the Gaullist Right to score off the reactionary Right of the *colons* and the capitalists, thus maneuvering their countries into the Community which they hope will benefit them in the long run more than any other feasible association. Certainly they mean to give it a chance, and it is the concoction of this chance which we have witnessed in the past year—with seven of the eight former states federated in French West Africa (Mauritania, Sudan, Ivory Coast, Upper Volta, Senegal, Dahomey, and Niger) and the four territories of French Equatorial Africa (Gabon, Middle Congo, Ubangi-Shari, and Chad) choosing the Community over independence. (In January, 1959, four of the states of FWA, Senegal, Sudan, Dahomey, and the Upper Volta, decided on a subsidiary federation, Mali, with a capital in the Senegalese metropolis of Dakar. Only the first two ultimately joined up, and in September, 1959, they asked out of the Community altogether.)

Very well, but where do we go from here? This political picture incites in us hopes of miracles, considering the turbulence and grudges of the past, but how many "empty bellies" are there in French Africa, and what is the Community—which in this department means France—doing about them?

At first glance the French have good reason for pride. Since

World War II the French have regularly expended more than 1.5 per cent of their national income in public and private investment in underdeveloped countries, compared to about 0.5 per cent for the United States and 0.6 per cent for Great Britain. (As Miss Tillion is quick to remind us: "The United States, which has undertaken to save the world . . . has devoted to the Point Four program a mere quarter of what France has distributed in North Africa alone since 1947.") On top of this sizable investment, which runs France a total of about $600 millions a year, there have been the severe, and perhaps lethal, costs of her "imperial defensives" in Algeria and Indo-China. Most of the pure development money has gone naturally to North Africa, but since 1947 about $1 billion has come to FWA and about half that sum to FEA. These funds, plus a fairly steadily holding market for French Africa's coffee, peanuts, cocoa, cotton, and lumber, have been enough to induce the same spectacularly ostentatious progress that we noted in the Congo and the Rhodesias. The appearance of the major cities of the coast has altered entirely in the past decade. And in the three years from 1953 to 1956 the iron ore production of FWA nearly doubled; diamond production more than doubled; for the decade, the ports of Abidjan, Dakar, Pointe-Noire, Conakry have increased their handling totals by factors of ten to twenty. As we have seen, the population of French Africa is more than keeping pace.

But once again we find that these glittering modernisms have been pile-driven down into a society without regard to whether they were hitting sand or rock, whether the society could digest such injections of "joy-juice" and metabolize them in a healthy way. The outstanding example of an improper development by France is not actually in Black Africa at all, but in Algeria, which the French conquered in the late 1820's. Here, what are estimated to be a dozen Frenchmen have come to possess as much money as all the rest of the population put together, and these fortunes were made without the slightest backward look at the havoc left by their making; in the most notorious instance, a vast pile was heaped up on the profits of turning tens of thousands of farm acres over to vineyards, although this has helped to wreck the agricultural balance of the country and although the Moslem Algerians do not even drink wine.

Similar laissez-faire practices, but on a more modest and slovenly scale, also prevail throughout French Black Africa. Understand that 90 per cent of the French Africans still live on their back-yard farms—and therefore that nothing which improves any one sector of the economy at the expense of the agricultural (or, rather, to put it more precisely, any policy which is not directly aimed at curing the deep-seated ills of the agricultural sector) can be considered to be progressive or even tolerable. But despite this overwhelming dependence on the agricultural sector, characteristic of all primitive societies, 60 per cent of the total French investment in Black Africa has gone into new urban projects, or into mining, electrical, processing, or port facilities, or communications—in the useless expectation that the profits from large-scale cash cropping and what industrialization is possible on these terms can somehow pay the doctor's bills of the rest of the society.

The development projects proper in French Africa are the responsibility of a special agency of the government, the Investment Fund for Economic and Social Development in the Overseas Territories (or FIDES, the initials of its French title). This agency has, of course, taken its lumps in Africa as all investors must be prepared to do; for example, on at least one occasion it contracted for huge quantities of agricultural machinery which was inoperable in the climates and terrains of French Africa. Even in their ventures which have been relatively successful, like the twenty-year-old development in the Niger Basin, the authorities have from time to time been tempted into making grandiose publicity disclosures which have never been quite substantiated. But these are things that one must expect in connection with enterprise in Africa; it is part of the old black virago's reluctance to soup up and modernize; I mention them here only because we Americans, when our time comes to shoulder these developmental burdens, must be prepared to subsidize failure upon failure, for the simple reason that many of the things which need most urgently to be done no one knows precisely *how* to do.

But unhappy accidents and miscalculations are not the really serious objection to the activities of FIDES. What is are its systematic, though unintentional, fosterings of the imbalances which we described at some length in Chapter 1. We have already mentioned the sacrifice of the agricultural sector to the industrial. Then there is "urbanization," which has led to a high rate of unemployment (and that almost worse thing, underemployment) in Senegal, Guinea, and the Ivory Coast, where it found an outlet in savage riots in November, 1958, against Togolanders and Dahomeyans who had immigrated into the country in search of work. (Remember that, despite a population density of about 10 per square mile, "over-population" is a reality; the bulk of these lands is unusable, and these people are heavily concentrated in the remainders, the coastal strips and river valleys, this on top of all the other causal elements of African overpopulation.) An increasing proportion of the new population is not being put to work, and this—plus a slackening in the prosperity prices of the great postwar years—has resulted in a drop in the average real income. Already the self-subsistent agricultural system has been so disrupted that two specialists (Virginia Thompson and Richard Adloff, on whose *French West Africa* I have leaned heavily in this chapter) surmise that only two of the seven states of FWA now are feeding themselves; the others, Senegal for example, are subsisting on rice imported from abroad. The perils of this kind of a dependence in a rural, backward, and *agricultural* society hardly need any underlining of mine.

Undernourishment is universal throughout French Africa. Over wide areas soil exhaustion and deforestation have so injured the watersheds that engineers are now wondering about the feasibility of some hydroelectric-*cum*-irrigation projects which have not yet been taken out of the files or off the drawing boards. In FEA, which earns 30 per cent of its foreign credits with its lumber, the fragile soils of the equator, denuded of their natural cover, have been degraded to total worthlessness. No conclusive, or even important, research has been done in drainage, irrigation, and reclamation problems. All these holes in the balloon exacerbate the manifold factors which we have looked at in connection with other African regions: the vulnerability to price fluctuations in marginal commodities, the rising costs-of-living in urban areas, the changes in consumer habits, and so on.

Tragic to say, in at least one way the promising new political arrangement has not helped the chances of these poor countries. The French government had originally planned, especially for FEA, to take fairly strong measures against soil deterioration and erosion by organizing "settlements of peasants" who would work on a mixed agricultural system, and could be compelled to fallow their land properly and to conserve their forests. But the makers of schemes like this have to be ready to juggernaut through a solid wall of peasant resentment. The African smallholder, like his American and European cousins, never can be persuaded that from time to time a bureaucrat's sweeping reform must be undertaken which interferes with his immediate crop and income. Now, of course, the French government has surrendered its right to juggernaut; it has gladly turned the job over to the same African leaders who so agitated in past years against similar juggernautings, and these leaders are now in an obvious condition of embarrassment.

As a result of all these misconceived measures—which, as I say, "jest growed" in the odd, directionless atmosphere of French politics of the last century—neither FIDES nor the government has come near accomplishing their objective of making French Africa an area of sound, self-sufficient states. Only the Ivory Coast, prospering on a successful culture of cocoa and coffee, shows a substantially favorable balance of trade. The rest of French Africa almost invariably submits deficits, which in recent years have shown an alarming tendency toward engorgement.

In addition to the fiscal drains associated with rationalizing these deficits, the French economy has also been chained to the economics of French Africa by a system of legislative market-supports slightly analogous to our American farm-price-support structure, which both increases the instability of French Africa and constitutes an irksome millstone around the neck of the French taxpayer. For example, 80 per cent of Senegal's export trade is accounted for by peanuts, and toward the purchase of this huge annual crop at price levels well above those on the world market every Frenchman contributes part of his tax dollar. To the ordinary Frenchman, this constitutes a clear case of imperial charity; and he thinks it reasonable enough if, in return, his government insists that the bulk of the territories' imports come from or through France. But to the African the system institutionalizes a deadly hypocrisy: the imports from France are in their turn purchased at prices above world levels, and here therefore is a sort of reverse subsidy which wipes out the effect of the much needed agricultural subsidy for French Africa. There has also recently been the same slowing down in the price rises for French African produce that we have found in other African lands, reflecting the gradually changing and stiffening world price picture in respect of raw material suppliers.

In other words, French Africa is a model of the runaway multi-deterioration process which we have also examined in the Belgian Congo. And again, as in the rest of Black Africa, this process—now critical, but not yet in its paroxysm—has communicated itself to the outside world in the form of those little rumbles and temblors to which the antennae of holders of capital are so extraordinarily sensitive. The French government, itself, is sadly handicapped by the costs of the Algerian war—and, for that matter, the lingering effects of the Indo-Chinese fiasco. She cannot finance any really grand-scale projects in French Africa, despite the tremendous paper ambitions of De Gaulle's program. Also, despite the alluring epiphenomena of the African Revolution—the giant cargo cranes towering over ports which, a few years ago, were nothing but sand bars among the brakes of the Guinea Coast, and so on—the French have not been able to attract any substantial capital from foreign governments or capitalists, and almost none at all for the vital tasks connected with rehabilitating the agricultural economy. The French share—$311 millions—of the half-billion dollars allotted by the six members of the European Economic Community to the development of underdeveloped countries falls far short, of course, of what is needed.

And African leaders are now proclaiming, with a great deal of right on their side, that the government is slowing down its encouragement and construction of big developmental projects which it has already promised, in order to concentrate what funds it has in furthering the narrow-focused, industry-oriented kind of project which we have described, that goes down easier with the voter at home. Of the many major dam sites surveyed by a government team in 1947 in FWA not one has yet seen the erection of a complete installation. The one dam that seemed surest of realization, on the Konkoure River, was indefinitely postponed when Guinea withdrew from the Community. And other revolution-makers, like the giant Kuilu scheme of the Congo Republic—are loitering in the lobby along with Konkoure, Inga Falls, and a dozen others. The world's holders of capital—public and private alike—are waiting for the nonexistent guarantees of a nonexistent superpower before they will risk money to save lives in Africa. And, to repeat what we have already remarked about the Congo, African leaders may display a superficial understanding of their multifarious problems when they count so heavily on these hydroelectric mastadons; but the irrefutable fact is that they do so count on them, because they have nothing else to count on, and because the conservative critics who object to this outcry for Big Dams have not come up with any more effective or less expensive methods of modernizing the countries—or, indeed, any methods at all.

If French Africa is still tied to the economic apron strings of the motherland, so in a sense is she politically. As mentioned, political life *per se* in French Africa began in the 1920's, in Senegal and the Ivory Coast, under the benignant sponsorship of the libertarian parties of the French Left—first the Socialists, then the Popular Front, then—particularly after Vichy's blundering attempts to put the clock back and in the confusions of the early postwar years—the Communists. These parties contributed not only funds, organizational experience, and the metropolitan ideological nexus, but also a mood—of private deals, double crosses, personal rancors, expert rhetoric, and so forth—which was borrowed and slightly revised for the uses of French Africa.

But in Africa the tendency of the political hurly-burly is not toward rubbing off the trustworthy features of all the participating parties and personalities—making them like pebbles tumbling over each other in a stream bed—but toward the exaltation of a single charismatic leader. The same belittling and leveling forces abroad in France are abroad in Africa, but the African people's need of a Man is even stronger than their distaste for eminence—as, indeed, France's is as well, every two generations or so. In Africa, after all, there are no sacred cows, no constitutional precedents, no memories of the *tiers état* and indissoluble loyalties to family and class. The populace is not roused, or convinced, by a political program unless it issues directly from the lips of a Man whom they recognize and countenance—and then it is the honor and career of this Man which they accept as a pledge for the fulfillment of his promises.

One hundred years ago, in France, the future Napoleon III wrote in his *Idées Napoléoniennes* about the "tutelary and democratic power of the plebeian hero": "Aristocracy requires no chief, while it is in the nature of democracy to personify itself in one man." What Napoleon meant by "democracy" is not of course what we mean by it; and because Napoleon was not a systematic thinker it is perhaps risky to guess what he did mean by it. But part of what he meant was that a politics which requires enlisting the mass support of the people ("democracy," to him) is necessarily a politics of crisis; that is, the traditional hierarchies of loyalties—or what Sir Lewis Namier has called the "acknowledged superiorities"—have been washed or eroded away by years of breakdown, so that the people at large come to take a more active and at the same time less deliberative part in the governing process. They want to embrace their Ruler, rather than simply accept their rulers. The application to Africa is clear enough. It is a Man to whom the peoples of Africa wish to turn over powers of a magnitude measured by the gap between their hopes and their possessions. They are committed to Him, because they have none of the comforts of life that allow a personal noncommitment. And how remarkable it is therefore that the repositories of this commitment—the leaders of French Africa—have so far been so willing to consult not only their own vanities but also the real welfare of their people (in this respect they are a long step up from Louis Napoleon). For years, every politician in French Africa has been engaging in vicious infighting with his rivals over the issue of reaching an accommodation with France, and with the exception of Touré of Guinea the men who have come out on top in every case are those who have gradually *moderated their own views.*

The most important political party in French Africa is the African Democratic Rally (RDA), a sort of political holding company which in the winter of 1958, when the territories were accepting and resolving their status under the new Constitution, had achieved a dominant place in four of the seven states of FWA and three of the four states of FEA. For many years the leader of the RDA has been one of the big-mover politicians of Africa, Félix Houphouet-Boigny, fifty-five-year-old doctor and wealthy landowner, who has experienced in his own career the whole cycle of politics, from Socialism to Communism to purging his own party of the Communists. And for years Houphouet has been a steady advocate of the French connection; in 1956 he wrote: "Today Africa is the fortune of France, as France is the fortune of Africa." And this trimming view of things, plus a long residence in Paris as a government minister, has never shaken the source of Houphouet's power in the prosperous Ivory Coast, of which he is the Big Boss; when the time came to vote in December, 1958, on the De Gaulle Constitution Houphouet told his people to vote Yes—and 99 per cent of them did. But it goes without saying that Houphouet is as much of an opportunist as most other politicians (and people), and he will be ready to experiment with something else if the Community turns out to be a failure.

Next to the RDA ranks the African Regroupment Party (PRA) long associated with the name of the Senegalese poet-statesman Leopold Senghor and that of Lamine Gueye. These men's minds were primarily architected by the French Socialist tradition of Jaurès and Léon Blum. They accepted the Community—and for a while even viewed it with enthusiasm—but always with the proviso that the new institution must prove itself in the economic betterment of lands that are far poorer than Houphouet's Ivory Coast. The home base of this party, Senegal, is now a member of the "Mali Federation," and, as we have noticed, in September, 1959, the leaders of Mali informed President De Gaulle that they wished to withdraw altogether from the Community. True, Gueye, president of the Senegal legislature, did say, "We are not rushed," but it is to this pass that the indifference and distractedness of the West has already brought the French Community, less than a year after its commencement.

Obedient to the French parent-model, a host of other parties thrives in the other parts of French Africa in addition to local branches of the RDA and PRA; and each of these possesses its own set of initials, its own conspicuous Man, and its own platform. Many of them are hardly parties at all in our sense, but rather mutual benevolent societies of urban friends, or loosely disciplined protective associations of tribal chiefs and African professional men. They all tend to follow the same rules of structure, centering on a man who is at the same time a slick tactician and a polished orator, progressively binding to himself a front line cadre of office workers, schoolteachers, and clerks. "The mass-party," writes Mr. Thomas Hodgkin in *Nationalism in Colonial Africa,* "must continually keep itself, its central ideas, its symbols, before the public, in the bush as well as in the towns. It therefore requires a party newspaper, or newspapers; party colors, emblems, and badges; a party flag; party slogans; party rallies and *tam-tams;* party songs, ballads, or hymns; and above all in Africa, party vans. It depends for its strength not on the backing of traditional authority but upon propaganda, designed to appeal particularly to the imagination of the young, to women, to the semi-urbanized and discontented; to those who are outside the local hierarchies, and those interested in reform and change."

What Mr. Hodgkin has described here, of course, is the typical party of a society-in-midflood, anchored firmly neither to bank sides nor bottom and without much control over its locomotion. Recently, in Europe, we have seen how a society that in one way or another was torn loose from its moorings—motivated by an amalgam of need and shock and self-pity—experienced the most unexpected and disastrous accidents. Without the stabilizers of tradition and good faith —without the guidance of calculations of self-interest, which cannot be made in a whirlpool—leaders have no way of telling when they have reached that point of no return where they become as enslaved to the flood as everyone else. Consider the dissimilarity between the governments of Caprivi, Stresemann, and Hitler, all comprehended within one lifetime—not so much contrasts in philosophical essence, for these were perhaps not as clear-cut as they ought to have been, but in public conduct, tone, and morality, and in their degree of rational control of events. Unless a wise and generous major force is injected into the African situation, we may anticipate many similar "Hitlerian" developments there. And the African is shuddering not only from emotions and shocks analogous to those complained of by Germans, but from the far more jolting shocks of the Technological Revolution, which has banished the present generation of Africans from the fellowship of all the Africans of yesterday.

We can depend upon a man like Houphouet to keep his footing in his party and his region; that is, after all, his own affair and his own profession; but it will be almost impossible for outsiders like ourselves to know when he starts keeping his footing at the expense of his leadership: that is to say, when he ceases to guide the aspirations of his people and merely utters their emotions. When this time comes, it will mean that the small dowry of hope and faith in the Community has been used up; and that the people—with their constantly churning "empty bellies"—are driving themselves, and their titular rulers, into the channels of less hopeful experiments.

In this the states of French Africa are not entirely without alternatives. They do not after all have to be responsible alternatives, from our point of view. A pauper-state which has been abandoned to the toils of despair by the food- and capital-holding nations of the world does not have to balance budgets, manage inflations, or conduct a balanced and rational foreign policy—all it has to do is to give voice to the howls and hatreds of hunger. And then there are the various schemes of superfederation which are bruited around Africa that proffer a chance at least of temporary relief: Nkrumah's "West African Federation"; the idea of one of the leaders of the opposition in the Congo Republic for an independent federation of the four states of FEA; Nyasaland's Dr. Banda's project of a federation of former British East Africa with his own territory, and so on. Without question a working Community is far superior to any of these designs, but only if it is working. A starving man lives just as well under any political jurisdiction, and he usually develops a taste for variety.

If the Community fails—that is, if the West and France do not make it the ark for developmental enterprise of the right kind and in the right proportions—it will mean the end of the concept of Eurafrica forever. And perhaps—though I do not myself believe this —that is all it deserves; perhaps "Eurafrica" never was anything more than a vapid phrase like one of Haushofer's "pan-Regions." It is curious that the master geopolitician of them all, Adolf Hitler, entertained the gaga old Pétain for hours at the Montoire Conference, in October, 1940, with his version of a supergigantic German Eurafrica, the French contributions to which were to be paid for out of British colonies elsewhere in the world. (A far cry from the classical German colonial policy set by Bismarck, who one famous day, after being prodded by a visitor about Africa, rolled out his map of

Europe and snapped, "Africa! There is France, there is Russia: that is my Africa!")

Perhaps the Eurafrica dream has been hopelessly corrupted by the "worldliness" of strategist-fantasts who are somehow trying to whistle up strength from Africa to compensate for the European weak spot of the Polish plains, across which so many armies have marched both east and west in the past 500 years. For if the umbilical connection between Europe and Africa is significant only because, in the words of a French general, "the whole area constitutes one single and indivisible theatre of war," then it is not worth believing in or working for—and certainly worth nothing from the point of view of the African, who has little indeed to gain from a war fought in his "theatre." But even at this late date there may be something more to Eurafrica; a whisper of greater days, of the old Mediterranean "universe" of Plato and St. Augustine, of the highfalutin Victorian era of Livingstone and Coillard and Faidherbe. There may still be enough Europe left in Europe for her to reach out her hands one last time. To quote a saying of Sir Thomas Browne's in a sense quite different from that which he intended, "We carry with us the wonders we seek without us; there is all Africa and her prodigies in us."

9. East Africa

One day every man gets worn out, bored, and hungry for a holiday, and a certain number of our compatriots have the money, time, and inclination to take their holiday in Africa. What an American in this category, usually a businessman, is searching for is an Air-Conditioned Xochimilco: efficient, low-keyed hotels; cleanly linen, restaurant, and staff; sun, water, flowers, and places of interest to visit in a hired car. If this man is wise, or well advised, he will go to Ruanda-Urundi, perhaps the little town of Kisenyi on Lake Kivu, easily reached by plane, where the swimming is ideal, where the Belgians have laid down an esplanade of luxury pensions that serve delicious food, where government-licensed curio shops feature all sorts of African mementos at fixed prices, where the guests—including plenty of pretty young girls—more or less dress up for dinner and then go on to dances, where the surrounding countryside is a spectacular scenery of volcanoes and green-black woods, where an easy two- or three-days' drive will land him among herds of elephant and buffalo—the route supplied with way stations nearly as comfortable as the ones he has left behind.

The sociological reporter travels round Africa with a different angle of vision. He is concerned about the statistics of the "shortfall" of wages below living costs, or in political usurpation and constitutional queerness, or in the art of sinking in liberalism, or in confirming prophecies of race annihilation. He must find his way to the Union. True, the government of South Africa has done what it can in the line of brochures to whitewash, or ignore, its reputation; perhaps it is barely possible for an American tourist to spend a week or two in that country, motoring along the "Garden Route" east of Capetown, photographing the lions in Kruger National Park, climbing up into the Voortrekkers Monument, riding the lift down a mine shaft, without wincing at what he sees around him—but these days this happy faculty must be growing scarce among even the most determined fun lovers.

The man who wants to glimpse marvels none of his acquaintances have seen must venture, I suppose, into the interior of Portuguese Africa, or Southwest Africa, or perhaps Ethiopia. If he is interested in sport he will here run across some of the rarer species of game— and perhaps as well a few of the bones of the strange old Africa, relics of forgotten empires abandoned and half-buried, like the village of Gondar in Ethiopia, where white-walled castles of the Renaissance settlement stand deserted, like totems, cinctured by a rubble of modern shacks.

Few men will desire to travel to the Congo Basin, the Guinea Coast, most of French Africa, Bechuanaland, or the East African deserts unless they have business there. These are the hot, smelly, buggy, dirty, unhinging Africas—and everyone one meets in the street, white or black, looks as if he were on the verge of knifing his companion. But if he is exploring for oil, or a consultant to a planter, or surveying for an international commission, or completing an anthropological field study, a man must make the best of it. And, in West Africa particularly, it is also possible to hire a boat and paddle up the slow-moving rivers, portaging around the shallows and rapids, until a man at last stumbles on traces of the paleolithic, the pre-Europeanized, Africa. Everything that paddles up the river must float down, but even a brief abstention from the Age of Space acts like a tonic on many of us. One finds only a highly qualified Stone Age in Africa, of course, because the few small tribes that rub up against European-style administration only at second or third hand subsist in a state of social ossification, like dragonflies encased in amber. The "real" society of prehistorical Africa, where a tribe energized by one or two genius-generals could heave itself out of the bush, lay claim to the dominion of a half-million square miles, and crumple back into total oblivion within a single generation—that Africa has gone the way of the companions of Alexander the Great.

Every man has his own tastes in Africa, but the common favorite is East Africa—the Africa of royalty and big-game hunters, movie-makers and novelists. Its flavor is still distinctive and not long ago, at any rate, must have been quite wonderful.

East Africa is the Africa of Speke and Grant, young Britons who in the 1860's tracked down the source of the Nile, and who on the way spent six months at the court of Mutesa, the king of the Baganda, near the waters of Lake Victoria. It is the Africa of the irascible Samuel Baker, who took his wife along with him into the wilderness, and who in 1864 discovered Lake Albert. It is the Africa of Joseph Thomson, the youth who tarried with the Masai on the plains of Kenya twenty years later. These "noblemen" of the Bantu, the Masai, are dying out now, more than one-fifth of them infected with syphilis, but no race will ever rival them in the affections of Africa-lovers. They are famed the world round for their imperturbable courage; their red-painted bodies; their skill in spearing lions; their indifference to the European, his weapons and his will; their diet of milk mixed with blood drawn from nicks in the veins of living cattle, with whom they dwell in a peculiar symbiosis; their whimsicalities (for instance, they sometimes forced the first Victorian adventurers that came among them, boys fresh out of Oxford, to strip in front of their womenfolk, who were curious to see what manner of male creature the palefaces might be); their straightforwardness, often expressed by man-sticking; their social structure, hunting- and battle-cells composed of male contemporaries parted only by death.

East Africa, the great "King Solomon's Mines" Africa, was all this and more—the horizonless plateaus of central Kenya, Uganda, and Tanganyika, a landscape of great presence which if for Americans is not perhaps quite overwhelming (because for us it is not unique; the East African plateau resembles the Mogollon region of western New Mexico and the highlands of southern Arizona) certainly struck the average nineteenth century, London-drenched

Englishman an almost physical blow, as a virgin universe of sense experience: the sun-soaked savanna, the pure air, the heady aromas drawn by the heat out of acacia and euphorbia and bush grasses, the magnificent fauna (of which, indeed, there is no peer anywhere in the world), the quaintnesses of the Bantu, the exhilaration of man-against-thorn and man-against-rhinoceros. And, last but not least, the observation that the plateau was not only high enough, and therefore temperate enough in climate, to render a safari enjoyable, but also high enough for ranching and for growing rich.

But the bush, and the people of the bush, are only the first page of a travelogue on East Africa. There are also the slave trails, for centuries the route of long, sinister caravans; the East African littoral has been inhabited, and governed, by Arabs for 1,000 years. And the countryside itself was the connective tissue between the nonpastoral, nonwarrior agricultural tribes huddled in the shelter of the deep forests on Kenya's mountainsides (or, as we mentioned, concentrated in larger villages, like Mutesa's, which could defend themselves). And Kenya is the fatherland of tens of thousands of Indians (now numbering about 150,000), descendants or countrymen of coolies who poured in to labor on the great railroad from the sea to Lake Victoria in the waning years of the last century. These various peoples have conglomerated into town types which anyone will recognize who has ever seen a Tarzan film: there is the English farmer who has motored up for his fortnightly gossip and "sundowner" with a set of old buddies; the supercourteous Asian, speaking nearly perfect English, running the hardware-and-grocery store; the occasional furious Arab; the wealthy German or American tourist, perhaps in the wake of a white hunter; the Savile Row-outfitted colonial officer and his bony wife—these characters zigzagging across a kaleidoscopic palette of Africans of every shape, size, and shade, dressed in every kind of garb from the Queen's coat to a torn sheet.

This is the East Africa of our memory and dreams, and in some points East Africa has retained this memory and dream—yet something has occurred which has drastically altered the essentials and given them new weights. It is as if a box of oil paints possessed magnetic properties, so that after a portrait was finished the pigments continued to creep around on their own, coalescing into little foci here and there about the picture space, until what finally took shape was a corruption of the artist's intent, and in fact an independent message of mutiny. To illustrate this let us look for a moment at a hotel in Nairobi, which for convenience we will call the Hotel Addison. The Addison was constructed in 1923, on a prize corner on Delamere Avenue, at that time the main, and almost sole, avenue in Nairobi, named after the redoubtable Lord Delamere, one of the first Englishmen to settle in Kenya and a man who earned the perennial leadership of the settler community by virtue of rank and an insatiable appetite for litigation. When it first opened the Addison was the biggest and best hotel in town, but now the pressure of the postwar building boom has shifted the center of Nairobi onto more splendid, wider streets. The governmental and commercial edifices that line the new roads off Delamere Avenue are all in the latest glass-and-girder mode; they are *chic*—stark concrete walls adorned with suspended medallions of abstract design—and when a man walks in this part of town he could as well be in Brasilia or Vancouver as the capital of East Africa. At one time the Addison was owned by a British syndicate, but now it is owned by a Greek, the narrative of whose personal history it would be extremely interesting, and exceedingly troublesome, to reassemble. The walls and floors are still solid, the place is comfortable, but everything is run-down and moth-chewed: the rug in the dining room has been replaced by linoleum; dust storms lurk in the curtains and towels; the bellpulls are holes in the wall; the elevators and water closets perform to horrendous orchestrations of protest.

Probably one will encounter no Americans in the dining room of the Addison. We prefer to stop at the new Norfolk Hotel two or three blocks away. But one will spot a few old-time settlers wearing khaki shorts, talking about the rains, which are slow to come this year, doing their best not to broach the topic that really grips them: the damn blacks. Then there will be a few older English couples, who out of minute budgets have contrived somehow to eke an East African jaunt. It is an effort to recollect that these are representatives of the commercial class—the ruling class, if you please—of the greatest empire in the history of the world. Naturally Englishmen are never at their best in a dining room, for they cannot help thinking that there is something indecent about the mouth-and-throat movements inseparable from the taking of nourishment, but even overlooking this food-shyness these middle-aged visitors from Imperial Headquarters have about them a dog-in-the-manger, what's-happened-to-us air which reflects a permanent if mild melancholia. There are a few Germans, in short shorts, who in the afternoon plan to pedal off to take snapshots of the Rift Valley. There are a dozen or so voluble and gesticulating Asians, busy with deals having to do with the shops lining Delamere Avenue and the crowded alleys behind it in the market place district.

Then one notices that he is seated also amongst a sprinkling of Africans—well dressed young men, obviously lawyers and political organizers, putting their heads together over lists of some kind or other, bubbling with self-confident laughter, the result of whispered gibes at that old booby, the Governor, whose latest address they have just skewered with a fiery pamphlet. And last, one day while I was eating my lunch, into the dining room of the Addison strode no less a personage than Tom Mboya himself, the head of the Kenya Federation of Labor and the African Elected Members Committee of the Kenyan Legislature, a forceful spokesman for the Kenyan African and for "Africanism" in general, world traveler and propagandist, at twenty-nine the best known politician in Africa next to Nkrumah, whose friend and protégé he is—a serious, impressive, intelligent, ambitious, and hard-driving young man. Our Greek host met Mboya at the door, embraced him with fervor, pounded his back, conducted him to a table where three of his colleagues were awaiting him, loudly called him "Tom" a half-dozen times, with an accompaniment of arm-and-eyebrow rotation for the benefit of the other diners, grandiosely grabbed two or three waiters and dispatched them hither and yon, and personally served the African leader his fish. (I must in fairness record that the fish which was served to Mboya, and to the rest of us, was that same abominable piscine freak which one confronts wherever Albion has conquered, that nothing can shame the English out of preparing and feeding to subjects, allies, and enemies alike. The hard conditions of Africa are no excuse; one can find no better food anywhere than a man gets in the Belgian Congo. Besides, the time previous that I had been presented this saffron-colored creature to masticate, in its pink sauce, resting on its couch of dead and dusty cucumber, I was riding on a train in northern Scotland.)

It is clear—offensively clear to many Europeans who intensely
loved the Africa of yesterday—that all in all the picture I have drawn
here no longer corresponds to the East Africa of Thomson or Lord
Delamere or Tarzan; and that the obstinate settler society chronicled
by writers like Elspeth Huxley has now been decisively if subtly
undermined by forces which, like armies of termites, it is hard to
locate and harder to challenge. Political upheaval is partially responsible, of course, but the changes in the objective political situation
are not yet broad enough to explain the striking alteration in *tone*.
When one strolls down the street in Nairobi, for example, one iden-
tifies European, African, Asian, and Arab—as the old days—but
the street crowd is noticeably denser than one anticipated finding in
the heart of the East African plateau. Nairobi is no longer just a
crossroads, where a man headed for the bush might stop over for a
few days to stock up on Purdy shotguns and Scotch whisky. It is a
metropolis, but the metropolis of a society which has not jelled into
a describable form. The Mau Mau business cost the British government millions, and discouraged them mightily, but it could not slow
down the upraising of new buildings in Nairobi. Yet these new
offices are not going up in answer to business confidence and programs for Kenya's future (the Kenyan Chambers of Commerce are
forever bewailing the lack of this confidence), but simply because
the administration *must* erect ever more housing for the minimum
functions of its duty to this fecund and fragmenting colony-in-mid-
flood.

Again, on the outskirts of Nairobi, past the brilliant daubs of
the bazaar section, where the Asians work and live, lie the terrible
African slum towns, swathing Nairobi as they swathe all the cities
of Africa in a shirt of Nessus. These junk-farms have alarmed the
British for twenty-five years, yet nothing that has been done has
decelerated their proliferation or their deepening depravity. It is not
a new problem, but it is one that is rapidly worsening; today there
are perhaps 300,000 Africans living in Nairobi, tolerable accommodations and employment for perhaps one-third that number. The
regulation that Africans without jobs must depart the town after
thirty-six hours proved to be absolutely unenforceable; and another
government measure to cordon Slumland, the razing of native quarters where Mau Mau were suspected of harboring, was equally

unhelpful. Not long ago the Colonial Office published with some pride a report that most of the captured Mau Mau had registered a substantial gain in body weight while they were in prison—that is, the Africans physically prospered despite monstrous overcrowding in the detention camps, brutal floggings, and a daily diet that cost the government less than 15 cents per man. How had they been surviving before they were caught? And these native towns keep swelling and writhing, like blind blobs of insensate protoplasm that mean to devour the world. It is not East Africa any more; it is Harlem with gigantism.

Looked at end-on, in cross section, Kenya conforms to the shape of an inverted V, with one leg, the inland leg, short compared with the seaward one. A slender coastal strip, on which is situated the port of Mombasa, constitutes the "Protectorate" from which the Sultan of Zanzibar derives a regular annuity and separates from the Indian Ocean an unwholesome low-lying inner region of a few hundred miles' width. Then the country begins its climb up to the apex of the Highlands. Nairobi itself, more or less on the eastern margin of the Highlands, is up 5,500 feet, and therefore comfortable all year round despite its being only a few score miles south of the Equator (the English complain of the heat from January to April, but most Americans will not find it trying). North and west of the capital city the land continues to rise, up to the great ranches that lie at 6,000–9,000 feet, and then beyond the altitudes of ranching and farming country to Mount Kenya at 17,000 feet and the Aberdare Mountains and other features associated with the Great Rift Valley at between 10,000 and 14,000 feet. On the far, westward side of the Rift escarpments, the shorter leg of our inverted V, the country dips down to the plains of Nyanza Province, finally running out on the shores of Lake Victoria, 3,700 feet above sea level. In northern Kenya our analogy to a V gives out, for the Northern Province, occupying nearly half the country, is a vast arid desert and semi-desert, peopled by nomads and their chattels who wander back and forth, without hindrance, between Kenya, Somalia, and the Ethiopian Ogaden.

Only about 7 per cent of the land area of Kenya has been alienated from the Africans, and this 7 per cent is nearly all accounted for by the 13,000 square miles of the "White Highlands" and the 4,000 square miles of "forest reserve" that march with them. No one has ever contended that this is not the best agricultural land in the country. And it is, moreover, the only land which has been cropped scientifically and is therefore not deeply compromised by the bitter dynamics of African soil degradation. Erosion in the native sectors of the Highlands, and the effects of overgrazing in the lower pastoral belts, have been uneasily watched and desultorily combated by the government since the First World War. Sprawling districts in the Kavirondo region, near Lake Victoria, were deemed to be hopelessly deteriorated as long ago as 1933, and the Royal Commission of 1955 confirmed the extension and intractability of "hopeless" areas into the other regions of Kenya as well.

We have said that Kenya is in many ways a Specially Favored Colony, and there is no dearth of studies of its society and economy and no reason to dispute their reliability. But it is curious to find that up to about 1930 the British apparently believed that the over-all African population of Kenya was falling off, even as the Masai are still declining. It hardly matters whether this deduction was a responsible one even in its own day, for in the past generation any lessons that might have been extracted from it have been plainly superannuated. Today the population in Kenya is exploding: there are approximately 6 million Africans in Kenya, an estimated gain of more than 1 million since 1946; about 60,000 whites; about 150,000 Asians; about 35,000 Arabs. And the bulk of the population, more than 70 per cent, lives in the so-called "Central Highlands" region; that is to say, clustered around the 17,000 square miles which have been alienated outright to Europeans or reserved for them. Therefore, it is in these territories immediately adjacent to the European farms (and, indeed, interspersed among them, for 200,000 Africans "squat" in the White Highlands) that the African population is booming the fastest, that the inroads of soil decay are the most severe, and that the influences of the Technological Revolution—emanating from European ranch houses and, for that matter, from Nairobi—are the most galvanizing.

Kenya became part of the British Empire in 1886, as a result of an Anglo-German agreement which also demarcated the German dominion over Tanganyika and the Sultan of Zanzibar's theoretical jurisdiction over the ten-mile-wide strip of the Kenya Protectorate, to which we have referred. Two years later the charter of an Imperial British East Africa Company was issued. This enterprise was intended to purchase valuable goods from the Kenyans in exchange for their acceptance of less valuable English goods, but the scheme failed, and after a few prodigal years the Company collapsed in one of the epic smashes of Victorian finance, turning its responsibilities over to the government in 1895. That same year, 1895, the first tracks were spiked down on the famous Mombasa-Lake Victoria railroad; the history of the building of this line is the quintessence of the romance of East Africa, but we must content ourselves here only with noting again the mass-importation of Asian laborers.

Now the English began to pay serious attention to their new acquisition. Reports from Thomson in the 1880's about Masailand, reports from the railway surveyors ten years later, raved over the limitless highland plateau which the iron horse would render as accessible as Hammersmith. And, marvel of marvels, this glorious realm was uninhabited, or—as it was asseverated at the time—"untenanted." The theory was, and still is in some circles, that Arab slave expeditions of the nineteenth century and the man-killer sweeps of the Masai (a race, however, decimated by a smallpox epidemic in the 1880's) had chased off "passive" tribes like the Kikuyu who would normally have occupied the Highlands, frightening them back into the heavy forests that ringed the great mountain ranges, where their numbers were presumed to be sparse. Therefore, when the authority that had shouldered the government of Kenya scheduled this highland country as "Crown Land" it believed, or stated that it believed, that it was taking possession of land neither owned in any meaningful sense nor worked in any functional sense by the indigenes whose interests the imperial architects steadily pledged themselves to defend. And when in the early years of the new century the government began to sell and lease these Crown Lands to European settlers, it did so on the assumption that the white immigrants would modernize and prosper the colony—and, indirectly, the Africans as well. And it was also assumed that, if the government mistakenly sold or leased land to a European which he subsequently discovered was either the site of an African village or the pasture of an African tribe, the lessee would void his contract.

But clearly this was asking too much of the human nature of the brusque and excitable settlers who in 1903 began to flock into Kenya, settlers in most cases backed by substantial funds and connections at home, and therefore embodying a stiffer order of pretension than the "pioneer" of American myth. It was asking too much of the sagacity of the bureaucracy in London—no matter how philanthropic they may have been. In other words, although an exhaustive retelling of the Kenyan land problem is too formidable an undertaking for this essay, not only has it always been impossible to persuade the Kikuyu and the other major tribes that any part whatever of their plateau was "untenanted," and hence free for the settling, but from the earliest years there accumulated a massive docket of cases of plain dispossession on the part of overeager Europeans which found a way into the colonial courts, almost invariably to the frustration of the African plantiffs. Also, we must notice that as early as 1908 the government made a public policy of not selling or leasing any part of the Highlands to Asians, a proviso that community angrily resented at the time and has continued to resent. In any case, the game was more or less bagged by 1919; the 17,000 square miles of "white man's country" were staked out and reserved, and the story of land merges into the story of politics.

The political tale begins thus: already in 1913, only a decade after the railroad was finished and white men began to move into the Highlands, the English settler colony was petitioning London for what it called Responsible Government. As a clause in their argument they cited the granting of Responsible Government to the Cape Colony in 1872 and to Natal in 1893—in addition, they made all the points familiar to Americans about the hardships of deferring to remote parliaments which have no first-hand experience of frontier life and problems. At the time the white Kenyans started this self-government campaign the Colonial Office was suffering pangs of second thought about premature power turnovers to settlers before the Office itself had obtained a clear notion of the circumstances of the aboriginal society—and had nailed down some ironclad assurances about aboriginal welfare. However, this creditable providence was not as efficacious as it ought to have been, because the settlers of Kenya had been seating a representative on the governing Legislative Council since 1906—and the natural solidarity of Englishmen thousands of miles from home more than sufficed to keep the ideas of administrators and ranchers running in the same grooves most of the time. In any case, during World War I London instituted settler elections in the country, and the genial promotion of white Kenya to the status of white self-government seemed to be only a question of time.

But now there burst onto the scene one of those amazing surprises which show us how truly complex the old Empire was: the issuance of the Devonshire White Paper of 1923, declaring in part: "Primarily Kenya is an African territory, and His Majesty's Government think it necessary definitely to record their considered opinion that the interests of the African natives must be paramount, and that if and when those interests and the interests of the immigrant races should conflict, the former should prevail. . . . In the administration of Kenya His Majesty's Government regard themselves as exercising a trust on behalf of the African population, and they are unable to delegate or share this trust, the object of which may be defined as the protection and advancement of the Native Races."

In all the years of aftermath no English or Kenyan government has ever been able entirely to inter, dehorn, or stultify this extraordinary declaration, composed over the exalted name of the master of Chatsworth and Bolton Abbey—a declaration extraordinary not so much for what it asserted, for it reiterated, almost paraphrased, the principles of the earlier Empire we sketched in Chapter 4, but extraordinary because this wanton whiff of the earlier Empire was reviving principles precisely the contrary of the principles under which affairs in Kenya had been conducted for twenty years, in respect of the alienation of land in "white man's country," and principles precisely the contrary of what the Kenyan settlers were demanding in 1923: namely, the right themselves to determine whose interests were "paramount" in Kenya and on whose behalf His Majesty's Governments were exercising their powers of "trust." Actually, the moral position of the settlers received a blow from which it could never recover, and nothing turns a modern settler's face ruddier, or impels him to call more peremptorily for the bar boy, than introducing the subject of the Devonshire White Paper at cocktail time. The standards of the White Paper gave birth to few practical implications, for, as we have seen, the Highlands were already consolidated

and later Colonial Secretaries hastily climbed down from Devonshire's lofty plane. For example, they emphasized that the "immigrant races" referred to in the White Paper were the Asians, whose
agitation against discriminatory legislation involving themselves presumably menaced the Africans. And it was explained that the colony
ran at all only because of European enterprise—in 1945 it was calculated that 72 per cent of the agricultural cash sales in Kenya
derived from farms owned by Europeans. But the stark simplicity of
the Devonshire conception never can be forgotten, even by the men
who loathe it the most, and it is an ever-gleaming, ever-razoredged
Excalibur in the hands of African politicians like Tom Mboya.

White Paper or no, the "settlers' reich" established itself in the
interwar period; the indifference of the Colonial Office, the African's
backwardness, the Asian's indigestibility, and the European's cocki-
ness conspired to funnel the real power in the colony into the clubs
of Kenya, where it was wielded by the governor and his cronies, a
few thousand landowners. The representative aspect of these governments was a Legislative Council, of the form that we have run across
in other parts of British Africa, an improvisation for later-stage
dependencies which attempted to mold a bit of everything into a
manageable instrument of government. A typical specimen of Legislative Council is that installed by the Kenyan Constitution of 1927.
This body consisted of twenty "official" members (eleven ministers
serving *ex officio;* nine nominated, one of whom represented Arab
interests) and eighteen "unofficials" (eleven elected Europeans, five
elected Asians, one elected Arab, and one nominated member representing the interests of the Africans; it was not until 1944 that an
African actually became a member of the Legislative Council).

Here we do not have the time to analyze the juggling, over the
years, of these racial and "official-unofficial" proportions on successive Councils. The original scheme, not only for Kenya but also for
the rest of British Africa, was gradually to increase the ratio of
elected members over nominated members as the colony settled
down, and gradually to increase the ratio of members representing
the "backward" majority race over those of the minority races as the
former advanced in "civilization." But in Kenya, as in Southern
Rhodesia, the theory was shipwrecked because it never was, and it

never will be, possible for the leaders of the white settlers and the leaders of the Africans to agree on a Freedom Day when the community with the overwhelming numerical superiority will finally express its preponderance in the political government. So far as the African leaders are concerned, the time is always *now:* an African politician who informed his people that they were too immature to govern themselves could not long depend on their constancy. So far as the settlers are concerned, the Africans will be ready for F-Day on the Greek Kalends. So far as the Colonial Office is concerned, there is little to choose between the puerility of African and settler, so the Office must hold itself in readiness to intervene as "impartial arbiter," a role especially exigent in Kenya because of the large, kibitzing Asian community sandwiched in between Africans and Europeans—and disliked by both. The idea of an "impartial arbiter" in such a tricky, potentially calamitous situation as Kenya's is, of course, a sensible one—even Protestants cling to the hope that *Someone* will explain our shortcomings to the Creator—and advocates for the Colonial Office have little difficulty converting Americans to the view that affairs would be very much worse if the Office surrendered its responsibilities. But in daily, on-the-spot routines the Colonial Office *has* surrendered these responsibilities in Kenya. In Kenya the "impartial arbiter" is really only an irritating spinster in the back seat, and the society is being hustled down its dangerous road by the men with the local social position and the East African know-how: the white settlers.

Probably the most "advanced" of the natives of Kenya were the Kikuyu who, as we mentioned, were supposed to have been sheltering in the mountain forests when the white man first appeared on the Highlands but who promptly emerged, began increasing spectacularly in numbers, spading up little farm plots round the English ranches, and drifting off to Nairobi. The Kikuyu account for no more than 20 per cent of the African population of Kenya, but it was this tribe—with the satellite tribes of the Embu and Meru—which became involved in the Mau Mau outburst of the 1950's. Let us review a few of the occasions of this sad business. We have previously mentioned that by the 1920's the white settlers had sealed off for themselves the 17,000 square miles of the White Highlands, the

first-class farmland of the colony more or less in entirety. Recall that
more than half of Kenya is desert, and a considerable portion of the
remainder situated in lowland belts which the Kikuyu cannot farm.
Now it became a grievance to the Kikuyu that not only had the
White Highlands been subsumed under European land law—which
it was hopeless for him to contest and under which it was illegal (as
well as unthinkable) for him to purchase—but that for years about
half of these 17,000 square miles were not actually planted by the
Europeans to whom they had been reserved; the Kenya Land Commission of 1934 reported that in that year 27.5 per cent of the White
Highlands was lying fallow, and another 20 per cent was occupied
by African squatters, mainly Kikuyu, of whom there are presently
estimated to be about 200,000 in an area where they are allowed to
reside so long as they sell part-time labor to the English farmer on
his terms but whence they can be, of course, summarily evicted. In
other words, the English were making provision not only for themselves but also for their children's children, at the expense of the race
whose country Kenya was, according to the Britons' own code (the
Devonshire White Paper).

What was more, the government of Kenya enforced a body of
statutory restrictions on the African farmer's production, notably of
coffee, which he was forbidden to plant without a license that it was
virtually impossible for him to secure. His pauperdom seemed to be
a matter of deliberate policy. The money crop he *was* encouraged
to grow was cotton, which exhausts the soil, before either the African or the government had any notion how to conserve its value or
the will to expend funds on doing it. In the field of social services
next to nothing was done. In 1944 it was reported that while the
government spent 46 pounds annually on each European child's education (an allotment generously supplemented by parental indul-
gence) only 2 pounds was being spent on the African youth's
schooling. And right into our own day only one institution of higher
learning had been erected in the whole of British East Africa,
Makarere in Uganda.

"Middle-classification" was as impracticable in Kenya as elsewhere
in Africa. In 1956 the wage scale for Africans on farms was about
$5 per month, in the towns about $15 per month. (In 1956 Mboya
made the grave accusation that the Kenya government was spending

20 per cent of its revenues on the "maintenance of law and order" and only 25 per cent on all social services combined. It would be instructive to hear his comments on the American budget, where the disproportion is at least as eccentric.) The so-called *kipande* institution—a system of labor passes—has always been hated by the Kenyans. And until 1946, when it began to be squeezed off (it was not thoroughly, legally plugged until 1949), the immigration of Asians into Kenya kept the Africans in a state of chronic ferment. If there was not enough room in Kenya for the Africans and Europeans already there to subsist in amity and comfort, the African view went, how would matters be improved by the entry of tens of thousands of Indians as hungry as the Africans yet much better equipped to find themselves a warm nest in the Europeanized society? On top of all this, remember that for three generations missionaries and missionary-schoolteachers had been moving among the tribesmen, sending many of the outstanding youth, like Kenyatta, off to England for their higher education—perhaps to such a school as the London School of Economics, within whose precincts a young man's doubts about colonial justice were soon laid to rest.

And when the scales had fallen from his eyes what did the young Kikuyu observe when he looked about him in Kenya—or when he returned to his home from England? Was there a chance that the refractory Council setup, by which regular redistributions of seats gave the appearance but never the substance of "democratic" progress, would ever respond to the African's new status and hopes? Could a sensible man anticipate the voluntary abdication by the white settlers of their prerogatives? Not a prayer. Here, for instance, is the sympathetic reply to the Kikuyu hunger for land by a Major A. G. Keyser, at the time of his writing a member of the Legislative Council: "There seems to be an impression among Africans that because a man is black he is entitled to hold land. . . . He must get the idea out of his head that he is entitled to own land—he must earn his living some other way." Other specimens of settler feeling can be culled from any letters column of a settler paper, like the fairly well balanced *Kenya Weekly News*. Here a correspondent admonishes: "After reading your article on Corporal Punishment in Tanganyika, how utterly, despairingly disgusted I feel at the sweet, motherly attitude of our Government towards this excellent form of punishment." (Needless to say, this man is referring to the beating of Africans, not children.) And so on and so on.

After the Mau Mau had begun to startle the world, among the other observers who swooped down on Kenya was an English psychoanalyst, Dr. J. C. Carothers, who subsequently wrote up his notions of the causes of the catastrophe. The answer, as Dr. Carothers summed it up in his book, was Frustration. And it is hard to see how anyone, no matter how lacking in training or faith in the techniques and theories of psychoanalysis, can disagree with this conclusion. We have watched in other parts of Africa these typical sociopolitical conjunctures of mischiefs. It is like a maze into which a sadistic psychozoologist places a mouse, after taking the precaution of sealing up all the solutions. The mouse is eager to cooperate, to show the scientist how clever he is, and so he charges aimlessly around for a long time before he realizes that the experimenter has cheated him —and that he is not to be allowed either to solve the problem or to escape from it. Could anyone deny the mouse his right to gnaw the scientist if he got the chance? Degraded land and corrupt, deracinated tribalism; a fast-multiplying population flowing into stinkvilles; political impotence; social humiliation—and the ineluctable hopelessness, because of powerlessness, of finding the exit from this labyrinth, of somehow innervating the gross, smug Master-man imprisoning and insulting Africa. Do Frustration and Rage strike you as abnormal?

The Kenya African Union, a welfare and political organization among the "citified" Africans, had been in existence for years before anyone thought of associating it with violence, although the government always insisted that it obtain permission before holding public meetings. Until 1950 everyone assumed that Jomo Kenyatta, the best known African in the colony and the head of the KAU, was confining himself, like the leaders of the African National Congress in the Union, to appeals to the liberal feelings of London Englishmen for relief from the illiberal acts of Nairobi Englishmen. True, his book, *Facing Mount Kenya*, was a seditious document, for in it he attempted to prove the natural rights of the Kikuyu to the White Highlands and to rouse in them a higher vision of their racial dignities—but the few Westerners who read the book concluded that

Kenyatta had sacrificed good anthropology to good politics, and they let it go at that. However, in 1950 the English settlers—through the media of remarks casually dropped by indiscreet houseboys and the hints of informers—began to hear of a secret society among the Kikuyu, the Mau Mau, which had for a target the obstruction of orderly government by intimidating those Africans who were employed by, and therefore collaborating with, the English. There did not at that time exist, nor has such ever come to light, any real proof that Kenyatta was bossing the Mau Mau; he was in his fifties, and a somewhat donnish rather than Napoleonic type of politician. Nevertheless, the English assumed that the Mau Mau could not exist without the consent and complicity of the Kikuyus' most beloved figure. (In the perspective of common sense, if not of jurisprudence, they were doubtless right. But this is a far cry from maintaining that proceedings in criminal courts should be governed by common sense, not jurisprudence. Surely we have learned the fallacies of this short cut. But it is one of the emasculating exasperations of politics in Africa that neither Law nor Reason supplies a clear-cut guide of conduct to the individuals who are personally enmeshed in them.)

Whatever the personal role of Kenyatta was, the reality of a Kikuyu secret society dedicated to force was soon past mooting. In the first few weeks of 1952 a number of African workers on the government reserves and in the Nairobi suburbs were savagely attacked, and in February the government responded by rounding up hundreds of supposed offenders. At this early stage of the affair the English had not yet had the benefit of Dr. Carothers' psychoanalytical diagnosis. For a few months, therefore, they held to the view that the raids were a recrudescence of traditional Kikuyu blood rituals, so they assembled certificated "medicine men" and presented them with sacrificial goats, purchased at the government's expense, to be beaten to death in "cleansing ceremonies." But the anthropological-theological approach failed, and the summer's speeding up in tempo of the Mau Mau offensive, now aimed occasionally at outlying English farmers, warned the government of the seriousness of the crisis on their hands. On October 20, 1952, a state of emergency was proclaimed and Kenyatta and all the leadership of the Kenya African Union were arrested.

From the beginning the ensuing trial of these individuals, in the

first months of 1953, was a famous farce. The proceedings were conducted along lines which would not have been tolerated in England
itself for a single day. There was no jury, and the lone, blundering,
and inexperienced magistrate, himself a white settler, foundered in
invincible confusion because of the coexistence of two systems of
law in Kenya, English and Anglo-Indian. Stupendous obstacles to
presenting his case were placed in the path of the barrister who flew
out from London at his own expense to defend the African leaders—
witnesses for the defense, for instance, often mysteriously disappeared. Not that all this delayed a conviction. The defendants were
sentenced to long stretches, and in June, 1953, their organization,
the KAU, was formally proscribed.

Oddly, the immurement of what was reputed to be the whole
managing directorate of the Mau Maus not only did not cripple them
but on the contrary seemed to inspirit them. On March 27, 1953,
they pulled the worst of their raids, the "Lari massacre," in the
course of which more than 200 Africans of all ages and sexes, living
in a compound whose chief was a friend of the British, were murdered and mutilated hideously. And with this horror the Mau Mau
war entered that grim phase which was so graphically described in
Mr. Robert Ruark's *Something of Value*—the gruesome and obscene
initiations; the mad, hyenalike assaults on helpless pregnant women
and infants; the eerie treacheries of old and trusted servants. And,
as counterbalance, the whites began to direct their determination
and their superior weaponry into complementary savagery: torture,
subversion, and bribery of captured Kikuyu; morbid floggings at the
prison camps, where African soldiers were instructed to use Mau
Mau methods on suspected inmates, often supervised in these out-
rages by English officers; the berserker mania that seized the minds
of so many "civilized" Europeans, the "slit the guts of the bloody
wogs, every last one of 'em" sort of thing—all charges which have
been amply documented in the reports of English judges and investi-
gating commissions. After five years of this, during which time the
colony sank from a gladsome jewel in the Queen's diadem to a fiscal
and moral suppuration, the Mau Mau were reduced to a desperate
and pitiful remnant of 100 or so crawling around in the thickets—
plus others pining in detention camps. By the end of 1956 the number of civilians who had been killed by the Mau Mau came to

2,856—of whom 2,739 were Africans. British military casualties, killed and wounded, totaled 1,167, of whom 988 were Africans. It is estimated that more than 10,000 Mau Mau lost their lives in the fighting, another 1,000 were executed. Nor is it yet all over. There are still about 1,000 "Mau Mau" detainees in Kenya, living in conditions of scandal which provoked the sharp Hola debates in the House of Commons. And there is little promise for the future in the government's plans to pass permanent legislation for imprisonment without trial, although the British have promised to end the "emergency" in 1960.

I should like to add a final word on the extraordinary animal fury at the Mau Mau which permeated Mr. Ruark's popular novel, an emotion that author shares with many another admirer of the "white hunter" Kenya. In my opinion, this raging hate is the most callow and brainless response to the Kenyan problem that can be conceived. A famous English judge once wrote that it is not only important that justice be done, but also that it be *apparent* that justice has been done. Surely it is clear howsoever one looks at it—commencing with the initial English settlement in 1902 or examining only the circumstances of 1950—that nothing like "justice" had been rendered the Kikuyu. And, to follow through with the next thought, that it would be psychologically unimaginable for a modern Kikuyu tribesman not to deem himself the victim of an especially noxious *injustice*, and not to feel that the only means of self-defense was to break up the society of which this injustice was an integral part.

In this generation of greatness and prosperity, why are so many Americans losing their instinctive national compassion—in particular, their compassion for people who annoy us because their lives and opportunities are so much ruder than our own? In allowing these sympathies to coarsen do we not risk clogging an avenue of communication which might serve us when all other means of communication have failed us—are we not maiming our political sense organs, not to speak of our spiritual ones? If it makes any sense to retrospect attitudes, it would seem that many contemporary Americans must be sought for on the sides *against* the Irish rick-burners, *against* the sans-culottes of 1789, *against* the Athenians, *against* the poltroons who sniped at the brave redcoats marching back from Lexington—for so many Americans do now find their passions inflamed *against* juvenile delinquents, *against* African nationalists, *against* thieving slum chiselers in Mexico City or Bombay, and (we are forced to add) *against* 700 million Chinamen. *Why?* First in the rank of kings and princes of the Earth, by virtue of our ancestors' hard work and the bounty of God rather than our private deserts, must we now adopt pseudo-aristocratic affectations like contempt for paupers and underdogs and a dandy's scorn of flicking them even the tailings of our feast? Are these affectations not the first symptoms of political paresis? Is there a straighter road to national disaster in plural dimensions than to permit greed, instead of rational Christian idealism, to dictate our national policies?

No one claims that the whole blame for the Mau Mau mess falls on the white settlers, for their closeness to the emergency, their personal stake in the *status quo*, extenuates their stupidity and cruelty in considerable degree. "I have been more inclined to blame," Miss Margery Perham writes, "not so much the individual settlers who have made their beautiful and productive farms on these Highlands but the British government and governors who allowed them to build up also a political position which contravened British ideas of justice and democracy." This is a wise, humane judgment. In these "multiracial" imbroglios a person cannot refrain from sympathizing with both sides—often, in Africa, with three or four sides at once. Another problem is that amid the ructions the human qualities we care most for, like Faith, Hope, and Charity, the open doors that make life endurable, slowly strangulate themselves: the town African metamorphoses into an infantile, manic atavist; the bluff English colonist into a merciless bully; the Asian into a greasy, twitchy vermicule. In other words, as if social and economic disintegration were not bad enough, the world must also stand by and witness the concurrent deterioration of Africa's human raw material —until at last this process hits bottom at a point where the ordinary outsider, be he black or white, English or American, bishop or commissar, ceases to sue for grace, succumbs to the temptations of hatred and inertia, or founds all his expectations on the phoenix powers of the Bloodbath. But it seems to me that it is these Despairs —the handmaidens of Death—which we Americans must shun at all costs in thinking about Africa. And we cannot shun Despair by acting out little secret melodramas in our overheated imaginations, attitudinizing: "Here I stand! Here are my pals, the manly, hard-living pioneers of Kenya—with their welcoming verandas and impeccable bushcrafts. And here are the bad apples—the slobbering, syphilitic, lying Africans, who are all going over to the Communists betimes whatever we do."

What are the prospects for Kenya?

The constitution of 1958 provided equal representation on the Legislative Council for the African and European communities. This was a bivouac, and during the summer of 1959 the government was forced by the pressures of African dissatisfaction to promise yet another constitutional conference, to take place at an undisclosed date; when men like Mboya get their teeth firmly into the principle of popular government they cannot be expected to let go until they have brought it home. Moreover, by the 1958 rules the government has kept control by increasing the number of nominated members on the Council, and further tried to temper the shock by continuing many of the restrictions on African political activity which were proclaimed during the Mau Mau emergency.

The new dispensation included an interesting innovation, a "Council of State" composed of representatives of the four races of Kenya, nominated by the government, which has the power to classify any legislative proposal as a "differentiating measure"—that is, detrimental to the welfare of one of the communities. When this happens the Legislature must either add reassuring amendments to the bill or reserve it for the decision of London. At first glance, this Council of State is a model of the institution which the Africans of Northern Rhodesia and Nyasaland are vainly struggling to secure for themselves; we do not have to enter into the objections which have been lodged against the present method of selecting it. But for Kenya the mollifying liberalism implied in the Council of State has come too late. It has come after raw emotional tensions and frozen social ideologies have turned the field of political maneuver into a narrow defile; and when the obduracy of an unreconstructable white-settler minority ensures that social progress must be in one direction down this defile—and that direction downhill.

And the fatality of this business has crystallized in but a few years.

In 1956 Mboya produced a significant pamphlet for the Fabian Society. As he sets them forth in this paper it is impossible to cavil at any of his aims, unless one is prepared to call into question all of the fundamental documents of the United States as well. He explains that he is for "law" and "equality." He convincingly demonstrates— if it needed demonstration—that in practice the "fancy franchises" of the "multiracial" colonies where white settlers have powerfully entrenched themselves do not turn out to be rungs of a ladder leading to self-government, but elaborate schemes for indefinitely bilking the African of legitimate political aspirations. In an introductory note to Mboya's article, a Fabian Society official suggests that perhaps Mboya has revealed a defective idea of the ignorance of his African countrymen, but Mboya replies to this well worn gambit too. There is no way of learning but to practice. And, we must interject, it is independence-plus-apprenticeship that the British have brilliantly engineered in Ghana, Nigeria, Tanganyika, and elsewhere round the world—but not in Kenya. Despite this difference in opinion, if that is what it amounts to, the tone of Mboya's paper is mild, reasonable, and dignified; there is no hint, for example, that Mboya held that the white man must prepare himself for the eventual evacuation of Kenya.

But today all is altered. Mboya no longer trusts the English and, what is more important, he no longer likes or respects them. They have compounded selfishness with hoaxing, and doctored the gruel with doses of Podsnappery, just once too often. These days the Mboya motto is "Scram!" And this particular politician is in the enviable position of being able still to denounce "hate and violence," because Mboya, alone among his confreres, possesses bouncers for silent partners. During the winter of 1958–1959 the Kenya government began to hear rumors of yet another secret society among the Kikuyu, a successor group to the Mau Mau called the Kiama Kia Muingi, or KKM. Naturally the governor hastened home to England to assure the Colonial Secretary that this time the outbreak would be disciplined without the blood, squalor, and costs of the Mau Mau operation. But this optimism would seem to be exaggerated; I am told by Kenyan friends that the managers of the KKM possess a professional flair which was wanting in the Mau Mau leadership— they mean to replace *pangas* with poison, and scarifications with sabotage. But Mboya personally has nothing to do with the KKM. Until the tribesmen have discouraged the British government into pulling out, or firmly overruling the white settlers on constitutional matters, they require no contributions from him, and it would be bad tactics for him to proffer any. Throughout the oncoming crisis he can afford to play the agreeable and profitable double role of World Statesman-*cum*-Cheshire Cat—roaming from one capital city to another saying "I told you so" over major television networks, while in Kenya reposing in a corner waiting for the old structure to fall in ruins and the necessary conscription of his administrative talents and overseas connections. Such is the fate that haunts one of the most modern and beautiful countries in Africa.

Is there then no fair hope at all?

In my judgment there is this small one: perhaps Kenya's precarious isolation in East Africa may so daunt the white settlers that they accede to a compromise on the basis of a comprehensive new arrangement, which in addition might be rigged out as a face-saver. Concretely: Kenya's two neighbors in British East Africa, Uganda and Tanganyika, both are slated to become self-governing within (relatively) a few months. Why not, then, combine the three territories into an East African Federation, to remain within the Commonwealth and partake of its benefits? Problems this East African Federation certainly will have, but they will not be racial problems—and whatever they are perhaps they can swallow up the tiresome racial stalemate in Kenya. Now it turns out that a union of this kind has in fact been the object of English speculation since the First World War, and some departments of a merged East African administration—for example, a joint customs service and a common currency—have been in operation for forty years. Moreover, on January 1, 1948, an East Africa High Commission, attached to which is a "Central Legislative Assembly," composed of members elected by the Legislative Councils of the constituent territories plus nominated members, commenced to regulate matters pertaining to aeronautics controls, income tax, pest research, and so on, in addition to money and customs. In other words, here would seem to be the articulated skeleton of an EAF, languishing for a touch from Merlin's wand.

What of the other potential members of the new Commonwealth partnership? Tanganyika, of course, is the former German
East Africa, mandated to Britain after World War I. It is a poor
country, largely overgrown with scrub, though in the north it rises
to a delightful highlands region in the vicinity of Kilimanjaro,
Africa's highest mountain. Here there has been some European settlement (about 23,000 Europeans live in Tanganyika; 8.5 million
Africans; 80,000 Asians), but neither the European nor Asian
community has ever been permitted to cherish dreams of domination. The British guidance of the territory toward self-government
has now, in fact, reached the stage that within the year Mr. Julius
Nyerere, an extremely intelligent, winning, moderate African, will
become the first Prime Minister of Tanganyika. Two-thirds of
Tanganyika is infested with tsetse flies, but the Africans there are
not notably poorer than Africans in nearby countries, and they are
noticeably happier; one cannot help attributing this to their smooth
and visible political progress.

Of the major components of our projected East African Federation the third has political cankers as well as those of "pauperization,"
"urbanization," and the rest of it. Unfortunately, the datum about
Uganda that is best known is that it is the country whose chief
province is Buganda, inhabited by the Baganda, who speak Luganda
(but the king is the Kabaka, and his council the Lukiko). Uganda
is also an impoverished, disease-ridden, agricultural countryside.
But, as we have seen, Buganda was one of the few indigenous semi-
civilized "states" which the European encountered in Black Africa,
and the country's modern difficulties stem from the desire of the
Baganda to preserve beyond the departure of the British this superiority of status over the tribes of the other three provinces of the
Protectorate—which is an artificial conglomerate like Nigeria—or,
if this proves impracticable, to withdraw from "Uganda" and set
up shop as a sovereign nation. With only about 9,000 whites in a
population of 5.5 million Africans (and the white population is
said to be rapidly melting away, as settlers and company officials
wind up their affairs), there is no appreciable European resistance
to independence, and there would be small delay in instituting
Uganda's self-government if only the political aims of the Baganda—
and the force with which they are ready to insist on these aims—

were clearer than they are. In addition to the separatist movement, in which the reigning Kabaka has dabbled since his accession, an involvement responsible for his temporary deposition by the British a few years ago, there is also an uproarious Ugandan National Movement, sections of which maintain cloudy connections with the the U.S.S.R. and with Cairo. In the summer of 1959 the leaders of the party, which is periodically proscribed by the governor, joined forces with the Kabaka and organized a boycott of the Asian merchants of Kampala and Entebbe; the plan here was to convince the British that the Baganda are serious about a sovereign Buganda, rather than a calculated enkindling of anti-Asian feeling.

Here, then, are the players in our game of East African Federation—with the Sultan of Zanzibar perhaps destined to join the board. And it goes without saying that neither Tanganyika nor Uganda, both of which possess a full view of independence in the immediate foreground, would entertain for an instant an association with a Kenya where the white settler occupied a position of fixed privilege. Hence the whole project must fall to the ground unless a combination of forces—fear of endless reincarnations of the Mau Mau and/or judicious Colonial Office nudging—suffices to seduce or coerce the Kenyan whites into surrendering their proud status, embracing all the risks that this implies, before it is too late.

Before we leave Kenya I should like to glance at a pair of issues that always emerge in discussions of Free Africa—and which will certainly be thoroughly debated if an East African Federation ever gets beyond the stage of reverie. First, it seems to me that the franchise problem excites an anxiety out of all proportion to its denseness in many of the wisest students of Africa, of every political predilection. Over and over it is recalled, for example, that full universal adult suffrage did not come to England until 1928. How then, we are asked, do we expect this system to work in Africa, where the people have been denied political memories and training, in our sense of the word; where they will be blithely conned by chiefs and demogogues; where they inherit no codes or apparatus of check-and-balance, "loyal opposition," and forgiving spirit?

As I see it, the clue to this riddle does not lie in the all-out dogmatic defense of "universal adult franchise"—for its many drawbacks, and the hidden perils it traverses, are patent enough. But perhaps we can resolve our doubts if we realize, once and for all, that it is impossible to come up with a viable alternative in modern Africa. The principle of No Vote at All—depositing the government of the African with scientific administrators, the system employed by the Belgians for fifty years—no longer passes currency. The "multiracial" principle, whereby each distinct community in an African country is somehow represented, but the whole machine is steered and lubricated by the "impartial arbiter" of the colonial power, nowadays functions only so long as everyone frankly concedes that this is a transitional state of affairs, and that within the near future the majority community will find itself in full possession of the majority voice in the government. In other words, the "multiracial" principle works in Tanganyika, where Mr. Nyerere knows that he needs only bide his time a few months to obtain peacefully the full honors of sovereignty. The "multiracial" principle does not work in Kenya or Southern Rhodesia, where neither the politicians nor the great tribes have been shown a Promised Land that they believe in.

To get down to cases of theory, the British themselves admit that they are stumped when it comes to affixing workable "literacy" and "property" qualifications to the suffrage in Africa, of the kind that limited the English franchise within our century, because the structures of English and African society differ so radically—and the "politicization" process plainly cannot be reined in until "literacy" and "property" come to mean the same thing in East Africa that they mean in Middlesex, even if this were conceivable or desirable. And the error in this analogy carries us forward to the second issue I wish to mention here: namely, land as personal property. Most experienced colonial officers now seem to agree that the concept of the private ownership of land—the "freehold"—which lies at the very root of the political philosophies of the West, does not enhance the prospects of an impoverished territory. For example, with the best of intentions the British apportioned huge districts of India into peasant freeholds, but soon they found that most of the new proprietors—too poor and too inexperienced to defend their freeholds—were heavily mortgaging them. Hence they became the tenants—and because of the abysmal poverty of India, hampering personal mobility, and so on, the virtual serfs—of urban moneylenders. Not least among the evil consequences flowing from this degradation was the degradation of the land which it was now in no one's immediate interest to build up or conserve.

And if personal landownership does not work, then we must think out forms of the collective principle—and we discover that corporate enterprises of all kinds, from tribalisms to secret societies to politicosocial trade unions, lie far closer to the heart of African practice and tradition than they do to Western. Imitations or modifications of the "group-farming" projects already under way in Tanganyika are obviously destined for a very broad application to other parts of the continent. But the point here is that the political customs and institutions which will rise round these African "cooperatives" in many different fields on an immense scale are as yet unknown—both to Western students of Africa and to the Africans themselves.

To sum up, there are two main rules to follow in the Africa of the 1960's: first, nothing worth-while can be done which is unacceptable to the African masses; second, what these masses will accept—and therefore what it is sensible to essay—must in the nature of things lie in the order of experiment, because of the unique multileveled pathology of contemporary African society. With these rules in mind the "one man, one vote" principle, pooh-poohed by the best British writers on Africa for more than sixty years, comes to seem no more of a gamble than the intricately equilibrated franchise systems that sophisticated British jurisconsults have been evolving for a half-century—and tied to the "one man, one vote" principle is the inestimable bonus of the approval of the people involved. The Belgians, who suffer from at least as many internal qualms about the Africans' ability to govern themselves as do the British, seem to comprehend these crucial political factors much more clearly; as we have noticed, in their constitutional experiment in the Congo they have leaped in one movement from total disenfranchisement of everybody, white and black, to universal adult (male) enfranchisement. But, in any case, the Ugandans and Tanganyikans will buy nothing less, so that it is a closed issue so far as our "East African Federation" goes. Again we see that the future of British East Africa returns to rest on the stoops of the *patres-*

familias of the White Highlands—the 10,000 or so hard-shelled *colons*
who if they do not grow up will soon find themselves dwelling
in houses where one African sits in the parlor quoting Burke, Blackstone, and Bagehot, a second out on the range rustles the stock, and
a third in the kitchen is setting fire to the place.

* * *

I am sorry to appear to scant the great country of Ethiopia,
and its ruler, the Emperor Haile Selassie I, but as I have firsthand
experience of neither I have thought it best to confine this account
to a superficial enquiry. As everyone knows, Ethiopia consists chiefly
of a massive plateau (the capital at Addis Ababa lies 8,000 feet above
sea level, and other parts of the country rise up another 2,000 feet
or more), so stoutly armored by lowering escarpments that, save
for a "Prester John"-seeking Portuguese mission in the sixteenth
century, it remained a blank on the map of the world until the
other day. Long reputed amongst earth's fiercest and finest warriors,
a fame they more than sustained in the Korean War, the Ethiopians
by themselves were able to ward off the Victorian Partition of
Africa, definitively routing the last haphazard Italian attempt at
colonialization at the Battle of Adowa in March, 1896. That same
year the European powers recognized her independence, and this
remained her status until the now-mechanized Italians occupied her
capital in May, 1936. Five years later, in May, 1941, with the aid
of British and Belgian legions, the Emperor returned to his palace,
and for nearly twenty years has been hard at work on the very
tenacious social and economic problems of his people. Today he
rules over about 15 million subjects, almost all of them peasants—
though not necessarily paupers—farming the comparatively hospitable, healthy Abyssinian plateau. Their major money crop is
coffee.

Dozens of fascinating anecdotes are circulated about the Emperor
himself. Examples of his pride and bravery. Or his struggle to en-
graft democratic political institutions on his ancient military absolutism by way of a promulgated constitution. (But the novice
legislators present their humble duty, declaring that they are
sublimely content with their lot and desire His Majesty to understand that they will not disturb him.) His family quarrels with the

Coptic hierarchy, an incredible squadron of hoar-encrusted prelates. (The Abyssinian Coptic Church was founded in the fourth century by the "monophysite" Church of Alexandria, and with the exception of the aforementioned Portuguese expedition, expelled in 1632, it has been left entirely to itself for 1,600 years. Thus it has had time in which to nurture, and mummify, numerous articles of faith that strike the onlooker as exceedingly odd; for example, in the Coptic calendar a day is set aside for St. Pontius Pilate, who presumably earned this guerdon with his speech, "I am innocent of the blood of this just man," made while washing his hands.)

Then there are the moving accounts of the Emperor's sponsorship and close personal supervision of the European educations of likely Ethiopian youths, his subsidy of universities at home, and the "unmodern" loyalty and fondness of the bright young men for their old-fashioned master. And witty tales of Selassie within his polyglot entourage, playing the advisers of one nationality off against those of another. But one finds himself attracted most of all to the recountings of Selassie's nobility of spirit—his behavior on his re-entry into the capital in 1941, for instance. The Italian occupation of Ethiopia had been conducted in maffia fashion—so had the war that preceded it, for that matter, and the Italians' slanging of the Emperor's person at Geneva. Among other scandals the Italians had scoured the country for the few hundred Ethiopians whom the Emperor had by then managed, at enormous trouble and cost, to send through high school and college; they took the boys up in planes, and pushed them out. Naturally, when the Italian Army vaporized it was impossible to keep the Ethiopians from the throats of all of the artisans and settlers whom Mussolini had dumped in the country and then deserted, but in Addis Ababa, at any rate, where the Emperor himself was on the spot, their persons and property were spared; and he made a wonderful speech a few hours after the return, reminding his countrymen of the "obligation to forgive" that belonged to a race which had vaunted its pure Christianity for 1,600 years. The last small story I will put down here illustrates this same quality in the man. In Africa it is said that, although it is not unusually difficult to gain an audience of the Emperor, the experience is frequently awkward, ending with interviewer and monarch inspecting one another in somber silence. But if the suitor can manage somehow to insinuate the phrase "collective security" into the conversation Selassie brightens up, and everything takes a turn for the better. The Emperor learned the concept of "collective security" from President Wilson after World War I, and ever since it has symbolized for him the kind of relationship that ought to prevail between the nations of the earth. Only the other day it was that the rulers of far more powerful states caught up with him.

Regretfully we must report that in this noisy, lie-cluttered Era of the Cold War the Emperor's splendid virtues have not won him any brass rings. In the past decade the government of Formosa has received from the United States in "economic aid" alone more than $1 billion. On the other hand, to quote *The United States and Africa*, the report of Columbia University's American Assembly of 1958, "Ethiopia has received very little external assistance to help her economic development. . . . Altogether, foreign private investment probably does not exceed $100 millions. Very little American private capital is invested in Ethiopia and Eritrea. The American government has given $11 millions in grant aid and $28 millions in loans—mostly in the last half-dozen years. The International Bank has made loans totaling $23.5 millions. . . ." Yet is it not conceivable that future historians will judge the Emperor of Ethiopia rather more of a heavyweight in the affairs of our time than Chiang Kai-shek, and also—what is perhaps more to the point—the Empire rather more important "strategically" than the offshore refuge at Formosa?

However this may be, in the spring and summer of 1959, in the midst of a Five Year Plan which is behind schedule because of insufficiency of funds, the Emperor finally wearied of the dull stares of the West and betook himself off on a junket behind the Iron Curtain, returning home with solid promises of technological assistance from Russia, Czechoslovakia, and Yugoslavia. The suicidal fatuity of an American policy which has succeeded in driving this marvelous skillful politician—a prince of the blood, an enlightened autocrat if ever there was one, the secular guardian of one of the oldest and toughest of Christian communions—to beg his bread of the men with whom we are competing for the future of mankind, or so we fondly hallucinate ourselves. . . !?

Apart from socioeconomic decrepitude there is another major emergency on the Emperor's agenda: the coming-to-independence in 1960 of Somalia, the former Italian Somaliland and up to now a United Nations trust area. Somalia is a miserable country of about 1.5 millions (among whom there is said to number not a single university graduate), most of them nomads ranging the heat-blasted wastes. Friends of Somalia and other optimists were somewhat disheartened in their hopes of her prosperity by the two outstanding events there of 1959: sanguinary election-day riots in the spring which required the intervention of the army and, a few months later, an urgent petition to the United Nations for famine relief. But the curious—perhaps not so curious—thing is that under the goad of Cairo, where most of Somalia's schoolmasters and mullahs are trained, the Somalis have conceived, or resurrected, the vision of a "Greater Somalia" which will incorporate not only the present Somalia but the whole "Horn of Africa" region inhabited by the Somalis and related nomadisms—that is to say, British and French Somalilands, a good part of Kenya's Northern Province, and the Ethiopian Ogaden right up to the foothills of the massif, about one-third of the Empire. Already the British have announced that British Somaliland will be promoted into self-government in 1960, and they have let it be known that they do not object to a union between their ex-colony and an independent Somalia. (But when the Emperor heard of this he dispatched a strong protest to London.)

There is, then, no question but that the first act of the independent Somalis will be to serve territorial demands on the Emperor of Ethiopia, and probably on the government of Kenya as well; and there is no question but that the Somalis in the disputed deserts have been alienated from the latter two governments and will enthusiastically cooperate in an irredentist program. Perhaps it is unlikely that the government of Kenya will consent to divest itself of the Northern Province, but this ponderability is overshadowed by the certainty that nothing whatever will induce Haile Selassie to cede one acre of his domain—especially as he still has hopes of an oil strike in the Ogaden. Therefore, the world will soon be improved by an evanescent, hit-and-run, Khyber-Pass kind of guerrilla warfare over these worthless dunes. There can be no major actions, for although the whole area now divided between five authorities that is claimed for "Greater Somalia" comes to some half-million square miles, the Somalis who range it amount to fewer than 3 millions. Primitive and scattered as they are they cannot defeat the Emperor, but they can drain his treasury, disrupt his plans for developing this quarter of his realm, add powder to the squibs of President Nasser, and generally reduce this part of Africa to wretchedness even more terrible than its present wretchedness.

10. Ghana and Nigeria

So far as most Americans are concerned, colonialism could have ridden into the twenty-first century—or, for that matter, into the twenty-fifth. It was certainly not we who asked to goad or galvanize the subject peoples of the world. True, President Franklin Roosevelt had inherited from his former chief, Wilson, some old-fashioned ideas about "self-determination," and part of the time seemed almost to regard the British Empire as a latter-day Austria-Hungary, without whose sepulture nothing could be put to rights. But his immediate entourage pretty effectively thwarted any practical expression of this outlook, and it was never shared by the bulk of the business and academic communities of America. Americans who knew something about Africa were far more anxious about the potential successors to Colonel Blimp than about Blimp's own quirks and derelictions.

Thus, it is only fair to say that—overlooking the conventional lip service we always pay to "freedom"—neither the American people nor government have been really interested in the contemporary events which naturally mean more to the African than all others. I think we delude ourselves if we assert that the coming-to-independence of nations like Ghana or Nigeria ever struck us as a substantial contribution to the peace and sanity of the world. It has neither calmed our fears nor made our hearts sing. If anything, probably most of us secretly miss the days when the British Colonial Office kept so much of this part of the world from getting in our hair.

But this indifference, not unalloyed with selfishness, puts a great strain on the politicians of the new African states, for all their programs and hopes are directly dependent on the sympathetic and abundant aid of the United States of America. For example, because he needs America the African politician sooner or later must come to America to woo us. When he gets here, he gains the ear not of the American community as a whole—or of its government—but only of certain parties who have for their own reasons appointed themselves the wardens of, and specialists in, African affairs. These parties tend to divide into two groups—vested financial interests, and a pernickety and theorizing band of liberal well-wishers—and it is through these cloudy filters that the African must try to convey his message. To keep the solid support of either of the two groups, the only support he finds here, the African politician is under pressure either to make economic concessions contrary to his social and political ideals—to enter into "arrangements," *à la* Liberia—or to ape the American Founding Fathers with a dogmatic chastity which exists nowhere in America herself. If he tries to explain or defend another policy, one which he has molded on the exigencies of African society and politics as they exist, he finds that the support of both camps hastily dissolves amid groans of disillusionment. He finds that people who know nothing—and really care nothing—about Africa harangue him about "irresponsible demagoguery" and "would-be Fascism" at one and the same time. More often than not he retreats home in some heat; tragically, without having learned any more about the real character of the American Republic than we have learned about him.

The problems, paradoxes, and potentialities of the Lion of West Africa, Kwame Nkrumah, throw some light on these considerations, and on the patterns that develop when any African politician starts treading a path through the murk of contemporary international relations. None of Nkrumah's answers to or evasions of the situation in which he finds himself is alien in kind to the customs of American politics—and so it is not impossible, or even difficult, to understand what he is doing and why. But the puniness of the tools at his disposal, the smallness of his maneuvering space—these *are* alien to American politics, and these things are decisive. Nothing is perfect in this world, and it would surely be impossible to defend the proposition that Nkrumah's government is the best of all possible governments for Ghana or anywhere else. At the same time, he is an amazingly competent and well intentioned man, and we will be very fortunate if most African politicians of the future bear his stamp.

Nkrumah's country, Ghana, is of course the old British colony of the Gold Coast, situated on the northern shore of that torpid, waveless elbow of the Atlantic, the Gulf of Guinea. Although it has been for twenty years or more one of the wealthiest sections of Black Africa, due to an extraordinarily successful (for Africa) cultivation of cocoa, for Americans it is still packed with intolerable squalors and discomforts. When the heat comes in the spring, it is breath-stopping; when the rains come, they are torrential and carry in their train the terrible molds and damps; when the dry winds come, senses and nerves begin to fray and a man wants nothing but his martini.

By a freak of geography, unique on the Guinea coast, a relatively dry coastal strip, fifteen miles or so in depth, separates from the sea the Ghana interior—the great rainforest belt, slowly rising to the "Sudanese" savanna. Up until the middle of the last century slave raiders preyed along this strip, and later still the forest tribes of the Ashanti Confederacy swooped down upon it for loot and workers. And it was here, in a little village fronting the sea near the frontier of the Ivory Coast, that Kwame Nkrumah was born in 1909 (the precise birth date he has never known). In his autobiography, *Ghana,* Nkrumah has told us something about his early life as a youngster of one of the coastal tribes, living between the limitless sea on the one flank and the limitless forest on the other, in a narrow slice of land cluttered with wrecks of ships, broken bottles, and memories of cruel and evil bygone days. But like many other Men of Destiny, he seems to feel principally indebted for his ambition and his success to his mother; it was she, for instance, who told him as a child that he was the heir to two chieftaincies; and she lived with him—keeping house for him—until she died, years after he had become the most conspicuous political African on the continent.

All African revolutionaries take off on their flights from the

schools built by the colonial governments—to this extent, the old
policy of restricting the curricula of these schools to the Bible and
a few garbled sentences of pidgin English or French was a circum-
spect one. Nkrumah was no exception. After he had completed
his own course he became a teacher, in his home town. Then he
moved to the Prince of Wales's College at Achimota, and began
here to develop a certain positive affection for things and institutions British long before he ever dreamed that one day he should
be in a position to decide their fate. Another spell at teaching followed this period of instruction, and then came the chance at the
adventure that cheers the heart of every ambitious young African,
the trip to America. In 1935, at twenty-six years of age, Nkrumah
took ship for the United States, supplying himself and purchasing
his passage on money borrowed from relations. Although he arrived with only $200 in his pockets, he remained in this country
for ten years, studying at Lincoln University in Pennsylvania, the
Lincoln Theological Seminary, and the University of Pennsylvania,
working in shipyards and as a seagoing waiter, making friends and
developing arguments, observing the world of the American Negro:
the pan-Africanists, the Urban League, the NAACP, Father Divine.

At the end of the war, in 1945, he left this country for England
and the London School of Economics. Here he encountered, and
carefully recorded, what so many travelers after him have also
done, the new winningness and kindness in English society and
manners—a new gentility which, surprisingly, they extend to one
another as well as to foreigners—that seem to be among the few
profits, but precious profits they are, of the German assault of the
Second World War. Nkrumah describes the pleasant smiles of English suburbanites and businessmen in the subways when he ostentatiously buried himself in the *Daily Worker;* the generosity of his
landlady; the reasonability of English drunks; the enthusiasm of
volunteer English girls working for "Free Africa." Nothing that
can be imagined would impress a vigorous, expatriated, impoverished, color-shy young man more than gratuitous and graceful
etiquette of this sort; and if the man is worth anything he stows
away in his heart a gratitude he is happy to remember and acknowledge when the opportunity comes to him. Nkrumah has done so, and
he displays it now in the form of an exquisite courtesy to the com-

mercial and official Englishmen who have been left behind in Ghana—and, one should add, in the care and deference in his allusions to the Queen.

During the London years Nkrumah made his first operational contacts with professional revolutionists: the Garveyites, George Padmore, Kenyatta, English sympathizers of the Labour Party, and of course the Communists—the party of those who looked forward to an African continent-nationalism and that which looked forward to an African race-nationalism. Nkrumah himself came to carve out a line somewhat more realistic and less clumsy than either of these, but at the same time a line distinctly broader than simply "independence for the Gold Coast." He envisaged various orders and combinations of federation: a "Union of West African Socialist Republics" or a "West African Confederation," ideas which he has never completely given up. Meanwhile, back home in Ghana, a group of fairly well-to-do professional people had organized a straight-forward "independence" party, the United Gold Coast Convention, and when they came to hear from their contacts in England of this young man with the golden voice they sent to supplement the meager income he had been receiving from his family and friends, and to post him on assignments to shops and prisons around England, wherever Gold Coasters might be in need of help. On these tours, and in speaking and writing about them, Nkrumah also came to the notice of the British police.

In the fall of 1947 Nkrumah returned to West Africa, to find that a substantial reputation had preceded him. A superb orator who had traveled, worked, and studied in America and England, who had at his fingertips the details of all varieties and personalities of the African nationalist movement, could rally an audience for himself anywhere in West Africa. He was still tied to the UGCC, of course, and indeed in a few months became its general secretary, in charge of propaganda and organization in the southern half of the country; this was the key step in his success. During this period it may be that he was also tapping a different, more sinister, more distinctively African source of strength. The British have often hinted that a secret society devoted personally to Nkrumah, and bound to him by inviolable ritual oaths, came into existence during the late forties. However this may be, the man's zooming popularity and eminence—abetted by the British police, who arrested him now for the first time on charges of complicity in riots, and similar charges—were too strong a medicine for his more moderate colleagues and sponsors on the Working Committee of the UGCC. They began to try to cramp his style; as, under their present label of the "Opposition," they have tried to do ever since; and in July, 1949, after great ruckuses and recriminations, Nkrumah pulled his personal supporters out of the UGCC and formed them into a new caucus, the Convention People's Party.

The principle of the CPP was "positive action," Nkrumah's version of civil disobedience, designed to impress the colonial administration with the necessity of pulling out by means of strikes, boycotts, mass processions, petitions, and other peaceful kinds of protest—and holding in shadowy, but visible, reserve the threat of revolution. What Nkrumah demanded from the first was practical, working independence for the country; he was always willing to accept dominion status. But although it had been two years since they had turned over power to the Indians, the British in West Africa had not yet begun to think in these terms. So when, by virtue of his prestige and skill, Nkrumah managed to whip up a wave of disorder that swept over the Gold Coast, the administration arrested him again, this time on charges of attempting to "coerce" the government; and, after a trial, sent him off to prison on a three-year sentence, of which he served fourteen months. But this temporary absence had no effect whatever on the energy of his party or his own legend; and in the election of February 8, 1951, held while Nkrumah was still in jail, the CPP won a working majority of the elected membership of the Legislative Council. In his own constituency the chief won 98 per cent of the vote. After this the British gave up. Upon the application of his party Nkrumah was released from prison, and on the next day—February 13, 1951—was invited by the Governor to form the first African ministry of the colony, at first as "Leader of the Government Business"; then, after March, 1952, as Prime Minister.

Thenceforth the tide ran fairly smoothly. A new constitution in 1954 provided for a totally African assembly, and virtual independence, with the exception of powers reserved to the Governor which he never exercised. And in March, 1957, the ultimate step was taken, when the Gold Coast became a full-fledged sovereign member of the Commonwealth. Nkrumah chose the name "Ghana" for his creation, from one of the medieval trading kingdoms of West Africa whose half-forgotten titles are playing the same role in modern African politics that the "Crown of St. Stephen" and the "Kingdom of the Jagellons" played in Victorian Europe. And in June, 1957, the first Prime Minister of the new Ghana attended a London Conference of Commonwealth Ministers, and dressed in his magnificent togalike garb sat down to supper with the Queen.

Only ten years after he had returned to his motherland from England, a penniless agitator in the second rank of African nationalists, Kwame Nkrumah now stepped out on the world stage, the undisputed Washington of the first free African state of modern times (Liberia and Ethiopia had been sovereignties for generations, of course, but Africans consider the first to be little more than the private ranch of the Firestone Rubber Company and the second, that strange and antique monarchy aloof on its high plateau, almost equally irrelevant to modern times). Ghana was not an exception to the rule, but the first proof that a new rule was operating—the emancipation of Africa—that might reform and redirect the politics of the world.

And as the first chief of this new state, Nkrumah faced the same task that all politicians have faced since the Stone Age, that of interweaving his personality into the social and economic dimensions of his field of work; in short, to find the right art for his canvas. Personally, the Prime Minister is a masterful politician and a renowned orator; an extremely intelligent, busy, confiding, and suspicious man; a craftsman of great virtuosity in the arts of infighting and stirring the emotions of his people—all in all, a figure built more along the lines of a Plantagenet warrior-king than a Western party chief. Both his most secret instincts and his objective assessment of the long-run interests of his people are continually beckoning him on to wider spheres than the administration of Ghana. If it ever is to be fully liberated, Africa requires a Liberator, a Simon Bolivar—and within Nkrumah's breast there swells a storm of affirmation which he disguises with difficulty from the outside world (and has no luck at all hiding from himself) that this is the

hour and that he is the hero sent by Fate to accomplish this
Great Work, to free millions upon millions of despised and enslaved Africans, and to compel the rest of the world to extend to
them the hospitality and the reparations which are their due.

Politically, Nkrumah stands foursquare on the unshakable base
of an absolute control of Ghana, admittedly a small country, about
twice the area of Pennsylvania, with a population of something less
than 5 millions. It is not of course a "state" in our sense—which
facilitates Nkrumah's identification of his party with the "nation"
rather than the government—but was originated by British administrators who tied together three different regions for their own
convenience: first, the coastal area, Nkrumah's birthplace, where
polyglot communities had grown up around European forts since
the seventeenth century, and which the British made a protectorate
in 1874; second, the loose alliance of tribes known as the Ashanti
Confederacy, in the great forest country, whose paramount prince
is the Ashantahene, the proprietor of the Golden Stool, a military
race which lived by raiding the coast lands until the British conquered them after a series of bitter wars; third, the so-called Northern Territories, peopled by a different race from that of the two
southern provinces and far more primitive, taken over by the British
to forestall French and German infiltration after the defeat of the
Ashanti.

(During their separate administrations, and after they were unified,
the British governed the Gold Coast lands on the principle of "indirect
rule," according to which, as we have mentioned before, all possible jurisdictions remain in the hands of the local, traditional
authorities. In Ghana, and elsewhere, this policy has eventuated in
far more palpable disruptions than its designers ever intended, and
some of its effects have conditioned Nkrumah's policy into shapes
which he otherwise might not have adopted. For example, while
the central colonial administration compelled the chiefs to submit
to a supervision which they never before experienced, it also by
officially recognizing and treating exclusively with them endowed
them with a strength in their own localities which they had, as well,
not known. It made the chief a vassal of the English, forced to
acknowledge the overlordship of the governor; but so long as
he did this it granted him the rank of a near-absolute baron in

his own dominions, free of the traditional encumbrances of chiefly rule. By turning semisacred figurehead ritual-figures, whose authority was hedged about by a hundred taboos, into feudal nobles with closely defined political responsibilities, the system of "indirect rule" infinitely complicated the matter of subsuming all these parochial jurisdictions in the kind of centralized government that modernizers like Nkrumah want to build. These complications took on a concrete form in 1955 and 1956, when the Ashantahene, employing his authority as paramount chief to depose and replace other chiefs in his region, challenged Nkrumah personally, and Nkrumah's concept of the future of West Africa, by trying to construct a personal machine to control Ashantiland.)

If all this does not read like very promising material politically, economically Nkrumah inherited a golden spoon unmatched in Black Africa. Ghana's treasury was bulging, with about $500 millions. This king's ransom—for such it is in West Africa—had been earned through the cultivation and sale of cocoa, a crop that accounts for about 80 per cent of Ghana's export trade. It is not an old culture; it was first introduced and encouraged by a British governor, Sir William Griffith, in the 1890's; but since then, as a result of changing taste and new processing discoveries, the popularity of cocoa has undergone an enormous growth, and Ghana and Nigeria together account now for more than one-half of the world's supply. In Ghana the crop is mostly in the hands of African smallholders, with farms of five acres or less, but the marketing and the pricing of the cocoa is handled by an unusual and highly effective government cartel, the Cocoa Marketing Board, which sets the price per headload of the beans, operates the marketing and manufacturing plants, and banks the profits in the Treasury for use in the expenses of government and to support the world price of the crop. The half-billion in his bank-account that made Nkrumah by all odds the world's richest African nationalist was the result of a headload price which the British consistently kept down to about half of that prevailing on the world markets.

Unfortunately, in recent years this world price has been increasingly unsteady and tending to decline; even more drastic falls are threatening, and in addition competition in cocoa growing from other parts of the world—West Africa, Southeast Asia, and Oceania

—is looming on the horizon. Meanwhile, the whole present industry, on which Ghana is absolutely dependent, is menaced with extinction by a disease of the cocoa tree, "swollen shoot" disease, which was first observed in the colony in the 1920's but which now is killing the plants at the rate of tens of millions annually. And as yet the only known "cure" for this malady is to cut out and burn the infected plant.

To sum up, then, the Liberator of Africa came home to a tiny country which until yesterday was one of the least popular and inspiring corners of the British Empire. Here he faced the opposition of former colleagues and of the traditional chiefs, but he had no trouble overriding this opposition by virtue of his charismatic hold on his people's affections and loyalties. However, if he wishes to retain this hold he must lead them into the promised era of progress and security—and the prospects of this era are seriously endangered by the vulnerability of an economy which hangs by the single strap of cocoa production, and that production under fire from declining prices, stiffening competition, and "swollen shoot."

Starting off with this sketch of his field of labor, how successful have Nkrumah's labors been—and what has he added to or subtracted from the social instability of Ghana?

To consider the economic quarter first. One of the Prime Minister's fondest and most urgent projects—to which he avers constantly in public addresses and to achieve which he has hired the best European economic and engineering advisers he can find—is to emancipate the economy of Ghana from her dangerous bondage to cocoa. Even if the "swollen shoot" affliction were mastered, even if the world price for cocoa miraculously steadied for a period of time, a healthy, middle-class economy—of the kind which Nkrumah is determined to create for Ghana—could never be erected on such a flimsy foundation. But what can he do? Take away cocoa, and Ghana reverts to what it was in the seventeenth century: a hot, poor, and dismal arc of the Guinea Coast.

The answer, of course, is other kinds of productive industry. Ghana already has a going manganese industry, but this is a minor thing. Her great hope is the exploitation of huge deposits of bauxite, which lie in the southwest, by means of a huge hydroelectric project, the Volta River Scheme, which would generate the power not only for the development of an aluminium center but also for the urban and irrigation facilities of a wholly modernized society.

To build and equip a dam and power stations here, and start them operating, will cost an estimated $700 millions. Prime Minister Nkrumah has done everything that he can—or everything short of assassination—to secure this sum as a loan from the Western world, but up to now he has failed. In 1952 the British administration itself published preliminary reports which seemed to indicate that construction on the project—to be paid for jointly by the British and Gold Coast governments, and British and Canadian aluminium companies—was only a matter of a year or so in the future. Later on the possibility of a contribution from the World Bank was canvassed; negotiations were commenced on the issues of ownership and control of the installation, now that Ghana was on the point of freedom. Still later, in the winter of 1957–1958, after an American group had desultorily wandered onto the scene and over the site, Aluminium Limited of Canada mysteriously started to blow cold on its part in the scheme. It was wondered—though not officially—whether the world's appetite for aluminium would stand up under another major producer; or whether Ghana could sell aluminium in competition with American and Canadian producers; or whether this would be a good thing; and whether greater returns were not in prospect in other parts of Africa, like the Congo. Finally, on his visit to the Western Hemisphere in the summer of 1958, Nkrumah put the question directly to the Prime Minister of Canada and the President of the United States. His reply came in the first months of 1959 in the form of a fact-finding mission from President Eisenhower to Ghana, to find out facts and review surveys that everyone has known everything about for more than five years; the mission was in the hands of the Henry J. Kaiser Company, which was slated to submit proposals for the work of an "international consortium" on the river project in December, 1959.

While he has thus been beating vainly at the indifference of the West to the rationalization and diversification of his economy, Nkrumah has also begun to be bombarded by critics of his domestic management. Some of this criticism—the expert part of it—deals with the agricultural sector, which Nkrumah has obviously subordinated to his long-range hopes of industrialization. For example, he has raised the headload price of cocoa: this, it is alleged, is unwise in the present circumstances, because cocoa credits are virtually the country's sole source of income. The Ghana government replies that the cost of living is rising, and therefore so must the smallholder's share of his crop. After all, a "democratic" government cannot be as arbitrarily prudent as was the Cocoa Marketing Board under British superintendence. Similarly, the charge has been leveled that the extermination of "swollen shoot"-sick trees is not being carried out as ruthlessly as it should be, and that the effects of widespread deforestation and erosion in the ex-forest lands are not being countered. Lastly, the Opposition has claimed that the funds of the Cocoa Marketing Board have been mishandled, if not misappropriated. Nkrumah's spokesmen declare that all these accusations are false.

A great deal more of the world's criticism has been aimed at the relatively minor matter of the "bearing" of Nkrumah's regime. Why, for instance, does he build statues to himself around the countryside? Or substitute his own portrait for that of the Queen on Ghana's stamps? Or abruptly withdraw his contingent from the Royal African Frontier Force? Or plan to proclaim a Republic, with himself as first President? Or assume the lifetime Presidency of the CPP? Why does he spend so much of his time traveling around the world—or holding confabulations of African nationalists—instead of buckling down to the all-too-knotty day-by-day problems of putting Ghana on her feet?

As the "plebeian hero" of the kind of revolution of which Europe has had much experience but we Americans—thank heavens—none, Nkrumah does not have to and does not choose to respond to this category of reproof. But more may lie behind all these things than egomania. Like any courtier—which in respect of the West, Nkrumah bitterly is—the Prime Minister knows that he must shun like the plague any pretext for boredom or melancholy in the Royal Mightinesses. Now neither the American people nor our State Department care one penny's-worth for the intricacies of the "destoolings" of Ashanti chiefs or of the "swollen shoot" disease. This is inconvenient, because these happen to be the facts of life in Ghana, but that cuts no ice over here, where nothing less than the "contest for men's souls" has occupied our exclusive attention for fifteen years. But if Nkrumah can puff himself up like a chuckawalla from a seamy little West African wardheeler into a Cold War Ally—if, in short, he can contrive to promote himself from Beggar to Blackmailer—then perhaps someone will listen to his supplications. And the best way to do this is to capitalize on the heroics of his own personality and those latent in the souls of the African people.

None of these foregoing idiosyncrasies of government and behavior has provoked anything like the hurricane of rejection and protest that has greeted Nkrumah's determination to alter the form of Ghana's government from that of a constitutional to that of a plebiscitary republic. This change, which he has now brought to accomplishment—at small enough cost to himself—we must look into in greater detail.

He has had the constitution revised, so that further amendments may now be made by a simple majority of the Assembly. Because his own party can depend on holding about three-quarters of the seats in this Assembly, and because it is unlikely that this plurality will be permitted to diminish much, this amendment is equivalent to a decision that all constitutional matters shall be determined at a party conference (or, to put it more precisely, in the head of Kwame Nkrumah). He has already employed the new procedure to veto the verdicts of the courts on several occasions.

To provide for a greater centralization of control, he has abolished the Regional Assemblies which had represented, and shielded, the local jurisdictions of the chiefs of Ashanti and the Northern Territories. The greater chiefs have been shorn of their right to remove lesser chiefs. Nkrumah has gathered the main powers of government around his own person by taking on two or three ministerial posts in addition to the Prime Ministership; and the other members of his cabinet are old trusted friends and clients. By means of a Preventive Detention Act the government may imprison without trial anyone it pleases for a maximum period of five years. The government has already employed this act against a few "Opposition" M.P.'s; and Nkrumah has publicly stated that he does not intend that one or two of these men now in detention shall be brought to trial in the foreseeable future. He has moved to shatter

the negligible, disorganized Opposition in other ways: he has threatened mass imprisonments and suspensions of the constitution; he
has had passed an "unlawful assembly" act that renders their political activities impossible; he has deported a few of their prominent
members as "undesirables," because they could not prove that they
were of incontestable Ghanaian ancestry; he has exiled others to
the Northern Territories; he has forbidden tribal chiefs to join their
party.

In June, 1959, he had a bill published in the Official Gazette, soon
to be passed through the Assembly, which authorizes the Attorney-
General to "direct any person to furnish information for the purpose
of detecting the commission of offenses against the state." And in
November, 1958, the atmosphere of the country took a practical
turn for the worse when a gigantic assassination-plot was "discovered"; forty-three members of the Opposition were arrested and
subjected to a peculiar, inconclusive trial. Finally, Nkrumah has
speculated publicly, in Ghana and in England, on ridding the state
of constitutional forms entirely by abolishing elections and by
confirming his mandate by plebiscites—or, in his term, referendums.

No matter how a man tries to explain away this record, it sticks
as a serious indictment in the craw of even-minded observers who
have learned that personal rule, however skillful and progressive,
cannot in the long run serve justice, because justice shelters itself
in a nest of statutory constraints that put ordinary men beyond the
passions of great men. Of course, the efficiency of a government is
an important matter, but efficiency does not bear directly on the
issue of justice, which is after all the end of government. A government can be outstandingly inefficient, yet preside over a thriving
civilization where social and legal justice are taken for granted;
probably the few admirable societies of the past fall into this category.
On the other hand, an efficient government can also be a just one;
but efficiency in a government is always a temptation to super-
efficiency, and then justice usually goes begging. In any case, it is
not a matter of Great Captains deciding what the people need and
then laying down their careers for this or that instrument of government; it is a matter of the people's maintaining a line of communications right into the consoles of power, so that their cries and
complaints are continually heard and feared—it is a matter of an

apparatus of response on which, in the long run, both justice and efficiency depend.

Nkrumah has made no promises about following the American or the British models of "democracy" and "democratic capitalism." How could he have done so? He has no idea of what the future holds in store; he has no control over even the smallest of possible disasters. Our American people will put up with incompetent and even ludicrous leadership for years on end, because the old familiar order of things is generally satisfactory to us; we believe that our laws make the best of feeble men and tame the worst of strong men; we do not judge our leaders on their inauguration of a new system, but on their operation of the old one. If a catastrophe overtakes us, like a pestilence or a thermonuclear war, we do not much blame either the President whose authority the Constitution has so deliberately limited or the Constitution which has proved itself so efficacious for 170 years. Nature herself, we will say, has struck us down.

But Nkrumah has no sense of this sportsmanlike community behind him—a community which is just as willing to blame its grandfathers as its contemporary muckers for its troubles. To the people of Ghana Nkrumah is the Lion of the Revolution—the new broom, which must sweep clean—and, we may be sure, their opinion has bitten deep into his psyche; the trust and love that his people repose in him is the best part of him. "Men do not become tyrants to keep out the cold," Aristotle wrote; Nkrumah must sleep too, and the revolution which he triggered is not like the Russian Revolution, where personal failures without number could be swallowed up in the march of the dialectic. The Ghanaian Revolution is a one-hoss shay. If the people starve, Nkrumah has personally failed. If the Volta River Project is never constructed, then he is a smaller man than he or his people dreamed he was. If "swollen shoot" disease destroys the cocoa industry, or the world market for the crop dries up, then Nkrumah has not come through with his part of his bargain with the people, who for their part have done everything he has asked them to do in the way of delivering up to him every atom of political power they have.

The disconcerting intensity of this political relationship—which the Prime Minister himself attributes to the political inexperience of his people (and also the "special circumstances" of West African society)—terrifies Nkrumah, as well it might. It does not extenuate his strong-arm tactics; it does not make them less vicious; but it does explain them. If Captain he is, of a nation-ship in the eye of a typhoon, then his control of his party must be absolute, his party's control of the government must be absolute; his own personal hegemony over the souls and bodies of his people must be absolute— and by these means, reducing his small craft to instantaneous responsiveness to the lightest touch, perhaps he can look forward to survival. For all the fatal flaws in this view, this is how he sees it.

In his own counsels Nkrumah has decided that Ghana's problems cannot be solved within the borders and resources of Ghana. She is too small; too off-center in her development; too liable to be neglected, or palmed off, by the Great Powers. Perhaps it is only a matter of a year or two before Fate sends her sprawling with a slash of the whip, and then Nkrumah will sink into an ignominious limbo, like some ex-president of a republic in Central America. What a prospect of intolerable futility! The creative afflatus of the days of liberation wasted, and Ghana herself and her people worse off than ever.

Hence, so it seems to the Prime Minister of Ghana, the Liberator must continue the God-given work of Liberation. Africans must continue to break free of the Berlin Conference, and to carve out their own frontiers and destinies; the outside world—particularly the United States—must be surprised one day with a muscular new Africa, preferably a United States of Africa, that will shock it out of its complacency, and that will inspire it to come running with many of the fruits of prosperity as a welcome-offering. This is, of course, the crux of the "Federation" idea. Nkrumah wants a larger stage, a Federation, in order to do for West Africa as a whole, Ghana included, what he cannot do for Ghana herself. It is for these reasons that he has so ruthlessly secured his home base, tried to maintain his eminence among the other African leaders and the propagandists of the world, and bowed to a studied moderateness in his dealings with Westerners.

And so far he has gone at the tides of history like a master, but he is so severely handicapped that he has registered but one small success at taking the flood. In the fall of 1958, led by the ex-trade union organizer, Sekou Touré, who declared that he would prefer to see his people go hungry than remain the vassals of France, former French Guinea orphaned herself by rejecting the constitution and Community of Charles De Gaulle. For his part, the General brusquely gave vent to his injured feelings by pulling French administrators and officials out of the country that very day, and by intercepting shipments of food to Guinea on the high seas and rerouting them elsewhere. For a time it looked as if the Guineans were going to be given an opportunity to measure their convictions against their stomachs, but then both Liberia and Ghana appeared on the scene with help—also, "gifts" from Iron Curtain countries like Czechoslovakia and East Germany. On May, 1959, a more permanent arrangement was formulated; Ghana and Guinea merged into a Federation, which cost Nkrumah a loan of $28 millions to his pauperpartner from the bankroll of the Cocoa Marketing Board. (But this is only the first of his troubles. Like most underdeveloped countries, Ghana and Guinea are competitively underdeveloped; that is, they both need the same things—food and money. Wait until some money does appear and Nkrumah has to agree with Touré on whether it is to go toward construction of the Volta project in Ghana or the Konkoure project in Guinea!)

Guinea is a start toward that "West African Confederation" which has been a dream of Nkrumah's since his student days. It is better than nothing; but it is when the Prime Minister looks around himself for the next brick for the edifice that he finds himself in a box. In fact, Nkrumah's career is stalling—and this due to no particular fault of his own. He has superbly calculated and managed his personal affairs, but the Liberation movement has made such swift strides that other Africans, in larger countries, have found themselves holding the reins of administration and bearing the name of Liberator before the Prime Minister of Ghana was able to consolidate his claim to the title of *the* Liberator. Theoretically, the West African Confederation could become an actuality tomorrow, but why should men like Houphouet of the Ivory Coast or President Tubman of Liberia desire to submerge their own aspirations in the profound energies of Kwame Nkrumah. A more or less casual West-Africabund, such as that concerted in the summer of 1959, yes; a unified, centralized nation, no. And now enters from the

wings the Jupiter of West Africa, Nigeria, seven times the size of
Ghana, by sheer weight certain to be the focus to which the affairs
of the region will increasingly gravitate—and yet almost certain
to remain, for reasons of internal dynamics, a member in good standing and in close association with the Commonwealth. And a new
generation of politicians is rising in soon-to-be African states like
Tanganyika, the Rhodesias, and even Kenya. Are these youthful
warhawks going to be willing to lend the earnings of their own
political labors to the Great Career? Hardly! Nkrumah is in danger
of stagnation.

This stagnation, or stalemating, of Kwame Nkrumah of Ghana
will not be a matter of regret to most Americans, because we prefer
a politician who minds the conventions—*our* conventions. We prefer
a man who tends his own garden in a businesslike fashion, and who
doesn't look over the wall at the other fellow's—even if that other
fellow is being buried alive by the neighborhood bully. We like
a nation that solves its own problems—without yapping. It goes without saying that it is our privilege as a community to like or dislike
whom we please, and to criticize as much as we please those whom
we dislike. But we do ourselves no favors if we forget that there
are principles, as well as errors, manifested in the career of Prime
Minister Nkrumah. For example, he believes that Ghana cannot
solve Ghana's problems; and he believes, furthermore, that Africa
cannot solve Africa's problems. In *these* beliefs at least it is he who
is right, and we who are wrong.

* * *

At first sight it will seem odd that Ghana should possess so commanding a share of the world's attention when her giant colleague in
Commonwealth, Nigeria, with four times Ghana's land area and
seven times her population, is so near herself to the rank of full and
independent statehood, to be achieved in October, 1960.

That the disparity exists is, of course, eloquent witness to the extent Nkrumah has been able to touch a few of the chords of strategy
and idealism that are motivating modern American politics. He has
become the firm, manly voice of languishing Africa. He embodies a
hint to the effect that the "colored races" may one of these days
suddenly spring out onto the world stage like Superman, throwing
off-kilter the familiar propaganda and European locale of the Cold

War. By incarnating the challenge which is unnerving the white settler regimes in southern Africa he is the forewarning of a future which will be, perhaps, even more troubled than the present. And, lastly, for most people Nkrumah's performance is the test of African political maturity and responsibility.

For a number of reasons contemporary Nigerian politicians are powerless to play a role of this grandeur, and it is likely that they will remain so for a long time to come. To begin with, they have no base anything like so solid as Nkrumah's. "There is no such thing as Nigeria," a young, cynical Ibo studying law in New York told me before I left for Africa. "Nigeria is not a nation; it is a mere geographical expression," said Premier Awolowo of the Western Region a few years ago. "Nigerian unity is only a British intention for the country," Prime Minister Abubakar Tafawa Balewa of the Federation of Nigeria has said. To some extent, as we have seen, all of the new "nations" of Africa are Europe-engineered conglomerates, but in the case of Nigeria the "unnaturalness" of the unity which was imposed on the country is so glaring that even Africans, as well as different sections of British officialdom, have speculated for years that dismembering the country may be in the long run the best way of promoting the people's welfare. Numerous alternative plans for this fragmentation process have been proposed and considered; none ever has been found satisfactory by a consensus of the interested parties. The foregoing remarks of the two premiers were both made in the late 1940's; and since that time these men, and others, have been both the subjects and partners of several constitutional experiments, varying the deeds of authority at the Federal, Regional, and local levels, all designed to discover whether "Nigeria" could or should work. In 1958 both these leaders sat down with their peers around a London conference table and came up with the constitution which will guide Nigeria out of colonial status and through the first days of her freedom; and it is a constitution that provides for a united, though as we shall see distinctively "federal," national government. In short, Africans apparently are as capable as the Colonial Office of appreciating the advantages of "Nigeria."

Like the other countries of the Guinea coast, Nigeria is banded longitudinally by two or three types of environmental belt: a coastal strip 100 to 200 miles in depth of swamps, marshes, and rain forests;

then the savanna of the interior, which except along the rivers rises up through drier country as it penetrates inland, terminating along the northern boundary in the outright deserts of the Sahara. It is a country possessing an enormous population, 34 millions, which makes it the most populous country on the continent of Africa. Of the three dominant races of this population, two of them, the Yoruba of the Western Region and the Ibo of the Eastern, approximating each other in numbers, live along the coast. In the Northern Region, which comprises more than 75 per cent of the land area of the country and about 54 per cent of the population, dwells the Hausa-Fulani, an Islamic fusion society still ruled by sultans and emirs who have more or less maintained themselves unchanged since the trans-Saharan migrations of the Middle Ages.

But this is only the beginning of a description of what is for the anthropologist a Happy Hunting Ground. Each of the Regions' populations is diversified by dozens of minority races and tribes, ranging in size from pagan village peoples of only a few hundred to huge groups like the Ijaws, who formidably rival the dominant races of two Regions—settled in minute, isolated enclaves or across broad belts, as in the Northern Region. Interregional migrations blur the picture even further, especially that of the Ibos into the Western Region, where the Federal capital of Lagos is situated, and of both Ibos and Yorubas into the so-called "Middle Belt" of the Northern Region. And the final element of confusion is added by Nigeria's experience of the slave trade (it was she who was the "Slave Coast"), which as we have mentioned mixed races and quashed social order as nothing else did. One of the early tasks of the British administration was to suppress ferocious old chiefs, like the King of Benin in his famous "City of Blood," who for centuries had been supporting themselves on this slave brokering.

In other words, the three Regions that make up the Federation of Nigeria are not homogeneous areas the simple coordination of which fulfills the aim of the Federal constitution. In each of the Regions there is one dominant race, but in each of them this domination is qualified by the existence of at least several large and innumerable smaller minorities; indeed, outside their own Regions both the Ibos and Yorubas also constitute large minorities. Nevertheless, because administrative procedures left by the British are already in working order, and because there is no conceivable gerrymandering that would really straighten out the checkerboard and make government any less precarious than it already is, the African leaders have simply more or less resigned themselves to the Regional structure as it now exists; and, indeed, because they have been used administratively and electorally, the Regions have come to have a life of their own. Therefore, paradoxically, it is at the bottom the coordination of three semiautonomous Regions that the new constitution is designed to accomplish.

For many years the Eastern Region, Iboland, has been the playing field of one of the best known and most colorful politicians in Africa, the veteran Nnamdi Azikiwe, or "Zik," newspaper publisher, agitator, Africanist—like his friend and ex-protégé, Nkrumah, an alumnus of American schooling. Although it is not easy to discern a system of coherent ideas behind his rhetoric, it is fair to term Zik the most radical of Nigerian leaders (but his critics say that he only says whatever comes first into his head). Generally he is opposed to tribalism and "regionalism"; he fills his speeches with rhodomontades about the role that a united and modernized Nigeria will soon play in Africa and the world outside, without intimating where the purchase price of these glories is to be sought. During the years of his greatest prominence and energy he was occupied entirely with bombing the Colonial Office, and now that this target has so unexpectedly sunk into the ground—with the Queen handing the keys of sovereignty back to her African subjects—Zik, like many other African politicians, has been deprived of the issue that he loved and knew and has been presented with baffling, brand-new issues for which he has no affection or competence. Until 1960, of course, he can devote himself to the infighting which will decide which Region, or combination of Regions, is going to have the dominant say in the new government, but his task here has been complicated by a government inquiry, a few years back, into certain irregularities connected with the operations of his personal bank. He seems now to have shrugged off this scrape with little harm done; he has rehabilitated his reputation, re-established his hold over his party (the National Council of Nigeria and the Cameroons) and his Region (of which he is Premier), and has plunged with undiminished zest into the prenationhood maneuverings.

In the Western Region, a prosperous, scholarly, thoughtful lawyer, Chief Obafemi Awolowo, has organized with a group of associates the Action Group, a party now in unchallenged control of Western affairs. So far as the British and the other members of the Commonwealth are concerned, this serious and responsible politician is by far the best liked leader in all of Africa. And Awolowo reciprocates this esteem by continually reminding his people of the advantages to them of the Commonwealth connection, even to the extent of publicly thanking the colonial power for what it has done in the country: "We Nigerian people are fully aware that the British people have given their wisdom and sometimes their lives to help in building the Nigerian nation." Like the best leaders of French Africa, Awolowo is extremely troubled about the social plight of his people. So far as correcting the causes of this plight, Awolowo's "responsibility" is no more effective than Zik's "radicalism"; once again, Africa's powerlessness to help herself renders the matters which are of the utmost significance in America entirely irrelevant in Africa, and renders other matters which are more or less self-adjusting in America the foci of life-and-death developments in Africa. In any case, what Awolowo hopes is that in the few years, or even generation, that the country has before its social troubles drown every peaceful prospect, the new constitution will be befriended by the West—who will then come to understand the necessity for, and to implement, the modernization of the land.

By our standards the Northern Region is far more backward than its southern brothers; it did not have the "advantage" of centuries of European forts and slave posts, and at a later date schools; and the sultans and emirs who rule it—it was the testing-ground of the "Dual Mandate," with its "indirect rule" principle—were never forced to surrender their old-time prerogatives to new fashions in political dispensation. As a matter of fact, it was these northern autocrats' absolute hostility to everything that both Zik and Awolowo stand for—their race, among other things, along with their eclectic storehouse of libertarian European ideologies, pan-Africanism, party programs, and so on—which was the biggest hurdle that the constitution-makers had to take. The emirs most emphatically do not want to be modern; they do not want a "Federal" government situated in the south interfering with their Arabian Nights judicial and punitive traditions; they do not want the Ibo, Yoruba, or other minorities in the "Middle Belt" of their Region disputing their hegemony; they do not want to have to engage in newfangled electoral campaigns, stump-speaking, and the like. The chief personality of the Northern People's Congress, the emirs' party, and Premier of the Northern Region is an austere Moslem aristocrat, the Sardauna of Sokoto, who brings himself with obvious reluctance into all discussions and controversies with his compatriots, the Negroes of the coast. After all, as the Hausa who happens to be the *Federal* Minister of Works recently put it, the Ibos only recently "emerged from the jungle and started to wear clothes"; perhaps they are better read (in English books) and technologically far more advanced than the northern people, but these are not things which signify; and it is better to have as little to do with them as possible.

In December, 1959, an election will be held which will determine the composition of the Federal House of Representatives that will legislate for the country after Independence Day in 1960. It is an assembly which will be made up of 309 members; 174 from the Northern Region, 73 from the Eastern, and 62 from the Western. The new institution, and other parts of the Federal government, will undertake the ordinary functions of a central government, foreign affairs, monetary policy, and so forth—and also the most important single problem in the country, the regulation and wardship of the multifarious minority-groups—but its authority in most matters of regional internal government is severely limited.

The tactics pursued by each of the major participants in this election in these preparatory days is what we could have expected from their characters and ideas. Before they accepted the idea of a free Federal Nigeria at all, the Northern People's Congress demanded and secured in the fall of 1958 the guarantees they wanted for the preservation of their way of life. Therefore, their only problem is to hold fast to nearly all of their 174 seats in order not only to perpetuate their domestic regime but also to control the Federal government. However, of these 174 seats about 74 lie in areas where the Hausa-Fulanis are outnumbered by minorities; most of these are situated in the "Middle Belt," into which immigration from the south has been particularly important. Therefore, Awolowo's and Zik's opportunity to overcome their structural inferiority lies in making themselves truly "national" parties, by picking up seats in the Regions outside their own. Following up this plan, Awolowo's Action Group vans and speakers invaded the "Middle Belt" in force in the spring and summer of 1959, and the nearer this election approaches the more energetic this campaign will become. On the other hand, Zik has embarked on a far more devious scheme. He has apparently concerted an agreement on a prospective coalition with the Northern People's Congress, whereby these two groups can exclude Awolowo and pretty much manage the Federal government by themselves. The idea works on paper, but it remains to be seen whether the sultans and Zik have anything in common on which to base a state policy. Meanwhile, Zik has also invaded Awolowo's Western Region trying to pick up support, and is vigorously defending himself on his home grounds against the counterattacks of the Action Group.

When you come to consider all these animosities and dissimilarities, these dangerous treadings-on-toes against the background of an extremely hungry country, it seems that any salvation for "Nigeria" is an almost inconceivable thought. But the new constitution has one great asset: everyone's eyes are wide. open. For so many years has the whole concept of "Nigeria" been scouted and scoffed at, and alternate plans of administering this part of West Africa been tabled, that even the hastiest and most reckless politician knows that nothing stands between "Nigeria" and total decomposition but a strict observance of the pledges of regional autonomy given at the constitutional conference in the fall of 1958. Powerfully situated as she is, the Northern Region can, and will, pull out of the Federation the moment that she feels her provincial interests to be endangered. Whether the future will develop powers in the Federal government that eventually will be able to circumvent and weaken this independence of manuever is dubious. In America, despite their superficial differences, the antebellum ruling classes of the South and of the North shared many things in common: they spoke the same language; they frequently intermarried; the South purchased manufactures from the North, and the North agricultural produce from the South. From the first a union was latent which it required only a steady increase in social complexity to develop to its present near-omnipotence. It is interesting that while the American Constitution has nothing to say about the Union's right to coerce states to remain in membership, which right was after all the crux of the Civil War, neither was it found necessary at the time the Civil War amendments were passed to propose one to take care of this oversight. Everyone—or nearly everyone—instinctively felt that the issue was settled; first by the naturally growing interdependence of the states, and second by the outcome of the war. It would be very hard indeed to find any analogy in all this to the situation in Nigeria. The Northern Region is not dependent economically, or affiliated socially, with the coastal Regions; indeed, in the short run the people of the Northern Region live at such a primitive economic level that they are not dependent on anyone; and we have seen the kind of aspersions with which the sultans respond to hints of a closer association with the coastal Negroes. If the Nigerian Federal government is to move toward power accumulation, after the fashion of the American Federal government, it will have to tread so softly that the delicately attuned ears of the sultans catch no whisper of the process. Considering that these gentlemen will handpick regularly about half the membership of the Federal assembly, this will be a real feat.

More than 90 per cent of Nigeria's people live in rural areas, on small farms. Exploitation of minerals and industry are not factors in her economy; and the problems of her great population concentrations are those of heavily settled farming areas rather than "urbanization" as such. She is of course a frightfully poor country, but compared with her past and—doubtless—her future she has known a fair prosperity in the past decade, the result of a period of high prices for her oil-palm products, peanuts, and cocoa (so far she has been spared really severe incursions of "swollen shoot"). However, though the diagram of her poverty is not so dramatic or easy to follow as that of a country like, say, the Belgian Congo, it is still a dynamic, morbid picture. Iboland, in the Eastern Region, is one of the most densely populated areas on earth; the pressure of people here is forcing Ibos to migrate into the other Regions, where they complicate the political puzzle, and into the cities, where they join the growing ranks of the urban unemployed and underemployed. As in other regions of West Africa, cash cropping and the unique kind of African "overpopulation" have exhausted her soils, large belts of the primeval rainforest have been laid bare for erosion; the tsetse fly is a familiar all over the country; and in the far north, where the Fulanis follow a pastoral existence, overgrazing has ruined whole domains of the already sparse range.

In all this we can notice again the most appalling single truth about modern African politics: that confined to the instrumentalities of Africa herself, the wisest and most virtuous sage—even of Solomonic dimensions—cannot cope more adequately with the community's problems than the most rabid and corrupt plunger. In a situation of this kind we can be sure that sooner or later a sort of political Gresham's Law will start its operations: since good men can make no more headway than bad men, it will be the bad men who will eventually predominate. And, with this in view, it is remarkable how many good men like Awolowo there are at the start of Free Nigeria, ready to try to integrate two or three hundred different races into a focal nationality—a process which will and must take in its stride all manner of obstacles, from communal riots in small villages; to secret societies like that one discovered in a remote district of the Eastern Region in February, 1959, which was quashed with the execution of the local chief and four of his henchmen; to the colossal minorities that irritate the three principal peoples and thus throw off balance the whole Federal structure; to housebreaking the Technological Revolution, which, for example, has already made the medieval, Moslem, blind-walled city of Kano, in northern Nigeria, for centuries one of the world's favorite "mystery towns," entrepot of all the sports and vices of the Near East, the seat of one of the busiest air terminals in Africa. Men like Zik will always be tempted to indulge in the kind of scheming he is now cooking up with the Northern chiefs, and no doubt protracted attempts to achieve parliamentary coups at the expense of long-run adjustments of interest would ultimately destroy the creative possibilities of the Federal government. But as it now is this is just a question of an early or delayed destruction; the creative possibilities of the Federal government are doomed anyway, so long as Nigerians are left alone with the problems of Nigeria.

For all these reasons the unanimity of Nigeria's African leaders about clinging to the Commonwealth association is one of the most reassuring features of the whole African picture. There is no substitute for what the English can contribute here. The "thin red line" is withdrawing, but it is leaving behind a host of civilian consultants, laboratory and agronomical technicians, anthropologists, medical workers, road-building engineers, entomologists, and so forth. The unparalleled and absolutely irreplaceable warehouse of administrative experience which the British have been hoarding for centuries, she is not only willing but eager to put at the service of her new Commonwealth partners. The Empire has vanished, but for a country like Nigeria the wisdom of the Empire is one of the few assets that she can call upon. So long as the former subjects of the Empire— like the Nigerians—can bring themselves emotionally to accept this wisdom and these gifts of their old oppressor, they will not be entirely without allies in their battle for survival.

11. The American Posture

This chapter should be skipped by readers who are weary of expostulations about the American Failure-to-Rise-to-the-Challenge-of-Our-Day. But I have included it here because it seems to me a practical impossibility to think constructively about the America-Africa couple without to a slight extent pondering the status of our own selfhood. Given the main conclusions of this essay—that Africa cannot save herself from social deliquescence; that the American Republic is the only power in the world that can save her, but that only a radical revision of our policy can accomplish the job—then it is folly to suppose that such a revision, amounting to a thoroughgoing reformation in all our thinking about the uses of Federal revenues, to take just one example, can occur along one front alone. Africa is not the only seething slum in the world. We cannot assume the physician's role in Africa without refurbishing our "ardours and humours" throughout, redefining our attitudes toward the whole world as well as toward the social problems of our own country. Hence this light sketch of our present posture.

The reverberating, soul-stirring victories of the Bulge, of Leyte Gulf, and of countless, irresistible air armadas over the towns and cities of the Japanese Empire now lie fifteen years or more behind us. The reaffirming, pioneering administrations of Franklin D. Roosevelt

—who understood that highly charged industrial societies simply cannot (and will not) endure the periodic trauma involved in the old non-self-regulating boom-and-bust economic cycle, but who believed despite the pessimism of a good part of the American business community that a "democratic capitalism" could be evolved by persevering experimentation which would go far toward satisfying simultaneously the material *and* the political needs of the people— these New Deal years of FDR lie twenty years or more behind us. Much of what was gained in both these national imbroglios has been firmly incorporated into the foundations of the Republic; but other aspects of what we won—and the changes that were initiated in them —have not been defined, or clearly comprehended, or still yet incorporated into policy.

For example, though we are proud of our strength, as manifested in the almost overnight creation of the unprecedentedly huge fleets and armies of World War II, we habitually underestimate our strength when it comes to the programs of peace. Like an old lady with gilt-edged bonds and a bad heart we are forever fretting about "overtaxing" ourselves in more ways than one. We have not yet learned to exploit the potentialities of the "democratic capitalism" which is so new to us. Again, although we are certainly happy to have won World War II rather than to have lost it, we as yet only dimly understand what a historical debt is incurred by a victory such as that one was; a defeated people can relax and vegetate, but victors must proceed from strength to strength, and must especially shun the temptation common to all victors of spending most of their time keeping a high polish on the aging weapons of victory rather than exploring the horizons of the territory that victory annexed.

In other words, through our own efforts and our lucky placement in history we have earned Power and Responsibility of a very high order, but we have not learned to live with them. We have not learned that special qualities like these demand special deeds—or they will atrophy with time, like unfertilized flowers. In the past fifteen years we have come up to "expectations"; we have done what we have been told to do by our elected leaders, a generally sincere and experienced body of men; we have been mulcted of fantastic billions of dollars, not to mention the lives of the men lost in Korea. And we are continuing to toil on and on, but all of this without a sense of the

Goal on which this Power and Responsibility (and this Effort) should be concentrating. Therefore, the toil is becoming ever more dispirited. We keep dragging our carcass down the trail of costly international political obligations, but is it not a trail that seems dustier, drier, and more hopeless of a conclusion with every passing year? Is our whole national performance not taking on the aspect of a mindless reflex? Tocqueville wrote once that Americans "conceive a high opinion of their superiority and are not very remote from believing themselves to be a distinct species of mankind." Is even this much true today? And if it is no longer true, can we cruelly hallucinate ourselves that the new "humility" is a profit of wisdom? The Superior Man is the man who knows what he has, what he owes, and what he proposes to attain; the Inferior Man is the man who drifts.

What we call a "goal" here, Benjamin Disraeli called a "community of purpose." "It is a community of purpose that constitutes society," he wrote in *Sybil,* his novel of the labor struggle of Chartist days: "Without that, men may be drawn into contiguity, but they still continue virtually isolated." The meaning here is plain enough. It is that there is a spiritual adhesive as well as "interest" which binds men and women living within the boundaries of the same political unit; that some societies possess more, and some less, of this spiritual adhesive; and that without it, much of the zest and significance of political life, and the effectiveness of a society, are frittered away on the petty, routine exchanges of existence. The problem of accommodating the claims of the "community"—which override everything in a society like, say, Japan's—to the ever-justified claims of individuals to a certain ration of privacy and self-ness has preoccupied political philosophers since *The Republic.* And, surely, the only resolution must conform to the near-absolute condition of everything else in life—an equilibrium of forces. Neither in our politics nor religion do we Americans believe that a man should surrender every value to the Big Picture, and retain no inner life at all. At the same time, if a man retreats entirely into a sphere of intimate satisfactions, playing no creative part at all in the Big Picture, acknowledging no debt to the "community," we say he is robbing his society of a portion of the strength and counsel which is society's due—if we hold at all to the concept of the continuity

of history. This man may have fellow countrymen, but no compatriots; and the former word is enough weaker than the latter that
we can observe—and have observed—the effects of the distinction
projected into very evil catastrophes.

That some sort of "de-compatriotization" or "de-communitization" process is actually under way in America can be confirmed
by nearly anyone who takes the trouble to attend a general meeting
of one of the school districts in this country. Next to the pleasures
of puffing on this or that cigarette, nothing in the past few years
has received more publicity than the delapidation of the American
public school system. So it makes no sense to plead ignorance of the
facts. Yet at meeting upon meeting, chaired by the head of the local
school board, man after man, woman after woman will rise, redfaced
with choler, to denounce new appropriations for which harassed
authorities armed with every kind of heartbreaking and indisputable
proof of their need have just been begging. And everyone in town
knows that every last individual of this obstructionist gang has
purchased within the past year a new automobile, washer, jewels
and clothes, and a dozen other new appliances and gadgets. And
while it perhaps would be unfair to state that these persons comprise the majority of the meeting, they are sufficiently convincing
that the final appropriation voted is invariably far below that asked
by the board. (After all, the experts tell us that 85 per cent of the
American public school system is obsolete, and Americans cannot
plead epidemics, war, or foreign occupation in self-defense.)

It is impossible to talk sense to nine out of ten of these people. It
does not do to cite the opinions and researches of a score of experts. It
does not do to ask them where America is going to end up with a demoralized, fourth-rate public school system. It does not do to ask them
what in the world they deem more important to our society than a
first-rate public school system. They do not care a pin for, and will
not abide by, any of the procedures of ordinary rational argument,
because they are simply not *interested*. They are indifferent to you,
to your arguments, and to the schools; these things are not part of
their lives, and in their bones they feel that they really mean nothing
to what counts in life. They have jettisoned the concept that everyone owes a great deal to everyone else in a Community, not least
to its children and grandchildren (but they have not yet lost their

idea of what is owed to *them*). They have forgotten that the American Republic subsists in a mystical space-and-time dimension of its own, and that in the political aspect of our lives we enter this dimension and do creative work in it. And what goes for the schools goes double for libraries, concert halls, theaters, slum-clearance projects (that is, those which end up with some improvement in *lowest cost* housing facilities), colleges, soil reclamation and reforestation projects, all the other forms of so-called "social investment"—all mendicants in the wealthiest epoch in the history of the wealthiest nation in the world.

To what extent the spirit of "de-communitization" that we have tried to suggest here with the "crisis of the schools" has pervaded other areas of community interest each one of us must answer for himself. We all have met college kids and young marrieds in their twenties and thirties who disclaim all interest in politics. They sneer at the old all-night dialectical *Kaffeeklatsches* of New Deal times as if they were the snake dances of naked savages; if they mention national affairs at all they refer, with a deadly calm, to the "they" in Washington, the "they" who direct the big American corporation, the "they" who run Madison Avenue and the television companies—all this "they" which is stultifying the "we." There is a certain membership of this group that eschews partisan passions of every kind; they will join neither a political nor an esthetic clique (nor a golf club); many of the cleverest of them—my friend Ed Fisher calls them the "New Brahmins"—with winsome sanctimony decline working for the United States government, for example, in any capacity whatsoever. Alienation and impotence are their ways of keeping in touch with themselves—or so they think. (The Beatniks might be termed the Anabaptists of this cult.) My own supposition is that the New Brahmins are clever enough to see how much time and energy-exhaustion is called for by the Power and Responsibility of the American Republic in the modern day—and hence they refrain from taking the first step into a sea of troubles. Considered as Americans—citizens of the world's most powerful state— they are following, without being aware of it, Marcus Aurelius's advice to "beware of Caesarizing," without remembering that Emperor's example, a sense of duty that welded Power and Responsibility into a long and melancholy lifetime's labor.

Then there was our recent rare brush with a Secretary of Defense, one of the government's movers and shakers, who ridiculed and hooted at the Conquest of Space the day after the first decisive victory in that Conquest had gained the admiration and excitement of the whole world; he was simply not *interested* in the ramifications of this fabulous new venture, its importance for the Republic projected in time. And the thousands of men, presumably among the ablest in the country (judging from the colleges they come from and the salaries they command) who work in advertising and public-relations concerns, who write what they are paid to write and say what they are paid to say without any personal investigation of the truth; they are not *interested* in the Republic's need of truth. Then, despite our possession of all the Bowl Games on earth, there was that dark day when we awoke to find that the Soviet Union—a plaguy backward country whose misery-hobbled peasants put oats in gas tanks because they don't know any better—leads us in the academic disciplines of geophysics and geodesy and oceanography and meteorology and nuclear-engine technology and space technology and metallurgy and chess and piano-playing and intercontinental missiles. The military implications of one or two of these deficiencies finally put a cork in even Mr. Charles Wilson's chuckles, but as a Community we Americans still do not realize that there is no rational explanation for or extenuation of them—except that we are not *interested* in the kind of society, and the kind of work and study, that produce results in fields like these. We still possess most of the world's telephones, cars, and refrigerators, but who is thrilled by these brags any more? That salt has lost its savor.

No one I know of contends that the self-infatuated inattention of our last ten years or so has wrought a decisive and irremediable injury on the Republic. I think that in the past year or two most of us have caught glimpses of a change in the temper of our people; after all, Republics like people have to survive Bad Times—and decades of intellectual drought must surely be classed as the worst of Bad Times—without giving way to hysterical frenzies of malediction and foreboding. I mention these things in this space because we Americans owe so much to fortune and to our Founders that we lapse less gracefully, perhaps, than any other people in the history of the world. That lapses like these—symptoms of a self-proud philistinism, a neglect of the "community," and perhaps an excessive popular egocentricity—will if carried to extremes eventually destroy the Republic's capacity even to defend our physical property from the hostilities of life goes without saying. That is to say, there is a Real World outside—on the other sides of the Atlantic and Pacific Oceans—ready to eat us up whole if we are utterly determined to put up no spiritual defense at all. Matters have not gone nearly so far as this. Still, they have gone far enough that the creative responsiveness of the Republic to the very complicated and mind-tiring challenges of this world of ours has already been seriously impaired.

In the seventeenth and eighteenth centuries, when the doctrines of "popular sovereignty" and the "rule of law" were receiving their modern formulations (I do not of course mean to imply that they are coincident ideas), no particular distinction needed to be drawn between the economic man and the political man. In all previous times, the ordinary man expended so large a proportion of his time and energy in earning his bread that it never occurred to the doctors of political science not to make this breadwinning the basic ground of all the paper reorganizations of society. And, to limit our discussion to English affairs, so far as the Stuart policies of this period were concerned, the attempts to perpetuate medieval molds into the era of liberated, heterogeneous instincts were deemed equally crippling to both economic and political progress.

Everyone agreed that on all fronts the Stuart system deprived society of numerous priceless achievements that would have come from freeing men's natural self-serving, money-getting energies of the pall of motheaten caste values and bureaucratic abuses like the commodity monopolies which used to be granted to royal favorites. But when the reformers cast around for another system than the Stuarts' to live by they discovered that they could find none without its own weighty disadvantages. Every other "system" presupposed other "custodians" or "judges" who must referee the game, perhaps in the long run no less selfishly than the Stuarts had done. And upon this consideration was born the new doctrine that "system" *per se* is wrong in these matters; that the good polity is the "wraps-off" polity, wherein the individual exercises what ingenuity and judgment he has been bequeathed by God in a flexible surround; the comprehensive resultant of all these individual judgments, translated into day-by-day decisions, will possess a strength and subtlety that no monolithic "system" ever can hope to match.

Crammed into a nutshell, what we Americans have subsequently learned in a national social experience of 180 years is that the doctrine of "systemlessness" also requires to be profoundly modified in order that the Republic may thrive—though the modifications are not at all necessarily directed to the erection of a closely-reckoned new "system." We have found that doctrinaire "systemlessness" does *not* work to the benefit of most of the people, and does *not* last once the people can get their hands on it; and that is that. And so the imposition of social controls on the wheeler-dealering instincts and appetites of talented individuals has come to constitute a main theme in American history.

This fact casts a reflection of hindsight on the intellectual environment of the Founding Fathers; a reflection which almost invariably escapes the observation of commentators on American society. And what is this? It is, I think, that the expounders of the "democratic" and "laissez-faire" doctrines of the Age of Enlightenment, which underlie our basic national documents, were almost altogether unaware of their dependence on a hierarchical, structural cohesiveness in society which had come down to their day by momentum from the Middle Ages—invisible to them because it pervaded the very air that they breathed. Rarely did they explicitly acknowledge—and the omission is particularly conspicuous in a mind as masterly as Jefferson's—the nonrational constraints, taboos, or customs which in their generation were always on hand to qualify, at least somewhat, the political and economic egotisms of individual go-getters. In a word, the Fathers did not know what they owed to that which they detested and overthrew. But then the Industrial Revolution came along, unhinging the structure and drowning the gasps of the Old Society, and men became less and less susceptible to the domesticating neighborhood, church, and clan influences. That the socializing assumptions of the eighteenth century had been largely unwritten then became a flaw as men ceased to remember them, and to be monitored by them. Egotism began to aggrandize Community, and no one remembered that this was *wrong*. It became necessary to call a halt—first here and then there—to try to refine and rephrase some of the nearly forgotten premises of "community," and to define other things like Proper Citizenship and Brotherhood.

So far as the Republic of our own day is concerned, this process of the definition of Community has hardly begun; nor is this anything to be regretted. Insofar as the Technological Revolution has hardly begun to revamp the physical concomitants of our lives we can hardly expect it to be otherwise. But in general terms what we are looking for is this: an "open society" in which there is more than enough room for dissenters and geniuses and eccentrics, and which also possesses the firm and *care*-ful structure to shield the helpless against the greedy and the psychotic. And now, as we look back at the attempts at defining this Community in concrete terms since the end of the Civil War, one very interesting feature strikes us at once: a gap has opened up in the urgency of this Community definition in respect of the economic and political sectors. That is, the vast majority of individuals in America who have permitted their egotisms to ride down their Community loyalties have made themselves—or tried to make themselves—economic autocrats rather than political autocrats. This is also true of England, but by no means true universally; for example, it is not true of modern Africa. The ordinary American really has no ambition to be a dictator, but most of us hanker to be monopolists; certainly we are prepared to be far more jovial and forgiving toward little financial peccadilloes than political ones. This anyone can prove to himself by studying the American statute books of the past 100 years. In a continuing, largely unconscious attempt to redefine and reform itself, the American Community has had to occupy itself almost exclusively with the control and penalization of overreaching entrepreneurs. With the exception of a few changes like the broadening of the franchise —and the great politico-philosophical episode of the Civil War— our political structure stands pretty much where it was, and at least as strong as it ever was.

Now the point I want to make here—which I will try to illustrate concretely in a moment—is that the differential development of the political and economic ego-instincts of Americans, which probably was latent in our system from the beginning but which now has blossomed into a full-grown distortion, must be brought out into the open if the processes of Community definition of our merger society—the "democratic capitalism" of our day—are to have a fair chance of success. It is not a question whether society has the right to protect itself against *both* economic pirates and political conspirators; of course society has this right—and if we have any faith at all in the Republic we can safely leave the pirates and conspirators of the future to our posterity. The issue is a much deeper one. It is a question whether time has not introduced a schism into the psychological surround of the Community—a schism which by no means necessarily renders the Community unviable, but one which must be faced and bridged boldly, candidly, and all the time. To quote John Strachey's terms, it is a question whether the dynamics of "latest-stage capitalism" are not inherently "antidemocratic," so that a marriage between the two can flourish only upon the labors of eternal vigilance. And to get down to cases, it is a question whether there is not something deeply antagonistic in the training and unconscious attitudes of American business to the extraordinary needs of American politics in our era.

We have room here to say very little more about this except to state—perhaps unnecessarily—that because the American businessman is such an important figure in the community, and the pioneering of a production-consumption nexus without parallel anywhere is so obviously the capital historical adventure of the Republic, it is perfectly legitimate for all of us to scrutinize the psyche and postulates behind his operations. He is, of course, just as loyal an American as a pipe fitter or a farmer; he has the right to work for what he wants for himself just so long as he does not injure the right in another; and no one is blaming him for the Cold War, the Inflation, or the Beatniks. Nevertheless, in only a few years we have had to travel a long road, from Coolidge's famous "The chief business of the American people is business" to John Kenneth Galbraith's "Beyond doubt, wealth is the relentless enemy of understanding"; we have traveled this rough road reluctantly, partly because for a long time it looked like an un-American road, and only because reality forced us to; it is a road lined with monuments to bitter experience and solemn reflection. We have traversed it for the reason

that American business *is* such a critical factor in the strength and
morale of the American Republic; and because a great many people—observing the facts before them as honestly as they are able—
have come to the conclusion that the political component of the
economic enterprise of American business is growing increasingly
heedless of and irrelevant to the basic problems of our time.

But what in the world has all this got to do with Africa?
It is very simple, and exceedingly ironic. Africa stands in dire
need of Business—but Old-Fashioned Business, roughly the kind
that popular movements had to struggle against in the nineteenth
century, not the kind that American businessmen purvey nowadays.
Africa needs to concentrate on the production of dozens of in-
dispensables; American business is concentrating on the "problem of
creating sufficient wants . . . to absorb productive capacity"
(Beckerman)—in short, on expendibles. Africa needs the stimulation
of a vast domestic market of consumers; we need a cure for inflation, at least partly caused by too much cash in the hands of too
many consumers. Africa needs people outside of Africa who have
the money and the desire to buy what she has to sell; we seek
some way to give away what we have overproduced to people with
no money to buy. Africa needs a genuine working class and the
social mobility wherewith this working class can through education
evolve itself into a genuine middle class; for purposes of practical
function, we Americans all lump together into a single gigantic
middle class (except for fringes like the Puerto Ricans in New
York, Mexican-Americans in the Southwest, Cabots and Rockefellers,
and so forth), and our ingrained middle-class habits of incurring
huge long-term mortgages and buying expensive apparatus on the
installment plan are one of the thorniest problems of our economy.
Africa needs rambunctious entrepreneurs to cut through Circumlo-
cution Offices, prejudices, and governmental indifference; the American economy is becoming increasingly concentrated in a score
of more or less tame "oligopolies," each with a blooming Circum-
locution Office of its own, run by managers so superconscious of
their "responsibility" that what they interpret as their political and
social obligations to society *almost* outweighs their sense of duty
to the stockholders. In short, what Africa needs is swashbucklers,

and what she gets from America are a gaggle of Junior Chamber of Commerce boys—calling themselves the New Capitalism.

As everyone knows, the chief structural difference between the New Capitalism and the Old has been the substitution for the business decisions of one individual, who possessed the resources he was hazarding, of the decisions of a group, hired to manage these resources in behalf of a faceless multitude of shareholders. The Parsifal's-vision of the old pirates has given way to the ethic of the "responsibility" of the director-manager. Henry Ford felt that he was personally guided by God as an instrument of Progress, and his secret soul whispered to him the directions for creating an empire. Today's director-manager feels—and so proclaims on innumerable public occasions—that his motif is "stewardship" and, of course, his "responsibility" which weeps down, like a crayon on a hot radiator, to tinge stockholders, founders, foremen, unions, and the whole country. The pirate made his decision in response to a dream of Organization and Production; the director-manager's decision is a meticulously arrived-at compromise chiefly orientated toward Sales, and within the compromise is comprehended not only the consensus of other directors' opinions but also the contrived "image" of the company which must be explicated and sloganeered by a public-relations corps to the whole world.

Over the past twenty-five years or so, in any number of books and reports, Adolf A. Berle, Jr., has brilliantly dissected and analyzed the actual mechanics of the decision-making process in the New Capitalism. Among his most important observations Mr. Berle has pointed out that a business policy which must be made intelligible, or at least acceptable, to tens of thousands of far-flung stockholders who know nothing whatever of the real circumstances of the business, who may possess only an infinitesimal share of it for only a month or so, and whose real concern thus narrows down to the size of the quarterly dividend (or various speculative possibilities) will inevitably in very many cases be a very different policy from that which would be arrived at by a "scientific" diagnosis of the best interests of the company. How this works out in practice is not affected by the even newer entry of titanic fiduciary institutions into the ranks of Big Ownership. It is doubtful that the management of any big American automobile corporation of today would dare to inform their "owner"—pension-fund managers or a hundred thousand or so of the "little people" of the legend—that all plants must close down for a year to retool, as Ford did in the 1920's, even though this were demonstrably and indubitably the best long-run thing for the company to do. To the extent that they are hamstrung from taking wide-ranging and unconventional measures such as this one by stockholder detachment, selfishness, and ignorance the director-manager of our time—for all his smooth façade and astronomical income—is not nearly the "responsible" and "creative" being that he would like us to believe he is.

This is all perfectly familiar ground. We all know that the mode of gambling engaged in by a man armed with naught but his own instincts is an entirely different mode from that he engages in after consultation with, and upon obtaining the approval of, a dozen or more self-interested parties. In this country, many historical elements have commingled into a general evolution which is placing a growing premium on just this kind of group approval. American business has stepped into this era without perceptible difficulty, and the ordinary successful businessman now perhaps rejoices in the protective coloration afforded him by his supersobriety, "responsibility," and annual popularity contests with the proxies. There is no intention here to apportion any blame; this is a complex development of attack and counterattack in answer to some unique stimuli within the Republic itself. And by opening up his profit records, the American businessman can easily enough prove to his own satisfaction at least that the American economy (and our "standard of living") has not suffered from the sea-change. But what he cannot prove, and what remains to be seen, is whether the New Capitalism—whatever its domestic triumphs—is a serviceable vehicle for the communication of America's pulsating energies to the political world outside.

Concretely, the "managerial-responsible" attitude has been flourishing in an epoch of such munificent domestic prosperity and social tranquillity that the "managerial-responsible" investment policy is to keep the investment here at home, where it can be safely hatched without fussing about expropriations, socializations, revolutions, and the rest of it. In short, our economic activity abroad is a minute fraction of our economic activity at home, and this means that the political tension between what is going on economically at home and what is going on economically in the rest of the world—from which we can in no wise isolate ourselves—has reached a point of such raw intensity that it must be considered a question of urgent national policy. What Lenin predicted as the March of Imperialism has turned into the March of Indifference. What has been happening we can read in this summary of Wolf and Sufrin's recent study, *Capital Formation and Foreign Investment in Underdeveloped Areas:* "On an annual basis, private investment abroad has been near the peak of the 1920's with the significant differences: 1. that post-World War II investment has been almost entirely in the form of direct investment rather than the portfolio investment which characterized the 1920's; 2. that the current rate of investment is considerably below the level of the 1920's in real terms, and represents a much smaller fraction of American national income than in the earlier period. Of the total, almost 40 per cent has been invested in Canada, 30 per cent in Latin America, 15 per cent in Western Europe and dependencies, and 15 per cent in the rest of the world. . . . The bulk of the latter is accounted for by investments of petroleum companies in the Near East. There has been little tendency for American private capital to invest in the Near East and Asia other than in 'extractive' industry, such as petroleum, for which there is a ready-existing dollar market. *There are apparently no signs of a substantial change from this pattern.*" (Italics mine.)

As we shall see below, the American investment in Africa is one of such a puny character that the authors of this study did not feel it necessary even to mention it in the above-quoted summation. And they go on to add, when stating the conclusions of the conference which gave rise to this report, that "the view was frequently expressed that private American capital would at best play only a small role, quantitatively, in meeting the capital requirements of underdeveloped countries." So reluctant, in fact, are American manager-directors to go out on the limb of investing in under-developed regions that although Congress about ten years ago appropriated some $200 millions to protect American private investors from accidents of expropriation and inconvertibility, up to 1958 the sum had not yet been completely subscribed.

On Africa the effect of all this is that so far as the American business community is concerned she simply does not exist. At the
end of 1956, the total private American investment in Black Africa
came to about $836 millions; of this $263 millions represented the
value of American oil tankers registered with Liberia; another $75
millions comprised the remainder of our investment in Liberia. And
more than half of the sum remaining, or $289 millions, was in-
vested in the Union of South Africa (and this investment in the
Union has perhaps doubled in the past three years). For purposes of
comparison, to show what we have been up to at home, in the single
year from December, 1957, to December, 1958, American personal
indebtedness *rose* by a sum of nearly $19 *billions* to a total of about
$240 *billions!*

Mr. Galbraith, Mr. Berle, and other invaluable commentators on
the economy have tried to explain why, even considering the home
scene alone, the "managerial-responsible" approach must eventually
injure the interests of the shareholders and citizens it has been so
conscientiously designed to cherish. This point of course is not
at issue here, nor is it within the competence of this author, so we
cannot argue it. But no one can forget his own hard times to the
extent of being incapable of imagining the *political* effect of all this.
How do we suppose these incredible disproportions look to the
Africans? How can the African interpret them except as signs of
a blinding selfishness on the part of blinding riches? And we cannot
afford to be blind in respect of Africa, because *there she is*—right
in the world with us—and it is impossible not to have a policy toward
her.

We have already discussed slightly Mr. David Rockefeller's African tour, during which he referred to the "problem of reassurance
and inspiring confidence" that faces underdeveloped countries who
want to get their hands on American investment money. If you want
Wall Street money you have to give Wall Street absolute security
plus higher returns than Wall Street can get from investing in California or Canada or some other orderly place, was the implication
of all his remarks. Upon hearing these consoling words Mr. Rockefeller's Belgian and South African auditors sank dejectedly back
into their soft leather chairs, permitted a self-pitying film to
glaze their eyes, and wondered whether they were sailing heaven-

ward on the isle of Laputa. But the real tragic-comic irony in the situation is that our modern Mr. Rockefeller's old-fashioned grandfather would have understood exactly what is needed in Africa, and probably would have gone right at filling it *and* getting himself a good profit. When we passed laws to curb him in the early 1900's we didn't know how much we'd need him in the 1960's. That old buccaneer was a real capitalist, an earthmover, a man who believed in producing things that change people's whole way of life, in the process freeing them of peonage and pestilence—not just coining money any old way, by, for example, stimulating the jaded appetites of overprivileged consumers for more and more useless adornments like an interior decorator. John D. Rockefeller believed in capitalism *and* in America *and* in God all at once; and therefore in an "American capitalism," a capitalism seconding and strengthening our over-all mission in history, a pioneering capitalism, a capitalism of opening doors and feeding hungers and pressing on humanity's surge to greatness and to the stars. Must we passively surrender the wonder-workings of our own Old Capitalism for the New Capitalism of Mr. David Rockefeller and his compeers, which may or may not suit America domestically but which is patently and progressively estranging us from the whole world? That is the question.

If the guts and gusto which more than palliated the severities of classic American capitalism have been overset by the Pecksniffian "managerial revolution," so also has American foreign policy of the last few years been following a false scent further and further into a blind cave.

The root of the trouble is an incorrigible Europe-centricity. When the war ended in 1945, the hard-breathing, novice masters of the world were left scowling at each other across a Europe which had always been for both of them the womb and switchboard of international affairs. Despite the "Open Door," the "Stimson Doctrine," and a half-dozen other half-hearted gestures on this order, American diplomats and politicians have always looked to Europe for the primary conditionings of our foreign policy—and have spent their lives traveling in Europe, and learning European languages. And this orientation was personally shared by Joseph

Stalin to the extent that for years, with an unbelievable want of foresight, he slighted and even injured the Chinese Communist movement which was to become such a formidable ally to his own country's power. Both America and Russia had won the war in Europe with the aid of European allies, and theoretically in their behalf; the main theater of war had been Europe; our postwar anti-Communist allies and Russia's pro-Communist allies (barring, as I say, the neglected Chinese Communists) were in Europe; even after Hitler, Europe was the richest continent next to North America; and, lastly, in pure physical terms, the problem of fixing Russia's western frontier, about which both sides enjoyed the strongest passions, was a European problem.

The consequences of these Europe-tugging influences we all know, because we have been bathed in them for the past fifteen years. The main aim of America's foreign policy—under Democrats and Republicans alike—has been to maintain the *status quo* in respect of the boundaries and alliances of Europe; and as each of these wearing years goes staggering off after the last our policy has come to focus more and more exclusively on this one subject, growing increasingly oblivious of everything else, even as a subject under hypnosis, as he grows sleepier and sleepier, focuses only on the shiny gold watch until it comes to look like the sun. All but a dribble of the Marshall money went to Europe. The key to our whole military-political system is the North Atlantic Treaty Organization, formed in 1949, with headquarters in Europe, designed to repel an invasion of Europe. When, in the spring of 1951, General Bradley criticized MacArthur's projected wrong-war-in-the-wrong-place-at-the-wrong-time, he added the qualifications, "so long as we regarded the Soviet Union as the main antagonist and Western Europe as the main prize." The implication was clear that this was just how the administration and the Joint Chiefs did so regard Western Europe, and there has certainly been no indication of a change in the ensuing nine years.

Now we have been astoundingly unaware of the shape which this institutionalized Europe-centricity, which could be illustrated with a thousand other examples, has imparted to our general policy. For example, if we always look at things the way we have been looking at them, the main antagonist must always seem to be Russia;

China, whatever she does, poses no threat to Europe, and therefore she must always be deemed only a secondary threat—and this judgment was made perfectly honest and explicit all through the Korean War and the "Great Debate" that followed it. Next, because the population of Europe is deeply committed to sophisticated prides and prejudices of its own—the legacy of a long and very superior culture—prides and prejudices of which anti-Russianism and anti-Communist Socialism are by no means unimportant ingredients, the problem of ideological persuasion became relatively insignificant once the despair left by the war had been put to rights; but of course Europe is as vulnerable as ever to *military* invasion from the east, and therefore we tend to think inevitably more about military than philosophical or moral defenses. Lastly, because the economy of West Europe is "over the hump" of the Technological Revolution, second only in health and prosperity to our own, the problem of keeping our European allies fresh and vigorous is not primarily a socioeconomic problem, but once again a *military* one.

But let me try to dramatize not only the effects of this Europe-centricity, but its dimensions as well; that is, the extent to which the special needs of the rest of the world have been passed over in our anxiety to shape our policy to the special needs of Europe. In the twelve years from 1945 to the end of 1957, the United States sent out as foreign aid of all kinds a total of $59.5 billions; of this sum $20.7 billions were allotted as military aid (the pattern is, in the early part of the period economic aid predominated over military aid, but since 1952 it has been the other way around). Of the $38.8 billions of economic aid, Western Europe received $24.9 billions, or about 64 per cent. Among the other shares, the island of Taiwan received $1.4 billions, which is about the amount represented by the *total present American investment—public and private alike—in the entire continent of Africa.* In the earlier survey of the Bolton Report it was shown that for the subtotal of $46 billions we gave away in the decade 1945–1955 Africa's share came to $71 *millions*—or about 0.15 per cent of the total—about twice the value of the shrimp that Mexico exports annually to the United States. Compare this $71 millions with the $100 millions that the new Grand Central City in New York will cost, or the $100 millions being spent on a two-mile-long atom-smasher at Stanford University. And of loans made to the world in the 1945–1955 period, totaling about $16 billions, Africa received $342 millions, or about 2.12 per cent, and of this nearly half went to the Union of South Africa and another $60 millions to the Rhodesias.

Despite the valiant, self-sacrificing efforts of Senator Fulbright and a handful of other Congressmen, no significant inroads have ever been made on the Europe-centered, military-centered assumptions and biases of American policy. Of the total of $3.3 billions allotted to foreign aid in the 1959 budget, some 2.2 billions went into either military assistance or so-called "defense supports," the bulk of it to Europe. (In fact, when the 1960 budget was passing through Congress, the Senate tacked on a stipulation that of the $1.6 billions requested for military aid $1.1 billions must be spent on North Atlantic Treaty members; this proposal was eventually dropped, but the trend of the thinking it mirrored is obvious enough.) We must also remember that on several occasions the International Bank has complained that our military-assistance programs are dislocating the economies of many of the countries which are supposed to be benefiting by them; capital that is not income-creating is always bad for the borrowers. Also, these indiscriminate funds tend in some cases to foist repressive regimes ever more harshly on the unfortunate recipients; the American taxpayer is being asked to suppress dissent, reform, and opposition in already misery-corroded lands. Lastly, although Senator Fulbright did finally manage to chouse his Development Loan Fund through the economizing wolf lairs of the spring of 1959, the present Administration has announced its distaste for the kind of program which the fund was set up to pay for—they dislike "long-term spending commitments," they explain—although everyone expert in the field is unanimous in saying that program continuity, over years and perhaps decades, is essential if we want to get any real value for this money. (The amount, too, is about a tenth of what it ought to have been.)

But even to *try* to analyze our "foreign-aid" programs as if they really signified something is totally to misunderstand the perspectives of the American Federal budget. Our total expenditures for foreign aid have been costing us roughly $3 to $6 billions per year, with a latter-day tendency toward economy, sponsored by legislators who rightly comprehend that this money is not really accomplishing anything, but miscomprehend why this should be so. During these same years our expenditures for defense, on the other hand, have been running about $40 billions a year—so that even if we were to defer to opinions like General Wedemeyer's that foreign aid is a "worldwide, indiscriminate giveaway," and cancel the whole program forthwith, the relief to the taxpayer would be practically zero. And this mind-numbing load of $40 billions a year, which we have been carrying for ten years or more and are apparently expected to carry for an indefinite number of years into the future (judging from anything to the contrary said by the leaders of either party)—an amount about five times the over-all annual budgets of the New Deal administrations which remade the countryside in so many wonderful ways—is being spent not on what the specialists agree is a really adequate program of defense (we are gravely behind, for example, in more than one area of military-technological research), but in the fabrication and strewing over the world of a military force-in-being whose size is as incredible as the treasure which buys it, and which is continually embroiled in a process of self-disembowelment and self-reconstruction as one part after another goes obsolete. In short, so mesmerized are we by the phantom of "security"—though no military program in history ever so failed to convey a sense of security—that we are trying to keep simultaneous, duplicate weapons systems of all kinds in all quarters of the world all revved up to the latest hot dope from the laboratory. Trying to spoon the Atlantic into the Pacific, in fact; but so long as we are as rich as we are and deliberately choose this method of expending more than half our Federal revenues we can to all intents and purposes keep at it forever. (At a certain sacrifice, of course, of things which perhaps it is not prudent to sacrifice. In any case, when we consider the shadow thrown by this behemothic defense expenditure, let us not even raise an eyebrow at the little annual "foreign aid" sops thrown to the "liberals"—or even, for that matter, at the total amount that Africa needs and could profitably employ from us, given the miracle that everyone changes his mind as a result of reading this book.)

Lest anybody complain that this is a wild cry from a tyro who should not presume to judge the military competence of the Ad-

ministration—and this is no captious criticism, for this author certainly puts forward no claims to an understanding of the $40 billion
defense budget, and, in fact, doubts that anyone outside two or
three Senators and perhaps a few maligned scholars cerebrating away
in their corners really does understand it—I would like to refer
everyone to the writings and speeches of General Maxwell Taylor,
who retired as Army Chief of Staff in the summer of 1959 and has
since delivered himself of numerous biting criticisms of the military
ineffectiveness of the machine he helped create with this money
which are perfectly conclusive. At least, no one has risen to rebut
him. The General's complaint is not that there are insufficient funds
spent on defense, but that what funds have been appropriated have
been improperly used by the Defense Department, who have not
been paying attention to the latest developments in military technique. And so we can go General Taylor one better, by asking
whether the value-proportion involved in spending $40 billions a
year to defend men who are not at war against $3 billion a year
to feed men who are starving to death makes any *political* sense at
all? There are few common-sense Americans who wouldn't like an
"invulnerable" (or near-invulnerable) "retaliatory force" as a platform from which to deal forth the American-Russian blackjack-
game—and this kind of force is exactly what critics like Oskar
Morgenstern and General Taylor say we have not got. *But, for the
love of God, what about the greater part of the world—which is
not playing blackjack?*

However, this essay has no more business delving into American
military policy than into the sins of the New Capitalism. Still, there
are a few reflections rising from these foregoing paragraphs which
do touch directly on the American-African relationship. I will suggest them here in the form of questions.

1. What if the post-Stalin governments of the Soviet Union have
no more intention of starting, or even risking, World War III
than we do? The kindest view that we can then take of our present
military program—a program, we must remind ourselves, whose
goal is nowhere in sight—will be that it is purchasing year-by-year
survival at the expense of mountain-ranges of obsolescent tanks,
planes, missiles, and so on; plus the time and energy which was

diverted from better things to fashion, ship, man, reship, and scrap them. (In many parts of the world anthropologists have identified a type of social custom which they have come to call the potlatch. Among the Kwakiutl Indians of British Columbia, for example, the chief of one tribe, accompanied by his entourage, will visit the chief of a neighboring tribe, bringing along with him all his most valuable pottery, bows and arrows, fishing equipment, and so forth. After the fiesta has gotten under way the first chief rises with great hauteur and destroys, one by one, all his own most valuable possessions; the idea is to shame his rival by this display of indifference to worldly things. Then, when a few months have passed, the neighboring chief pays a return visit with his own valuables and destroys them; this maintains the equilibrium. But I wonder if any scientist has run across a tribe which does not mind hosting a potlatch, while refusing to play the game itself?)

2. What if the post-Stalin governments of the Soviet Union understand that, because the United States never will attack them, they need not themselves maintain a massive force-in-being, or indeed a force even a fraction the size of ours? With the money and time they save economizing on military expenses they can then with their more limited resources still achieve decisive, superior concentrations of capital and manpower on other, preselected objectives; a space-research program, for example, or loans to underdeveloped areas. This capacity to concentrate is naturally enhanced by the authoritarian nature of this government. Meanwhile, back in America, we are spending tens of billions to stamp out this year's missiles *and* this year's Cadillac fins, *and* in rounding up and melting down last year's missiles and fins.

3. What if the center of historical disruption for the next century or so has shifted from the Soviet Union to China? Demographers predict that within 100 years half the population of the world will be Chinese. Now Russia is a "have" nation—as rich in physical properties as we ourselves, in the road of advanced and (apparently) self-generating modernization, with a bumptious and ever-growing middle class that has demonstrably exerted, and presumably will continue to exert, a conservative influence on her expansionist instincts. But China, in contrast, is a "have not" nation if there ever was one. Therefore, whatever she likes to label herself ideolog-

ically, the essential nature of the problems facing any government of China is something entirely different in kind from Russia's, a bleak fact which Khrushchev has obviously mastered for all his strident reiterations of the "solidarity of Communism." Naturally, China's responses to the fortunes of life must also be different from Russia's: for example, when the time comes—as it must come—that nearly 2 billion Chinese are inflamed by flood and famine, her government will risk next to nothing if she invites World War III by, say, an invasion of the Rice Bowl of Southeast Asia. Immunity to holocaust is not one of the realities of life in Russia at all.

4. What if what we have termed "pauperization"—after Miss Tillion—consumes the social order of the whole underdeveloped world? We have seen how this mingling of imbalances has already constituted itself into an inexorable, morbid, onmarching process in parts of Black Africa. Symptoms of it have also been noted—varying in virulence—in North Africa, non-Communist as well as Communist Asia, and most of South America. It means that the Technological Revolution is itself now combating our feeble efforts to harness it in eight-tenths of the world. And why do we not ask ourselves more frequently the question of what happens when "pauperization" has proceeded to such a degree that we can do nothing more about it, yet the paupers themselves will endure no more of it? Things came to this pass in China in the late forties. Do our experiences of this episode suggest that a similar conflagration might deprive us of the forbearance and even neutrality of more than eight-tenths of the world? Is this not a prospect we should be eager to spend $30 billions—or even $5 billions—a year to avoid?

All of these questions are not really fair questions because they are "loaded"—implying not "what if's," not ponderabilities but probabilities, so long as the one "random force" in the situation, the United States, is not exerting that force in a positive direction. A man could write a very melodramatic study on the changes which have overtaken the world—even the United States—in the past fifteen years; it is the Technological Revolution which has moved us, in a breath, from the Age of Buchenwald to the Age of the Astronauts, and soon, we may be sure, to the Age of the Astrocolonists. It is hard to believe that a never-to-be-ended one-sided "arms race," to which we Americans regularly devote 50-odd per cent of our national expenditures, has been designed with a view to coping with this Technological Revolution, which in addition to opening up glamorous superlunary doors to our bedazzled eyes is now storming into all the underdeveloped regions of earth. Has the "arms race" now not become an Article of Faith, something like Haig's conviction that bullets could never stop a well managed cavalry charge, and about equally dispensable for our health's sake?

The fact is that in the forties we did not anticipate the realities of 1960, and now that we are here we are not anticipating the realties of 1970 or 2000; and life has many humiliating surprises stored away to spring on men who are so deluded or comatose that they neglect the anticipation of reality. Another study could be conducted to determine the extent to which the ordinary American more or less unconsciously senses this failure of policy, and expresses his instinctive reaction with a bit more resentment and disgust and *malaise* than is our temperamental wont. We have elected to office the best men we know how to, and they are all "responsible," "mature," and "experienced" fellows, but they have not been able to figure out a way to put the vast strength of the Republic to better purpose, to create something more substantial and more in harmony with the aspirations of modern history than this endless march on the treadmill of producing nonconstructive arms that are out of date six months after their manufacture.

Of course, nothing is wrong structurally with the United States. The Gross National Product keeps growing; the population keeps growing; in the first months of 1959 the index of production made up its last recession losses and stood at 144 per cent of the 1947–1949 monthly average; in the previous year we added about $5 billions to our installment debt; and 150,000 new incorporated businesses entered the economy (the largest number on record). Also, the 1956 election was the largest in history. These are just figures, illustrating an undiminished economic and political virility which we are already aware of from personal observation, but when we look inside ourselves we still find that nothing fundamental is wrong—except for a lack of the wit to fashion an imperial American policy for the world that we happen to have been born into. We are still the one nation graced beyond all others in the history of the world with the blessings of Power with which to raise miseries, meannesses, cruelties, and the mutilations of disease off the backs of our brothers and to walk with them—cleaner and wiser and more open-minded —into the Golden Age of which the decade that has just closed, the 1950's, is but the first token. We all recognize only too well that the years since 1945 have been chock-full of disappointment, confusion, and discouragement to America; but a Republic is no password to an old man's way of life, and the frustrations and distractions of those fifteen years have stolen from us no really crucial gifts of strength or genius. It abides, as always it has, within the Union. "A hundred times . . . have I been disheartened by the facts I was stating," Lord Bryce wrote seventy-odd years ago about the Republic: "A hundred times has the recollection of the abounding strength and vitality of the nation chased away these tremors."

12. What Is Going to Happen in Africa?

Before we come to the end of this study, a recommended program for the American-African relationship, perhaps it may be worth while to see if the movements and dynamisms that we have already looked at conform to a predictable trend—a trend, that is, which will control events so long as grand-scale American efforts do not enter the picture.

Of course, only a very foolish prophet or one with a very exalted source of information will attempt to predict the future in any detail. In many respects history is like the sea: there are magnificent profound currents in it, which roll on immutably for millions of years and modify vast terrestrial phenomena like the Ice Ages, but man's affairs are of such a puny dimension that what really makes or breaks his commerce are usually waves which penetrate beneath the surface only a few feet. In short, the "accidents" of history—such an accident, for example, as the peculiar personality of the German Emperor William II, and the premature death of his father—often modulate the things which concern us to a greater extent than the "trends" which are the material the forecaster must work with. Therefore, the wise politician-forecaster aims at a policy that achieves a deep harmony with the "trends" which he can observe, and at the same time possesses an inherent power of accommodation to unforeseeable "accidents." And here the wise democratic politician-prophet comes to resemble the head of an established

257

royal house: the interests of Republics and Dynasties both have a continuity; it is not necessary for the men of one generation to built a seamless, changeless edifice for all time; we can depend—we must depend—on our children, our successors to our throne, to build on in their own time. It is all very different with those whom Burckhardt called the *terribles simplificateurs* of our modern day; men who emerge from the primal ooze of a society in the throes of disintegration, and in a decade or two of strutting must try to build for 1,000 years.

Several predictions of things to come in Africa are certainties. The African population's rate of increase will not only maintain its present high level (already high, we remind ourselves, for the specific conditions of life in Black Africa), but as medical modernization now begins to cut into the death rate in a big way, the over-all rate of increase will undergo a startling advance. This development can already be observed in parts of Africa such as Guinea (with a rate of increase of an annual 4.3 per cent); and in ten years or so will be observed the continent over. Second, the mechanisms which throw an increasing proportion of this population into urban concentrations will continue to flourish. And as the urban sector more and more dislocates the rural sector, we shall be able to observe in wilder and more exaggerated forms that whole schedule of symptoms associated with "urbanization" which we have discussed so many times in earlier phases of this work: the rise in the real costs of subsistence; an increasing dependence on food imports, and destruction of countryside; growing unemployment and underemployment; increasing need of a nonexistent stability in international markets and its concomitant, an increasing need of artificial subsidies and stimuli; alteration of social habits—including changing patterns of consumption and new and more exacting political aspirations.

To sum it all up, there will be more and more people in Africa growing hungrier and hungrier as they grow increasingly less satisfied with their lot. As they look around them, observing a progressively more senseless disarticulation of society, with abandoned industries and worked-out mines cheek by jowl with mud-acre patches of wind and water erosion, square mile after square mile of cardboard-and-corrugated-iron Hoovervilles, and perhaps one or two operating factories and a few branch offices of European banks, at first the desolation will strike them as hopeless, a bigger-than-mansized farrago of misfortune. But already the African has discovered that European "liberal reformers," "humanitarian philosophers," trade union organizers, and left-wing politicians view the mess as a something which must be treated, or a crime for which someone must pay.

1. One way out has been suggested by President Nasser of Egypt. His proposal: unite with President Nasser. It is always difficult to take seriously a leader whose ideas are as vacuous as President Nasser's—especially when his country is, if anything, even poorer than his ideas. For example, one cannot discern from reading his book, *The Philosophy of the Revolution,* whether in his secret soul Nasser is contemplating the Chiefship of Pan-Africa or the Khanship of Pan-Islam—or both. No doubt he has failed to make the distinction clear to us because it is of little moment to him; after all, what he is seeking is a *point d'appui*—any one will do—from which to astound the world into throwing him a few bucks. In this and many other aspects Nasser resembles our old friend Benito Mussolini. Mussolini was also unencumbered by anything like an intelligible or intelligent policy: on Monday he would speechify about Italy the Peacemaker of Europe and on Tuesday, from the same balcony, about Italy the Shatterer of False Frontiers. He poured ten times the money into his desert domains than they ever returned to him, and from a treasury so humiliatingly meager that when the time came for his staffs to disclose to the Germans vital statistics about the Italian army and resources—so that the Germans could compute an estimate of the total Axis potential—Mussolini ordered all the accounts falsified. And he had his heavy industry and his railroad stations; Nasser has the Helwan steel works, "A drain on the economic resources of Egypt, not a contribution to economic strength, since the cost of making steel in Egypt is very much greater than the cost of buying it elsewhere; it is simply a modern equivalent of the Pyramids except that maintenance expenses are higher," writes the American economist Milton Friedman. In military power, too, Nasser like Mussolini is utterly contemptible, but in peacetime the solvent power of the battlefield is only too gladly overlooked by men of good will, and no one sticks a pin in Caesar, even if he is visibly leaking sawdust.

Nasser is an African, by virtue of Egypt's location on the continent of Africa. And, as a Moslem, he is also the co-religionist of the substantial Moslem populations along the Sahara fringe in West Africa, in Ethiopia and Somalia, and even farther south. In his direct sponsorship of Moslem movements in these latter two countries—where the Emperor of Ethiopia and the present government of Somalia are carefully eying the Nasser contingents—he has shown an interest in playing this religious tune. In his domestic policy, his on-again-off-again flirtations with the Soviet Union and China, in his personal and representative delegations to the Bandung Conference of 1955, the Cairo Conference of 1958, and the two conferences held in 1958 in Accra, he has shown an interest in playing what other instruments he can reach as well.

But it is the firm opinion here that the Nasser threat has been magnified out of all reason in the United States. Whatever disturbances he can contribute to the Near East—and no one doubts his capacity to keep them in a permanent sweat—he cannot make himself a major figure in Black Africa. What are the reasons for this? In the first place, what does Nasser have to offer men like Nkrumah of Ghana and Houphouet of the Ivory Coast that they should want to hitch their wagon to an *arriviste* whose naked opportunisms are neither dignified by idealism nor veiled in seductions? What are his qualifications for organic leadership? That he has continued to operate the Suez Canal on his own terms—the sole achievement of his regime? He has miserably failed even to dent the social and economic appetities of his own people—and able, watchful Black African leaders like the aforesaid Nkrumah and Houphouet know only too well, and the knowledge is disconcerting, that *their* personal position rides on the relief of the social and economic pressure on their people. What can Nasser possibly offer any Black African? Even his luck at rallying the World of Islam has been nothing very striking. Nasser is a hot puffer in a flabby age; the creature of an environment so demoralized that even strong men do not dare to pick him up to see what manner of thing he is.

2. The stalling of "Nasserism," so far as Black Africa is concerned a red herring if there ever was one, is related to the stalling of a far more serious potentiality which, as we noted in Chapter 9,

has long excited the anxieties of the West. This is a "confederation of color," of the sort that for a time seemed to be emerging out of the Bandung Conference, where a large group of countries, almost each member of which was nonwhite and an ex-colonial victim, seemed to threaten forcing the West to its knees by the sheer weight of superior numbers. There was a great deal more talk at Bandung about "ideology" than was necessary, or profitable to the citizens of the world of color, but as it is our experience that countries in the economic circumstances of the participating states at Bandung almost invariably turn sooner or later to some form of authoritarianism—and as the overshadowing member of the conference and in the area was China—the prospect of a general "Communist confederation of color" was just strong enough so that even non-Communist members employed it to frighten the United States with. (Everyone knows that children will continue to push the button, making Jack jump out of his box, long after Jack is tattered and unsprung. So long as we Americans look upon the word "Communism" as a diabolical absolute we are going to have to listen patiently to the unbelievably tiresome litanies of exorcism prepared for us by moralizers like John Foster Dulles, and needn't expect the politicians of the underdeveloped world to spare us either. They like to see us jump up and say the same things over and over and over.)

The reason why a Confederation of Color has not materialized, and is never likely to materialize—unless the social disintegration of the pauperized world goes very far, and in a particular direction—is extremely interesting, and full of suggestive clues for a proper American policy toward these regions. It is that underdeveloped countries—despite their superficial community of interests—are in reality competitors for the one commodity they require more urgently than any other: Capital. For example, the principal obstacle to a policy of simply dumping American rice in the ports of India, and letting her famished people come and get it (this, after all, would be a cheaper program than the present one of warehousing-till-rot), is that the other governments of Southeast Asia, for whom sales of rice to India are one of the largest sources of revenue, violently protest. Basic conflicts like these show up very clearly in the United Nations, and often most surprisingly—between the states of Islam, for instance. The "have-not" nations cannot act in unison in any really important economic matter. Portuguese African coffee is competing with Brazilian coffee; Ghanaian cocoa with Ivory Coast cocoa; Gambian peanuts with Senegalese peanuts, and so on. These are competitions for markets, but how much more intense will the competition be for development capital, of which for all practical purposes the only source is the United States of America—with fringe contributions to be made by Western Europe, Canada, and the Soviet Union?

What this intractable capital competition, which tames even the most compelling of normal emotional reactions, reflects is a world-wide shortage of capital. Indeed, there has always been a shortage of capital since the barter system went out of general use; it is only in the last 150 years, in a few favored spots, by means of processes of "accumulation" which are still the objects of controversy among economists, that "capital shortage," in its widest aspect, was not the main limiting factor on the economic growth of a society. And this general shortage—plus the fact that most things of transcendent political and social importance can be done only with capital—imposes an obligation on the holders of capital to ascertain that their property is being used in the wisest of possible ways—that is, the way that will bear the maximum economic and *sociopolitical* return. (In the next chapter we shall tackle some of these points more extensively, but I want to say here that I hope I have nowhere in this essay given the impression of advocating dams, universities, farm-research stations—and all the rest of the "Point Four" instrumentalities—laid down like a barrage with an eye only to impressing the local populace. America's great reservoirs of capital are trusts—and must be carefully shepherded. But, the point is, we may have to liberalize our notions of shepherdship. For example, if our capitalists accustomed themselves to smaller returns in certain kinds of investment—if they become content to be paid off in thirty years, say, instead of ten, in African investments—perhaps twice as much or more of private American investment capital would find its way to that continent. But this will happen only when capitalists realize that they may on this system get a *political* return—in the form of the blood of their children, perhaps—that compensates them for the temporary sacrifice of 10 per cent annual money yields.)

In any case, countries like Ghana and Guinea can amicably enter into a political merger, deriving whatever comforts they can from it, so long as no field of competition exists; that is, so long as there is virtually no capital in Africa to squabble over. But if an American agency appeared on the scene with precisely $800 millions, empowered by Congress to subsidize the construction of one major hydroelectric scheme in West Africa, then the interests of Nkrumah and Touré would instantaneously collide. It would then be necessary for the money to be turned down; for the African governments to tack on so many conditions of acceptance that the American Congress would withdraw it; or for one of the African leaders to suppress the other one.

The competition for capital explains the sluggishness of what would seem on the surface to be the extremely alluring blackmail promise of a Confederation of Color—and the at first sight odd determination of former colonial areas to remain within the orbits of their oppressors. But as we have said so many times before, we cannot hope for everything from these unnatural affiliations. They can survive only so long as Africa is pinned together by a little reasonable orderliness; an environment in which men like Nkrumah can still find a modicum of hope for the orderly, statesmanlike modernization of their countries. But if the pump from Europe and North America has an insufficiently generous bore to keep the continent from drying up into pauperdom, then the superidentifications—Black Skin, and perhaps even just Colored Skin—will revive again. Indeed, these superidentifications are even now kept fresh by the two most colorful political personalities in Black Africa, Nkrumah and Mboya, at their conferences; as a last resort they are ready to play for Black Federations, with frontiers which do not need to be defined until the last moment, and—at the end of the road—a United States of Black Africa.

3. When and if the Black Federations come into existence—striding over the corpses of the superannuated Community and Commonwealth—we shall see the politics of Africa entering a lethal, foredoomed, terminal phase. Competing for scraps of chaos is not going to bring out the acumen and responsibility of Black African leaders. The whole premise of these governments—whatever their theory—must be something altogether different from the premise

of every present-day African government, free or servile. For the mandate of the rulers of the Federations will be entirely a mandate of driven emotions, reinforced whenever necessary by a ruthless police and army. Dealing in a rational manner with social and economic problems will not be thought of, and if it were it would have to be instantly dismissed as an impracticable notion. The West —private and public sectors alike—will recoil from these Black Federations, and the means by which they inherited and maintain themselves in power. It will not be in the interest of Russia or China to lend them more than a token hand; and so the Federations will be left to boil and bubble as best they can, amid unimaginable horrors.

Already, with the half-abandoned schemes of land reform in the old French Equatorial Africa, where the new African governments possess neither the force to extort the peasants' compliance to far-reaching rehabilitations, nor the funds to purchase it, we have seen the beginnings of the dangerously unstabilizing emotional biases which always creep into the deeds of governments of hungry people —deeds which, like the work of a Filipino mother, who polishes her rice all the more desperately the ricketier her son grows, make everything worse. But there is no time, no margin, for an African government to stop, to reconsider, to plan; acquiescence in superstition and peasant obstinacy is the only prophylaxis for panic and revolt. The African leader is in no position to be a statesman, but only a *caudillo*, a man whose care for the objective conditions of his country rides far in the wake of his personal careerism. In carving out his position, in the maneuvering period which will precede each of these Black Federations, our man shall already have forfeited the sympathy of the power interests of the West. Therefore, no act of violence or arbitrariness can lose him what is already lost. His demands for the enthusiasm and loyalty of his countrymen will grow in stridency as his measures for resisting the "pauperization" process grow feebler and feebler, and as his neighbor *caudillos*, deep in their own troubles, grow more hostile and menacing. Somewhere in the confusion—here and there throughout Africa—will be achieved that most dangerous of all political compounds, the amalgamation of Tribe and Party—which must at once light the fuse to wars of extermination, either the Tribe-Party aiming to extinguish the opposing minorities of the country or the government aiming to extinguish this new sinister rival. The trade unions, such a promising evolution for Black Africa, will be of course the first organizations subordinated to the government; and the fact that the Man of Destiny in many African countries is also the leader of the big trade union will facilitate the take-over. But none of these horrifying temblors—as one by one the pillars of colonial and industrialized Africa crack, leaving exposed to the elements a population far too large to live on the old nomad-subsistence system—will frighten off the "pauperization" process. One Federation will be driven into war with another—or perhaps, if a Black Napoleon emerges, into a racial war against the Union of South Africa. And, clear of the carnage, we Americans will stand by with pursed lips: "Those Africans are running amuck again! What is the matter with people in the world who can't settle down with their houses, cars, laundromats, picnics, travels, colleges, books? . . ."

4. Shifting our sights for a moment from Black Africa, what is likely to happen in the Union itself?

It is impossible to guess—or at least I find it so—whether the Union's Africans will organize themselves to the point of exploding against their masters before, or after, the liquefaction-federation-chaos process described in the preceding paragraph reaches their frontiers. I wonder if it matters very much. We have mentioned something of the handicaps of organizing the revolution of a serf class which outnumbers the masters by only four to one, and which into the bargain can lay its hand on no modern means of warfare. We have seen how the revolutionary leadership in South Africa has not up to now been able to overcome the divisions and inexperience of the Africans, or the vigilance of the Afrikaners. Some of their deficiencies of technique are, of course, being rectified by imported professional revolutionaries now hard on the job. And in the same thought we must remember that the Africans even now can any time destroy South Africa's existence as an industrial society—thus splitting the white population, and somewhat hampering the Afrikaner's ability to cut down the political revolt.

The unpredictable, yet decisive, factor in all this is the emotional physiology of 7 or 8 millions of Africans. All the viruses and

justifications for reckless revolutionary rage are already in their
bloodstreams; there is also the coagulant of a desperate despair,
a systematic and almost inhuman self-denial of hope on the part
of every African in the Union whom I met. The slightest success
anywhere against the Afrikaner police and army—and this success
must come one day—will transform these elements into mass blood-
lust, and three out of four Africans will literally fling themselves
at the throats of the white men who happen to be standing closest
to them. An outburst of this kind might or might not be coordinated
by a central headquarters with the campaign of industrial sabotage
which the more or less underground leadership of the African National Congress now is docketing. One cannot provide a timetable
for a catastrophe composed of so many variables; perhaps fifteen
years is a good guess at the time left to the Afrikaners; certainly
the labor to bring them down is already in progress.

But even if African apathy, and Afrikaner virility, hold off the
Day of Blood in South Africa indefinitely, there is no hope on earth
for the regime. Even if we console ourselves with forecasting events
against the longest possible time scale, and look off down into the
centuries, there is no possible way to stop the racial pincers that
are creeping down from northern Africa to engulf the Portuguese
colonies, the Rhodesias, and the Union. Perhaps the Afrikaners can
defend themselves effectively against the 10 million Africans of their
own country, but what chance have they against the hundreds of
millions who compose the arms of this pincers, and whose hate will
be riled and spiced by their failure to settle their own problems?

5. Revolution, genocide, and destruction come to South Africa and
the Rhodesias. The Commonwealth and Community collapse, giving way to shapeless federations dominated by self-appointed generals and corrupt demagogues. Trade unions, tribes, secret societies,
and everything else that might challenge the absolutism of the
Federal governments are swept away or enslaved. Fearful, raving
bureaucrats do what they can to infuriate the people. Warlords and
military gangs dragonnade the land unhindered. The government's
writ runs only so far as its regimental pickets; and beyond these
camp sites, a supine prey for all, lies the fatally wounded, eviscerated

countryside. *It is Chaos.* And when Chaos comes to the modern world, Chinification cannot be far behind.

Chinification is the political anti-Christ of our day—and not only in Africa—for it offers to the legions of the lost of the pauperized world their one last chance at twenty or thirty precious years of personal life—with the purposes and aspirations of life—rather than the lassitudes of living death. And we must be clear that we do not mean by Chinification the standard brand "Communism" of conspiratorial coteries which we American have so unnecessarily—or so at least is my opinion—rushed hysterically around about for so many years. It goes without saying that agents of the Chinese and Russian governments are already working long hours inside Africa—infiltrating unions, teacher groups, political societies, and the like; recently Mr. Victor Riesel, in his trip through Africa, chronicled some of these activities. (Presumably, also, we have our agents in Africa, and in China as well.) Doubtless these "Communist" agents will welcome whatever opportunities come their way; but the point that needs emphasis is that what is coming their way, and *our* way, is not simply opportunity, cracks in the veneer into which scheming termites may bore an entry, but a Storm of Rage far huger in kind than anything mere spies and *agents provocateurs* can be held responsible for. This is a tiger that is coming to Africa, and one which cannot be mollified by an invitation to tea at the White House.

Chinification is the last thrust of a society (through a hard-bitten, self-judging, fanatical clique of priest-politicians) to avoid the ultimate tumbling over into the pit of total social disintegration. It is therefore a completely different species of policy from anything which will ever come to Russia, an ancient state of vast resources, temperate climate, and relatively unshaken—even by the Revolution—historical, language, and religious customs. Chinification is not "Communization," and need never profess or adhere to any dogma. The key to Chinification is the iron-handed capture of the Technological Revolution for the purposes of civic order; in a word, a turning of the disintegrative forces of the Technological Revolution against itself. That is, the Technological Revolution puts into the hands of a country's leaders powers and weapons (and concepts) which have no parallel in history, powers of a magnitude no autocracy of the past, however absolute, ever came near possessing. Therefore, the logic of the thing asks, why not turn these unprecedented powers against the unprecedented disruptiveness of the Technological Revolution? Perhaps the very violence, novelty, and amorality of the Technological Revolution are the correct substitute for the familiar social ideas and structures that it has shattered. If a man is starving to death because of the erosion and flooding of his land, then force him at gun's point to build dikes and strew fertilizers, even if he still starves to death. At least, he shall have added reclaiming labor to his country's total reserves as well the minerals in his cadaver. Perhaps nothing has ever been seen in the world before just like these hundreds of millions of Chinese who are forced to work for nothing which they will ever see—it bears a resemblance to some of the phenomena of the insect world—but at least it is better than Chaos.

Judging from what we hear of them through the unsatisfactory filters of an information system long crippled by absurd ostrich policies of the American State Department, the leaders of modern-day China fully understand the purity of logic which is required of them, according to the lights of this construct of theirs. Only a homogeneous, all-embracing iconoclasm can free them for this try to catch up with the Technological Revolution and to subdue it. Only when the human substrate of China observes around itself a totally leveled cultural substrate will it accept the cost of the new principles of organization. Everything must go. And there must be no such thing as cost; nothing must count but the year-by-year accumulation of heavy industry, and a few indispensable effluents in the form of secondary manufacturing. To fulfill the capital formation and other requirements of the government's plan, flesh and blood must be forced past the limits of endurance; and when one group which has been so forced sinks into the ground the logic of Chinification tells us that it will be just so much easier to coerce the next. The hideous mass executions, the fantastic paramilitary agricultural communes being settled throughout Central China, involving hundreds of millions of peasants; the tens of thousands of unarmed infantrymen—or armed only with bugles—who were sent up against our machine-gun posts in Korea: these are examples of the "happy sacrifices" of a regime which needs the ultimate in breakdown in order to achieve the ultimate in responsiveness.

Former governments of China were always short of capital. They could never persuade first the mandarins, then the warlords, the hongs, the extraterritorial interests, the Soong family, *et al.*, to disgorge themselves even of their legal tax assessments, let alone taxes which would strike any American or Englishman as reasonable and fair. Without a backward glance the new government has overleaped this millennial obstacle. The wealthy, exempted classes of the old China have either been gathered to Buddha's bosom or chased across the China Sea to Formosa or America. When the Peking government needs $100 millions, it can obtain the sum simply by knocking that much gold out of 400,000 jaws, or rendering the gold leaf on 10,000 pagoda spires. And when it comes to spending this $100 millions the Chinese government can cherish its reserves by paying out no more, and no less, than it chooses in the form of wages; not only in the project immediately at hand, but in the production of all the components of any project, it possesses an enormous labor force which perhaps need be paid nothing at all. Therefore, while in the midst of recovering from one of the worst famines in her history, the Chinese government can—and soon will—construct nuclear fission reactors and intercontinental missiles (artifacts which would have been beyond the resources of the old Chinese governments for centuries to come), and construct these artifacts at a fraction of the cost we pay for them. Given casual technical aid from Russia—which will perhaps be superfluous after a few years—the Chinese can fabricate and man weapons systems every bit as potent as our own (or near enough to make the difference a matter of indifference), while at the same time not a single man connected with the development owns a pair of shoes.

And what will she do with these weapons systems when she has them? How this question appals us. To begin with, she is in the perfect bluffer's seat. We want to fight a war with no interruption of the movement of turkeys to the front lines twice a year, at Thanksgiving and Christmas. But it hardly matters to the Chinese whether they win or lose a war—what material damage could any bad risk inflict on the Chinese that would not be also inflicted by not running the risk? What do China's hundreds of millions have

to lose? When the day comes that China achieves an equality of
armament with us—and I take it that this equality will mean that
she possesses fifty, say, continent-busting multimegaton thermonuclear bombs, and appropriate up-to-date delivery systems—and
if on the same day that she achieves this equality she sends her army
into the Rice Bowl of Southeast Asia, does anyone seriously believe
that a President and Congress of the United States will declare
war on her?

But to frighten my readers about the outlook of the New China—
of which they are probably frightened enough already, or ought to
be—is not my chief business. For illimitably minatory as the Chinese
state will be for the rest of our lives—and as far ahead in the future
as anyone can see—"Chinification" is even more important and
dangerous, because it is a process which is rearing up all over the
world, Africa included. It is not a question of foreigners' perversity
or laziness. People do not *want* to be Chinified. No one *wants* to live
in the style of the modern Chinese—his life hardly even a statistic,
dehumanized, de-familyized, depersonalized. A regime like the Peking
regime can take over only when total despair has eaten away the
normal, healthy, psychological and cultural ego-resistances to mono-
tone and despotism; when despair has so far enfeebled the forces
of intellect and personality that the very bestiality of the regime is
accepted—even eagerly welcomed—as a talisman, a token of the
regime's faith and capability. Consider China herself. Americans who
in many cases have lived most of their lives in China report in tones
of amazement that the wonderful people they knew there—the
small-town shopkeeper, the cynical, gentle rice farmer, the exquisitely courteous scholar and physician, the family philosopher,
the progress-minded young clerk—that all these types and individuals,
so subtly intertwined with the legacies of a vast and ancient civilization, of empires and the devouring of empires, of peerless literary
and plastic arts, of intricate metaphysics, of the disciplines of the
Confucian family and clan—should have embraced the red-hot
manacles of a cult of "Marxists" (how absurdly unmeaning this word
is, and "Communism" too, when applied to China) who sear and
squander their lives and everything the society has prized for thousands of years as if they were no more than the droppings of so
many sea gulls. Why is this so hard to understand?

Why do we permit our imaginations to grow so sluggish that we do not see that nothing but "nothing-but" could drive a people into this course? What alternative to relaxing into the tortures of the New China had the majority of Chinese faced with the circumstances of the 1940's—especially the 300-odd million Chinese under twenty years of age: the criminal and bungling family cabal which controlled the Kuomintang, the desolation left by the Japanese, the population explosion, the inevitable misadventures of flood and famine? The Chinese are far from a stupid or insensitive or unaspiring people. They want hope; they want to be modern; they want missiles and bombs; they want colonies on the moon. (On this latter point I must break in to notice that one of the really disastrous miscalculations of our "propaganda" has been the emotional downgrading of the Age of Space. We proceed on the assumption that the world's people—50 per cent of whom are not beyond adolescence—view space travel with the outlook of the president of a real estate firm, as a sort of highbrow academic fad that has nothing whatever to do with the "good life" that "practical people" want, clinking a glass with a locker-room crony at the club or that shiny new station wagon. We used to hear all these admonitions about "realism" and "gradualism" from the pulpits of somnolent suburban churches; now we get them from every side. But we could not be wronger. I will never forget the evening I spent in a Hong Kong restaurant, surrounded by a dozen or more young waiters who were foregoing their own meals to listen to what paltry information I could give them about our progress toward the Conquest of Space.) The Chinese want the Age of Space—and all the rest of the principalities and powers which compensate modern man for his modern troubles. And if they can get them only by signing up with the Devil, then the Devil it is. And when and if they are reduced to the same monstrous choice, the Africans will do the same.

6. So far as Africa is concerned, is there no chance at all that "things will work themselves out" without this mysterious "pauperization," military dictatorships, bloodbaths, Chinification, and without we Americans having to stir ourselves up to drastic derrings-do?

There is no such chance. This we must understand if we are not to destroy our children's chances by default. We must recapitulate all the arguments first presented in Chapter 1. Jobs are not being provided fast enough; industry-making primary installations are not being constructed fast enough; health and agriculture are not being attended to; the growth of an educated, self-buffering middle class is not being attended to; none of these things is happening fast enough, or even nearly fast enough, to stem the submerging tide of population growth, the psychological and social dislocations and eccentricities of "urbanization," rural decay, and sociopolitical destabilization.

It is not even a matter of Something-Being-Better-Than-Nothing. In the case of Africa Less-Than-Enough will end up in the same place as Nothing-At-All. Whether we do anything to stop the Death of Africa is a collective test of our seriousness and determination as a historical people, but for the sake of our private souls we cannot afford to fool ourselves about it. Things are not going to work themselves out for the best in Africa—*unless we make them.*

7. Is there any real hope at all of checking these hostile polarizations, which seem to have sprung from the gloomy brain of a nineteenth-century dialectician—to register a Great Achievement in rehabilitation similar to those we have been registering in science and engineering, or is the real Africa a sort of Joseph Conrad-Evelyn Waugh bug-world, overheated, corrupt, red-eyed, ridden with stinks, souls enchained by wildness and jeopardy and darkness and lust?

Who knows, but why not hope? Africa is not Pandemonium; the individual African is an antientropic entity as much as an American, an organizing and metabolizing creature battling the frigidities of space. Why not build on his anomaly, as we do on our own? And the African has been to a hard school—no less than organizing and metabolizing in Africa. The Africans know that no wand can be waved over them; that they will not one day awake to find a doctor and a generating plant and a high school in every town; birth and death rates similar to ours; factories, highways, hospitals, farms, laboratories all equivalent to ours. They know what is possible in Africa, and what is not possible, better than we do. They ask only for someone to hold out a hand for a while, to arrest their progress down the dreadful slide they find themselves upon, so that they can catch their breath and start climbing up on their own, perhaps even improving on what we have taught them. If the Africans can hope, why can't we? If we are not prepared to hope then perhaps we all ought to follow the advice of a renowned investment counselor at the time of the Berlin Blockade crisis; he told the "holders of capital" who subscribed to his monthly newsletter that they should convert their funds into diamonds and bury them in concrete vaults in Kansas—in this way avoiding the fiscal and physical perils of the war that seemed to be brewing. Perhaps this advice made sense to somebody, using some extrasocial set of values, but it wouldn't have made sense to Jefferson or Lincoln or Franklin Roosevelt.

In the summer of 1843 Florence Nightingale wrote a letter to a friend that included this rare burst of agony: "When one thinks there are hundreds and thousands of people suffering . . . when one sees in every cottage some trouble which defies sympathy—and there is all the world putting on its shoes and stockings every morning all the same—and the wandering earth going its inexorable treadmill through those cold-hearted stars, in the eternal silence, as if nothing were the matter; death seems less dreary than life at that rate."

After revolving these sad thoughts in her head for a period, Miss Nightingale pulled herself together, came forth to save the lives of thousands of her countrymen and to reform the British Army, and to gain the love and respect of the whole world. An object lesson to us all.

13. Conclusions in Search of a Program

In a world that requires as much alternative warming and cooling as this one, and the constant availability of energy, the proper policy for the United States should be modeled on a key feature of mammalian physiology—the circulation of the blood.

Everyone knows that the heart pumps the blood, laden with oxygen and nutriments, through a system of ever-narrowing arteries and arterioles until at last it reaches the miscoscopic capillaries. Here, briefly, the fluid is liberated from the vessels and oozes out to bathe the tissues—it is in this phase that they respire and metabolize. Then the blood regathers itself into the tiny venous capillaries and returns in the larger veins for recharge by the lungs and the other organs, and to be recirculated by the heart.

But putting aside the contributions that are poured in from the organs and glands the circulatory system itself is far from being a mere mechanical loop with a life-giving discontinuity at the extremities. It is itself an extremely complex organ of adaptation. For example, the total volume of the arterial network far exceeds the volume of the blood in the body at any one time. This means that at all times large branches of the system may be nearly shut down while other branches are active; and by means of an intricate endocrine-neural instrumentation the mass of the blood can be shunted from one function to another—from the muscles to the

274

viscera, say, or vice versa—depending on the local, immediate needs of the body. Also, if a peripheral loop has been interrupted—severed in an accident, we can suppose—unless the affected element is a major artery the limbs beyond it are vascularized by standby vessels which now dilate—the "collateral circulation"—to take care of the emergency.

Here is a beautiful, sensitive, self-equilibrating apparatus within our own bodies—full of the "feedbacks" so dear to modern designers—with which Nature defends us from a thousand daily crises of which we are not even aware. Now let us consider the case of Africa, and her relations with the West. Of course, the heart of the West is the United States, the most powerful nation in the world and the only nation in the world with the power to plug the social and economic disintegration flood which is engulfing three-quarters of the world. (But the blood that we pump is not merely money. The reason it seems so is that it is so hard to get money, and the American people and their Congressmen are so fatigued with voting money, that even the most farsighted and philosophical "liberal," in his exhaustion, tends to leave the impression that it is only a billion or two more that he is coaxing for. Perhaps money is the matrix of this political "blood"; but money without intelligence, passion, and directed policy nourishes nothing.)

Now we have seen that this power—in the form of this composite capital-blood—is not getting through to Africa, although a great deal of it is going round and round inside the United States, without accomplishing anything in particular. But what is the actual system in Africa, the arterial reticulation, into which American energy might move? To begin with, there are the two great ancillary subdivisions of the Commonwealth and the French Community, both of which are capable of shouldering and properly distributing much more of the load than they are at present. Within these systems we find smaller, direct, bilateral, American-African connections: with Ghana, for example. We ought not look upon this second line of communication as a duplication or a conflict; it is supplemental to the main system—part of the "collateral circulation," which gives us another dimension of flexibility in which to get the job done. Into other parts of Africa the life-giving vitality has almost no entry at all: the Congo, for instance, but here we as the heart have another means of access, back along the main artery, in our NATO colleagueship with Belgium. So long as it is at all possible, surely it will be most effective for us to vascularize Belgium-Belgian Congo as a unit—trying hard to inspire there the same kind of tentative kinship that we hope to succour in the Community and the Commonwealth.

In the Rhodesias we run into the first signs of a pathological condition—to exploit this metaphor, perhaps, for more than it's worth. Here the small strength which is delivered from the heart—represented by the investments of American companies in the Federation —are not only not nourishing the society, but unwittingly are contributing to the society's inability to restore itself to health. And we find that the Commonwealth loop here is equally unproductive, as the Southern Rhodesians have refused the advice from London that would make this connection valuable. And farther south yet, of course, we encounter a firmly fixed embolus. Insofar as American private investments, purchases, and public support is assisting the present Afrikaner regime we are simply engorging a gangrene—and making all the more disagreeable the inevitable surgery.

And although we will return to Africa in a moment, let us not forget that the whole great African artery, with its dozen or so affluents, each with its special functions and problems, is only one sector—and not the major sector at that—of the over-all circulation for which the United States has made herself responsible. Our ally the Commonwealth, for example, sends out a tremendous shoot to India; we have already referred to the declining dietary of India, which must sooner or later undermine everything that is good there, when the present generation of unappreciated moderate leaders has passed on, or even earlier, in case of a massive failure of one or both of the annual monsoons. There are also our military alliances with forty-odd sovereign countries; there is NATO (certainly not unimportant merely because it is not all-important); the Organization of American States, SEATO, the United Nations, and so on. There are intangible, vertical circulations into the sphere of ideas: the "closed political system" of the Edwardian geopolitician, the "world economic solidarity" of economists like Frankel; the obligation owed to our posterity which we pay by pushing on with the Conquest of Space. There is the circulation by which the heart re-creates itself—the coronary system—the schools, music, literature, prosperity, and "social investment" that we need here at home for the fruition of America.

A formidable vision of a pumping, pumping never to be remitted, a labor of Sisyphus—and on top of the pumping an unceasing cudgeling of the brain as to where to pump, and what, a reckoning and rereckoning, regulating and regurgitating, revising and re-revising! A vision that strikes melancholy into the hearts of so many Americans, for at this rate Life looks like Work. So it is, of course, for the heart never stops until Life does. And, put this way, we perhaps are all still Puritan enough to pay lip service, anyway, to the notion that the Best Thing in Life Is Work. I remember the story of Senator George Norris bursting into tears at the ceremonial climax of the inauguration of the Tennessee Valley Authority, to which he had been invited by President Roosevelt. It was the culmination and the triumph of twenty-five years' ceaseless work and prayer, on behalf of a state and people not his own. Any engineer can tell you that building a dam is the glory of life; a painter, the same thing about a finished portrait; a pianist, the same thing about his finger exercises. All right, some of my readers say, Work is part of the human condition, and there is no need to belabor that point with *us*. But where in heaven's name is it all going? Is it necessary to rave about pumping as well as to feel obliged to do it?

I do not know where it is going. No one does. But I do draw attention to the omnipresent reality of the Force to which our Work pays tribute—the Force which is manifestly hauling our race out of the primeval slime toward greater and greater controls of the elements of existence and who knows what greater glories of comprehension. The young English astrophysicist, Mr. Fred Hoyle, calls this Force "The Thing"; we know not whence it came, or whither it conveys us, but its power—expressing itself in newer understandings of the microcosmos and macrocosmos, and philosophical formulations of wonderful usefulness and subtlety—is the climate and the color of our day as it was of no other age. "The Thing" is the central datum of all our lives whether we care to recognize it or not; it is changing us before our own eyes into masters of energies before which only yesterday we groveled as slaves.

It only remains to be said here that "The Thing," so far as we can yet determine from the evidence, is concerned only with material and intellectual *control;* so far as we can see, it has left us as free as ever we were in the spheres of ethical and political choice; "The Thing" is neither Communist nor anti-Communist. Therefore, *our* motive—that is, the motive of the United States—for this pumping of our health and strength through the world is not primarily to serve "The Thing"—which is amoral, or whose morality is transcendental—but to keep faith with the choices which we have been permitted to make, the intimate and beloved principles of our nationhood.

Let us briefly review the main failures of our present policy.

1. We have done virtually nothing to grasp or to halt the "pauperization" process, and therefore we are not prepared for the future political actions of the "underdeveloped" world.

2. We have failed to buy "security" with the arms race. We are not more secure in 1960 than we were in 1945; indeed, considering the dynamism implicit in Point 1, which has had this wasted interval to develop in, we are very much less secure than we were fifteen years ago.

3. We are unprepared for the inevitable half-maddened eruptions of China (though I do not want to leave the impression of underestimating the Cold War contribution of the "Thunder Tigers," a team of aeronautical acrobats which we donated to the Government of Formosa).

4. The American creative genius has not been able to find itself in this Era of Standpattism. Therefore, we are not leading the world in those endeavors in which we always have led the world in the past, like the Conquest of Space.

Now let us come down to Africa specifically. At the outset of the discussion let us discard the phrase "foreign aid" for keeps. We are not proposing in this essay just a highly magnified "foreign aid" program—a Point Four "with real teeth in it." Up to the present, except for what was done in Europe in the immediate postwar period, "foreign aid" has been a farce. It has nowhere accomplished the socioeconomic reformations which it must be our main interest to accomplish in undertaking this kind of an overseas program in the first place. And to the extent that "foreign aid" has failed in this, the titanic labors of a parcel of "liberal" statesmen have been tragically wasted; indeed, because these truncated appropriations sometimes give the American people the impression that something has been gained which has not been gained, that we are protected against a certain eventuality which we are not protected against, these labors can be said to have been perverted.

We must begin not with dollars, but with the acknowledgment that history has taken our hand and placed it in that of the African. Therefore, it is discreet of us to cultivate a profound affection for each other, an affection solid enough to withstand the pulls and stresses of countless irritants in the future. Perhaps we can evolve our new feeling for the minorities in our country into an encompassing, practical compassion for the underdog everywhere. In any case, the hoary old clichés—which are equally stale and unprofitable when mouthed by a fifty-years' resident of Africa or a brassy American novelist back from a six weeks' safari in Kenya—must go out the window.

Politically, one need look no further than Ghana to find a government which—despite a host of blemishes—is handling her unbelievably refractory problems a good deal more competently than, let us say, the government of Louisiana is handling its comparatively negligible problems. (And one need look no further than Germany to find a white, European, "Christian" people who did not handle their problems at all, but simply went berserk.) On the personal level, no openminded person can travel in Africa without being struck over and over again by the sweetness and outgoingness which flourish in the breasts of some of the most shockingly handicapped human beings on earth. One finds, also, a circumstance which I suppose was also characteristic of medieval Europe—illustrated, for example, in *Canterbury Tales*—of the intense pleasure that farmer-peasants who are rooted in their plots and villages their whole lives take in talking with and inquiring about strangers from the outside world who chance to cross their path, and the curiosity and sympathy with which these Africans will discuss your life and problems (no problems at all compared to theirs), and the hospitality they are overeager to press upon you. I will always remember a dinner (of horrible beans mixed with slimy lettuce) I was given at a young African artist's shanty-house in one of the "townships" outside Leopoldville, where he lived with his parents, a young wife, and his two children, all in one room. I brought the wine, and was almost turned away from the door. Then, having mislaid my manners for a moment, I said that I insisted on buying some ground beef for the babies when I returned to town; this so hurt the feelings of my friend's mother that she turned her back on me and never spoke to me again. Later my friend, the young artist, told me that it would be all right to buy canned meat; this he would bury in the back yard and in a few months his mother would dig it up and serve it. (Whether this camouflage was really to deceive her, or only to give her an easy out, I never discerned; anyway, this was the way we worked it.)

As I say, one finds these virtues—must we call them "primitive virtues"?—in many areas and places around the world, but the life-situation of the ordinary African is so debilitating, so dehumanizing (or, rather, we should have expected it to be dehumanizing) that one is prepared to find that good humor, friendliness, forgivingness, interest, and sympathy with casual tourists who can do nothing and will not even ever be seen again shall have totally evaporated. When a family must sit by and observe two of its four offspring die in childhood, when every member of the family suffers from worms, ulcerated legs, nutritional deficiencies, and so on (and when they look at you and perceive that you are not suffering from these things; that you have learned somewhere how to protect yourself against them, but have for some reason not communicated this knowledge to them); when this family is crammed into indescribably filthy slums, all the handier for the police (but again they perceive that you do not live this way, yet evidently can do nothing to help them)—given all this wretchedness and the blazing contrast between this wretchedness and your comforts one might prognosticate nothing but sights of red-eyed hatred and sounds of *pangas* being sharpened in the back yard on an African trip. Yet such is not the case. The African has been in many ways less damaged by what has been happening to him that we have been in complying with it.

What we must do is to step into Africa and break, by main force, the mighty vicious circle of "pauperization" and social disintegration, by planting in Africa—as surgeons plant tiny seeds of skin all over a badly burned chest—the mechanisms and installations that can then begin to run by themselves and weave into a sound social fabric. This is the "social mutation" which Miss Tillion refers to as the only hope of saving the underdeveloped regions of the world from chaos, and it is up to us to engineer this mutation.

Africa is a complex continent, and therefore we require for this task the services of something more like a college than a government agency—something that we perhaps can call the United States Institute of African Affairs, placed administratively under the Secretary of State, which will combine—and naturally vastly extend—the functions now distributed around the present Bureau for African Affairs, the Office of Dependent Area Affairs, and other liaison offices situated in the Departments of Commerce, Defense, Agriculture, and elsewhere. This African Institute should be built in Washington or New York; should be able to depend upon a regular appropriation of $6 to $8 billions a year (we shall discuss this figure in a moment); and over the years should build itself up to become the virtual world center of all things African.

What precisely must this Institute do? In the first place, its staff must recognize the prior claims of the agricultural sector in Africa over everything else: 80 per cent or more of Africans still live at least partially on food they grow themselves. Therefore, research must be subsidized wherever it can be carried on into all things concerned with reclaiming soils, stimulating the growth of protein-forming microorganisms, improving the nutritional content of food crops and forage crops, and so forth. A compensation agency must be established somewhere within the Institute, with ample funds to tide over large groups of peasants when they must be moved out in pursuance of indispensable reforestation or watershed repair programs. In parts of Africa these monies can be handled through existing agencies of the Commonwealth and the Community; in other parts the Institute will perhaps prefer to deliver them directly to the African governments concerned. (But in every possible case we should attempt to use the experience of and share the responsibility with the Eurafrican connections.) The Institute will actually have to construct at least several agricultural research foundations in Africa, as well as support those that are already on the field, such as the works going forward under the Commission for Tech-

nical Cooperation in Africa South of the Sahara, an organization
with limited funds operated by six of the white governments who
are interested in Africa. And the Institute must serve as the message
center for communications between these new stations in Africa
and all the other agricultural researchers in the world—particularly,
of course, those who specialize in the soil and crop problems of
tropical areas. Stock breeding experiments must be undertaken,
some in Africa and some elsewhere, and when a promising strain
has been developed a number of studs must be flown out to Africa
and their services donated to the Africans in the vicinity (something
along the lines of what Winthrop Rockefeller is doing in Arkansas).
All of these interconnected institutes, with their intercommunications
and interchanging staffs, will require the African Institute to maintain a huge fellowship program: with thousands of American
agronomists (or just farmers) going to Africa each year, and thousands of Africans coming over here.

Next in importance to trying to arrest the galloping consumption
of African agriculture is general education. The school that is most
urgently needed throughout Africa is a sort of high school *cum*
junior college. For some time to come a competitive examination
method of admittance will be meaningless; students will have to
enter on the basis of interviews, and almost without exception their
total living and educational expenses will have to be provided *gratis*.
In lieu of any more reliable guide to follow insofar as numbers of
the new facilities are concerned—except that they are desperately
needed—perhaps we should govern ourselves by a rule of thumb: one
such new institution for every 2 million Africans. Affiliated with
them, of course, will be experiment stations, information and coun-
seling centers, clinics, and so on. For years their staffs will have
to be imported from the West (here again we see the value of the
Eurafrican connections), and the salaries paid to these staffs must
be of an order sufficient to induce them to go there. (How we are
going to provide 100-odd institutes of this kind in Africa with teach-
ers when our own school system is crying for the want of them
is a poser; but we slid into Madison Avenue habits on our own, and
if we have to scramble like navvies to get back to where we should
have been all the time it is no one's fault but ours.)

The African Institute must maintain relations with other university study centers, such as the Centers for International Affairs at Harvard and Johns Hopkins, which are perhaps in the best position to work on some of the general issues of social and political "balance" that have such a crucial place in modern Africa—the city versus the country, cash crop versus subsistence, population control; these liaisons will also provide the Institute with an outside-the-government check on the efficiency and effectiveness of its operations in Africa—and also, incidentally, another informational check on what the Commonwealth and Community are up to. The Institute will also want to keep up a direct link with certain specialized research work in this country: with, for example, an American stockraiser's association that has been assigned the job of breeding the optimum strain for different classes of savanna, or a particular outstanding man who has been given the contract to study "swollen shoot" disease. And, of course, when any of this work has led to promising results, the Institute must be in the position to translate the findings at once into pilot projects—just large enough, and not too large— and then, if the pilot runs are also successful, to disseminate the news in a practical form throughout the appropriate regions of the continent.

Even though we are told that we cannot depend on American private capital to carry much of the load of investment in Africa, the Institute should nonetheless attempt to stimulate private investment. This it can do in two ways: by propagandizing the American business community and by increasing the guarantee reserves which have already been provided by Congress. (We notice that most of the private investment in Africa before World War I was also backed up by the colonial governments in one way or another— and, indeed, entrepreneurs were more often paid back from revenues than from profits.)

When the Institute comes to the fields of health and pest control it will discover that there are already dozens of Western groups in Africa, many of whom have made substantial progress to which the rapidly rising rate of population-increase is the best index. In every country in Africa there is at least a rudimentary network of mission hospitals and government clinics—dozens of small connections which the Institute can employ in preference to establishing a separate medical bureaucracy of its own. There are also the med-

ical research centers of the colonial development agencies, the
World Health Organization, the installations maintained by the
churches and orders like the Roman Catholic Holy Ghost Fathers,
and private research work supported by such philanthropies as the
International Health Division of the Rockefeller Foundation. In
this area the main function of the African Institute will be that
of a coordinating godfather; if they are short of funds, give them
what they need to do what they already know how to do, and help
them fill in whatever gaps exist. (Also, of course, medical education
will be one of the most popular aspects of the over-all education
program. Africans want to be doctors, and Africa needs doctors.)

Perhaps the worst of all health problems in Africa, now that the
great epidemics of past years have been more or less brought under
control, is chronic malnutrition over vast reaches of the continent,
which, in its turn, naturally lowers the African's resistance to
parasitization, tuberculosis, and all the other terrible things that
lie in wait for him. Malnutrition is incontestably the main cause
of the brevity of the African's life expectancy; in its worst form,
kwashiorkor, a combination of protein and vitamin deficiency, it
is almost always fatal. Now in combating an evil like widespread malnutrition we see how important the centralizing and coordinating,
rather than simply the dispersing, functions of the African Institute
will be. For here is not simply a medical problem; it is also partly
sociological. Teams, sponsored from the Institute, must travel over
the countryside teaching mothers the proper rules of diet, and
discovering and sending in the alarm from areas of general malnutrition as soon as they catch a glimpse of the symptoms. Then, too,
the stockraiser must be introduced to the sociologist—while they are
both introduced to the African. The Bantu must be shown how
to breed cattle in a "scientific" way at the same time that a huskier
stud is made available to his cows. (Perhaps, also, as no one else
seems to want it, the African Institute may be permitted to draw
upon our vast stocks of surplus, unused food—$3 billions' worth
of wheat as of 1959, for example, plus comparable quantities of
butter, eggs, and other staples. I think I have studied all the public
statements which describe the insurmountable obstacles in the way
of disposing of these decomposing stockpiles, but is it really too
much to expect that the same brains who penetrated the atomic

nucleus may one day find a way to get food which is worthless to us into the bellies of people who are starving to death?)

Here is a vague sketch of some of the possibilities of agricultural and social development, but America's principal, and most characteristic, contribution to the "mutation," the modernization of Africa, will comprise the industrialization of the continent. Industrialization is after all the only real hope for Africa, for absorbing her new population—more importantly, for absorbing them into a self-evolving, educated, and enterprising proto-middle class, which can then begin to handle its own problems—population control, for instance—far more effectively than we can.

The mines are presently the only source of really large amounts of foreign exchange credits, and there is no question but that this will remain the case for many years to come. But we have sufficiently investigated the liabilities and instabilities associated with an industrial development that is centered exclusively around "extractive" enterprises—perhaps the chief shortcoming is that such enterprises are never the nurseries of a middle class. At those sites where they are feasible, therefore, the answer is gigantic, multi-dimension development installations similar to the Tennessee Valley Authority, with integrated agricultural, irrigation, flood-control, water-supply, power-generating elements, paying for themselves in terms of generations rather than years.

The American African Institute must be in a position not only to fund the construction of these installations but also in a sense to plant them in the society; that is to say, the industrial hinterlands which are created simultaneously in the dams' ambits must produce something that can be sold; the workers in the projects, and in the factories behind the projects that employ their power, must be paid sufficiently, and must possess all the other rights of social and job mobility, so that our basic aim of middle-class creation can become a reality; the towns, housing, and public facilities that serve these new middle-class Africans must of course represent the new Africa —*our* Africa—not the Africa of decay and ruin. There must be an Inga Project in the Congo; a Kuilu Project in the Congo Republic; a Konkoure Project in Guinea; a Volta Project in Ghana—and a half-dozen more—not simply "symbols of modern industrialism," as a modern economist scornfully characterized Nasser's white-ele-phant steelworks recently (whatever else they are, they are also "symbols" of course, and the African's relief at seeing them finally going up must surely count for something), but as piles driven down solidly into the queasy mud of the African economy, providers of the power which the African then can expend on his own education and his health. Obviously it is absurd to spend billions on educating the African, and perhaps appending ten or twenty years to his life span, while at the same time expecting him to subsist in the old de-caying nexus of farms plus mine compounds. Modernization means Power—its generation and its deployment.

In other words, remember despite the abruptness in this word "mutation" that what we Americans really mean by "development" is the opening up of the opportunities a man has to develop himself *as an individual;* a widening of the life-platform he stands on; giving him arms against environmental tyrannies. When we work in Africa we should keep in mind that one day the African is going to resent us, tease us, and criticize us. One of the reasons that education is so important is that when this day comes we want this criticism to be rational—leaving intact the basis of permanent friendship. Nothing profitable can be done in Africa that slavishly defers to a dogmatic "social engineering"; let the overzealous planner who disagrees look into the shocks suffered recently by that apotheosis of plan-ning, the Belgian Congo, or the profit and loss sheets of the East African Groundnut Scheme and a hundred other lesser fiascos. It is a time for experiment, for failure, for stouthearted generosity in both failure and success. And the kind of work that has to be done—on grasses, on animals, on people—must be primarily the responsibility of men on the spot who possess the authority to admit failure, to start over again, to gamble large quantities of money in exploiting new lines and stiffening old ones that seem to be in danger of premature collapse. A few disheartened, underpaid public officers, in hospitals or botanical research spots isolated in the midst of the bush like the flotsam of an insane inundation, gnawing away like obsessed moles on one or two narrow specialties, perfectly aware that the elephantine troubles of the continent that submerges them are totally out of hand—this is not the kind of delegation of powers we have in mind. As "the unforeseen is the rule [in Africa]," wrote an old hand,

Marshal Lyautey, "and decision is an everyday necessity, one formula tops all others; and it is the right man in the right place." And ultimately the majority of these right men in their right places must be Africans.

But of course it is absurd to talk of "Africa" as if it were a clean canvas awaiting the master's brush, a monolithic jurisdiction which only needs to be acknowledged in order to become compliant. Unfortunately, the African Institute will not be dealing with "belts" of this or that kind of savanna or rainforest, or this or that general need of the Africans who inhabit these "belts," nearly so often as it will be dealing with obstreperous established governments. How do these fit into the prospects of a rehabilitated continent?

1. In the newly independent states of West Africa our African Institute can make use of the existing framework of the French Community and the Commonwealth—and their existing development agencies, FIDES and the Colonial Development and Welfare program, and others. What these institutions need are more funds, more coordination, and wider horizons. We need not fear that the African leaders of former French and British Africa will resent their interposition because it was the benefits which they expected to derive from them that caused them to retain the Eurafrican associations in the first place.

2. In the Congo the African Institute will find the embryo of a similar priceless Eurafrican connection in the administrative and social welfare services of the Belgian colonial government: the hospitals of the Queen Elizabeth Foundation, for example, the Medical Foundation of Louvain University in the Congo, the Kivu Social Foundation, and so on. If it is at all possible, this connection should be strengthened and put on a permanent basis. But political pressure must be brought upon the Belgians in Europe to accept our support on conditions of the same kind of emancipation and autonomy in the Congo that now prevail in the northern parts of West Africa. So far as we are concerned, we would rejoice as much as the most conservative *colon* to see Belgium and the Congo

remain in fraternal association forever, but we know enough to
understand that only on a free basis is this a practical possibility.
And the Belgians of 1960 seem to understand this also.

3. The situation in Kenya is now very dangerous, and another—
and this time much worse—Mau Mau-like outbreak could erupt
at any time. But here, perhaps, putting pressure on the British to
pressure in turn the 60,000 white settlers of Kenya into more reasonable attitudes (to save their own skins) is not the right way
to proceed. (Putting pressure on Britons is never the right way to
proceed.) Probably the only way the situation in Kenya can be
handled is through the intermediation of a compensation commission
which will simply buy out the white settler, or most of him, sweet-
ening his medicine a trifle. (As we have mentioned, in other parts
of Africa we must expect to compensate African smallholders for
permitting us to repair their countryside; this may seem like almost
too much to ask of the American taxpayer, but remember that these
people are reactionary because they are desperate, and there is no
use mobilizing this potent emotional force against us on top of
everything else.) Smiling on the inviting prospects of an East African
Federation is also very much in order. We are also fortunate in having in Kenya a politician, Tom Mboya, who has shown on many
occasions that he understands the primacy of "development" as over
against the purity of any particular political doctrine.

4. Dealing with independent African leaders like Nkrumah and
(we presume) Mboya, through the filter of the Commonwealth and
the suavity of London officialdom, will spare us Americans the
necessity of deciding whether we like them or not. Nkrumah may
then go on to take occasional caustic hits at the United States, or
erect a statue or two of himself, without risking the wrath and
disinheritance of the United States Senate. This is no mean gain.
But at the same time it is not unreasonable that America should
insist on the African's keeping up his end of the bargain. But what *is*
his end? To begin with, absolute honesty in the use of our funds;
our European allies and the African Institute can easily enough
check on this when we want to be reassured. But there is another
element which is even more important than fiscal probity: the

minorities—urban versus rural, educated versus illiterate, clerk versus peasant, "citified" versus tribal, Tribe A versus Tribe B, trade union versus government and professional clique—all the hard little divisions, universal throughout Africa, which are so vulnerable to the charisma of an overtempted Man of Destiny. In short, American compassion and good humor do not have to mean the same thing as appeasement. No state in Africa should get its dams, factories, schools, and so on unless its government enters into firm engagements, which we are prepared to insist upon, that it will treat all its minorities in the spirit of the United Nations Charter. These engagements will stand apart from the constitutional structure of the countries—which each African country will naturally want to decide for itself.

5. The policy outlined here will induce a much closer tie between the United States and our European allies France and Great Britain —we will, in fact, literally be in each others' pockets. I leave it to each reader to judge whether this is not a consummation devoutly to be wished. Is it not, indeed, the main aim of American foreign policy, as expressed now in the sacrifice of everything to the pampering of NATO? And is not a shoulder-to-shoulder partnership with a fattened-up Community and Commonwealth—with all their world-wide ramifications—a far more promising method of bolstering our local European alliance than the one presently in use, which features among other things squabbling with President De Gaulle about who has jurisdiction over American thermonuclear warheads stationed on French soil?

6. Not for an instant can the United States of America give the appearance of buying Sir Roy Welensky's hypothetical line of division across Africa, "north of which the concept of a multi-racial society will not predominate but south of which the concept of a multi-racial society will be the rule rather than the exception." "Multiracialism" is nonsense; it has been made nonsense by the same men who invented it, on the spot in Africa; it is like a rear-guard skirmish, which may or may not enlist the passions of the men under fire, but cannot effect the outcome of the battle or the war. In Kenya, it means something like the present constitution, where

6 million Africans and 60,000 whites send representations of equal size to the Legislative Council; this is patently a thumb-in-dike expedient, designed to hold back the flood for eighteen months or so, until the African politicians who were powerful enough to force even this much of a concession have regathered their legions for the next assault. In Sir Roy's home ground, the Rhodesias, we have seen that "multiracial" does not mean even this much. There is no effective African politics in the Federation, and no branch of the government for them to use in framing their views and demands; "multiracialism" in the Rhodesias connotes no more than a mood of paternal patience and kindliness on the part of the white masters. But we have seen that the mood of the white society has been moving rapidly in precisely the opposite direction from "paternal kindliness"—if anything, socially and legally the African is worse off in "multiracial" Rhodesia than he is under the outright patronization of the Belgians in the Congo; and, what is more, his social and legal status are rapidly approaching the nadir of total, Afrikaner apartheid.

But, mendacious in word and deed as "multiracialism" is, we are still left with the perilous plight of the Federation. If the United States can act in time, perhaps we can tactfully suggest to the British that they reassume their responsibilities in the northern territories—backed up, of course, by funds from our African Institute. In other words, if it is at all possible the Southern Rhodesian whites must be prevented from clamping down their rule on Northern Rhodesia and Nyasaland in the revised constitution of 1960. If the Southern Rhodesians succeed in doing this, it will be impossible to avoid disastrous trouble there in the future. But assuming that the northern provinces return to full protectorate status, then perhaps a full-scale boycott of Southern Rhodesian goods, and a systematic discouragement of private American investment in the area, can entice the white settlers into changing their social and juridical policies, if not their intestinal reactions. But this is an exceedingly delicate business, and any drastic measures of this kind should be preceded by confidential consultations with the Commonwealth authorities in London and perhaps even the Federation government (who tend to make sense when they are not expatiating on the stump for the benefit of their inflamed, frightened partisans). But let our African Institute not be too creep-mouse in these talks;

when all is said and done we are trying to save the lives of the white settlers, not hurt them.

7. A general boycott should be placed on all goods coming to America from Portugal or Portuguese Africa—*until* the Portuguese government agrees to the entrance of a United Nations Study Commission into Portuguese Africa with full powers of access to all sections and records of the provinces. So much about these territories is unknown that further recommendations for development should wait upon the submissions of this group. Then further negotiations can be commenced, with an eye, if it is at all possible, to retaining the Portuguese connection, under the same circumstances of political liberty which is to be the rule in the Belgian, French, and British parts of Africa. Such is the plasticity of the African—his *reasonableness*—that even this association might come to pass.

8. Southwest Africa should be invaded by a United Nations force, composed of contingents from African and Asian countries, *and* America; the Afrikaner government should be ejected and a U.N. administration installed. This is the kind of violent policy which the citizens of middle-class Republics always denounce as a "counsel of radicalism" until they embroil themselves in a mess from which they can escape only by means of a general holocaust. In other words, today's surgery forfends tomorrow's interment. The Union's occupation of the province is at least ambiguous, from a juridical point of view; the administration of the country is a notorious scandal; its chances of reforming itself are nil; and the ideals which it is obeying are an affront to the sensibilities of the whole world. It is a clear case for a United Nations Armed Emergency Group, a test whether on the international level Justice and Law are principles of action or merely insipid terminology, latter-day versions of Locarno and the Kellogg-Briand pact, something to fill out the newspapers in the *entre deux guerres* interim between more exciting reports of slaughter and carnage.

9. We should back to the hilt our British ally's intentions to keep the High Commission territories clear of Afrikanerdom at all costs,

and the African Institute should do what it can to make these lands showcases of free, modernizing Africa.

10. We come to South Africa itself. Here is one of the vilest and most irrational governments in the history of the world—and that is about all that can be said about it that is simple. The essential problem boils down to whether 2 million Afrikaners prefer to die horribly rather than to surrender the pleasures of *kaffir*-beating. It is a choice they have to make for themselves; and if they decide in the affirmative—as indeed they have decided—nothing can save them. A Third Boer War—a United Nations invasion of South Africa, for example—is impractical if for no other reason than that it would involve the killing of so many innocent Africans. All we can do is to isolate the country within her cordon of hate, and engineer the modernization of African all round her, remembering in our own interest that if conspiratorial Communism—that bogey of ours—is going to find a permanent foothold anywhere in Africa it will be right there in the Union. It already has found a home there, in fact, and thus it is in our interest to keep the death throes of Afrikanerdom as brief as we can.

Perhaps a general boycott and sanctions will complete the divorce between the Afrikaner and the English-speaker. Then the Political Department of our African Institute can ship in secret organizational and material support to the "democratic" revolutionaries inside the country—exercising the most painstaking care (but this will be a very tricky matter) to discourage the Africans from rising until they can really defend themselves against the machine guns and pursuit planes of the Afrikaner. And when the atrocious catastrophe comes we must be ready, in concert with our African and European allies, to move swiftly and massively into the Union—in order to save the lives of as many of the people as possible, and to set about the settlement and rehabilitation of the wretched country. (And we must keep reminding ourselves of the reality, the absolute inevitability, of this "atrocious catastrophe." It is no use repeating the phrases over and over again, or quoting the hundreds of citizens of the Union—black and white, Afrikaner and English-speaking—who see perfectly well what must happen. Even the most conservative report I have seen on modern Africa—and I mean "conservative" in a respectful sense, though I do not personally agree with this report's approach—that of John Scott, assistant to the publisher of *Time* Magazine, speaks unhesitantly of the "racial bloodbath" which is coming to South Africa. And so it is. But what no one knows is what to do about it.)

Does this brusque and gaudy power program—a huge new Institute of African Affairs; thousands of students, engineers, doctors, dentists, consultants, stockbreeders, and even political agitators being sent all over Black Africa, equal numbers of Africans coming by return passage to study here in the United States; hundreds of millions poured into the development agencies of Great Britain and France; dams and power plants by the dozen; a friendly nudge at Belgium; the intimidation of tiny Portugal; the ostracizing of the governments of the Rhodesias and South Africa—these free-wheeling, bronto-saurian, arbitrary projects, are they repugnant to the American way, or to any "responsible" way? I hope not. For it would be a shame to forget what it cost us so much to learn; namely, what words like "abrupt" and "arbitrary" can so easily come to mean in other contexts, the contexts for example of 1918 and 1943.

In other words, we can no longer afford the semantic dichotomy implied in the conventional verbal usages of War and Peace, because the traditional conditons of War and Peace, on which these conventions were founded, no longer correspond to the possibilities. Peace-time diplomacy's ideal—the type of standard that will most severely deprecate the suggestions of this chapter—has always been the ideal of the jeweler's balance: a long-protracted, skillful adjustment of gives and takes and compromises, postponements, deftness in hitting on just the right safety valve, just the right nuance in a note of warning; all to the desired end that out and out shooting is put off as long as possible, and that if it comes, as it invariably did, your side will get the best of it. But today we discover that it is nothing (relatively) minor like dynastic ambitions, or the vices of munitions makers, or the infatuated illusions of a warhawk club like the German Navy League that threatens the equilibria of Peace, but something so stupendous, so portentous, as the Technological Revolution's "pauperization" of more than three-quarters of the inhabited globe. This revolution, this all-pervading upheaval is nothing that can be put to rights with an offhand touch or casual correction here or there on the normal diplomatic balances—while 99 per cent of energy of the American nation is tending to the normal pleasures of normal life. You need a force of management that matches the force at large; that is to say, you need the industrial and social concentration which always in the past has been called up for the crises of war. (And, when we look about us at our rivals, Russia and China, we see that they are concentrating for their role in this struggle in just this spirit.)

On the other hand, the classic conventions of war are just as impracticable in this age. In the good old days, when a politician like Hitler kicked the scales off the table we put away our toddy and cookies and went after him with the carving knife. Then, when we had cut his throat and buried his body we returned to the kitchen and started up the entertainment again. But when carving knife means cobalt bomb, and war means uninhabitable desert, we have to anticipate our Hitlers, and stifle them before they settle down, rather than depending on our ability to destroy them when they finally make life absolutely impossible.

Does any more need to be said on this point? What it comes down to is that we must link in our thoughts of war many of the restraints which our fathers associated with peace, and in our thoughts of peace many of the labors which our fathers associated with war. Both the absentmindedness and sloth that are traditionally suitable for peace, and the all-out ferocity that is traditionally suitable for war, now pose critical perils to the survival of the human race. The traditional balance aims of diplomacy must be widened to a statecraft that comprehends the sculpting of dynamic forces in addition to the balancing of static power forces. Only our ultimate aims can remain the same: they are the enhancement of the American Republic and the freedom of mankind. Whether we have evolved something in this country that is of priceless importance to the men of all generations—which the author of this essay emphatically believes—or whether we are a flash in the pan, overwhelmed eventually by hostile, conglomerating forces which are too big for us—this is an issue which is still unsettled. We do not propose to compromise about it. What we do propose is the invention of new structures to carry forward our political and moral aims into an age of quite unprecedented challenges.

But can we afford the "New Imperialism"? That is the cry one always hears from every side. At the outset we predict that the same people who say we cannot afford a decent school construction program for our children will also denounce the costliness of the African Institute. But as the latter will be substantially more costly than the former this prophecy is something of an *argumentum ad hominem.*

The fact is that these people do not know what we can afford; that despite their smug injudicious minglings of this kind of carping with the most unexceptionably patriotic sloganeering, these poor-mouths are disgracefully bearish about the potentialities of the Republic they claim so noisily to love. In his book *The Affluent Society* Professor Galbraith has devoted a long section to the common delusions about the economic sacrifices of World War II. We did achieve fabulous production records in armaments, navies, transportation fleets, and so forth, but at the same time Galbraith is able to show that domestic consumption of nonwar-related items like elecrical appliances and gasoline for domestic travel rose steeply in those very same years. In other words, so packed with previously untested muscle was the American economy that we achieved our vaunted "miracles of war production" *and* very substantially raised our standard of living—both at the same time. It is almost unimaginable what we could have achieved had it been necessary really to concentrate our forces—as the Chinese government is doing today. Naturally no one suggests that we emulate Peking in this matter, but the whole episode is an adequate refutation of the old fogies who declare that we must not concentrate at all—especially if we believe, as I do, that not to concentrate is to injure the Republic very gravely. Even relegating the war itself to the background, to judge from the prevailing tone of modern economists, what they are worrying about at present is whether, with the changes due to automation, and so forth, the level of consumption can be kept somewhere near the level of production—*even if the vast defense expenditures of the government continue at their present level or even rise!* Such are the fathomless forces that we are tapping in this country—powers of society as well as powers of technology.

Specifically, these discussions of the proper level of overseas investment sooner or later always come round to the datum that at the turn of the century Great Britain was investing abroad at an annual rate of 10 per cent of her Gross National Product. If the United States were today investing abroad at this same rate, we would be sending overseas more than $45 billions a year. It is only honest to

point out that the high Victorian rate of British overseas investment
has been strongly criticized by some economists, notably John
Maynard Keynes, as representing an unwarranted diversion of capital
from domestic needs in Britain herself. But this point need hardly
detain us; nothing is less likely than that an undue proportion of
American capital will start leaving this country. The danger is
obviously all the other way: that American capital, and the energy
embodied in this capital, will continue along its present self-con-
cerned course, thus fatally impairing our capacity to handle the
political tensions of our time. But, to be common-sensical, an annual
investment of $45 billions—90 per cent or more of which would have
to be appropriated by Congress, which is as much a part of the real
world as Africa is—is rather more than even the most fanatical "devel-
oper" will believe feasible for this hard world. (Indeed, we have
already made the point that there is not nearly enough "development
capital" going into our own social investments; and there is no doubt,
in my mind at least, that these projects—school construction, slum
clearance, river valley development, conservation, and so forth—must
take priority over everything else, most emphatically including the
budgets of the Department of Defense.)

Therefore, after the most rudimentary attempts at a computation
which blends costs, needs, and practical possibilities, I have come up
with a reckoning of $6 to 8 billions a year which *should be made
available* to the African Institute. I emphasize "made available" because we have spoken of the difficulties of spending money wisely in
Africa, and there is no reason for us to spend it if we cannot spend
it wisely, which is not at all the same thing as illiberally. Perhaps this
sounds harsh to our African friends, but nothing is accomplished by
throwing nine or ten equivalents after the original groundnut scheme.
At the same time, as we say, we must take risks and cheerfully
swallow our failures; hence the criterion of appropriations must be
the needs of the African Institute as estimated by themselves, along
with the authority to engage in any project, large or small, or to
withdraw from or cancel out any project, large or small. In other
words, whether or not it is spelled out in the enabling statute, we
must assume a semiautonomous status for the Institute—something
like that of the Atomic Energy Commission, but *sans* (we hope)
that agency's tribunician functions. To give an idea of the kind of

expense they will have to face, the Inga Project, which should have been started five years ago or more, is estimated at a cost of about $4 billions, for which the investor should not expect to be repaid in less than 100 years. This is a gigantic sum; it will be the largest installation of its kind in the world; but on the other hand it is almost certain to be a resounding success. Some of the Institute's other projects will be much less costly but they will be operated parallel to, and dependent upon, research programs into very obscure fields, the pasture land and drainage problems of Bechuanaland, for instance. What we do in areas like this is much less likely to yield up a brilliant, heart-warming return. We may have to fail a dozen times before we discover what we need to know about these matters.

This is all very well, but where is this $6 to 8 billions a year to come from—not to speak of investments in other parts of the world when America enters the "development business" with the seriousness and concentration we are here demanding? The money can come only from one of two places: either from a new bite on the American pocketbook, such as the national sales tax recommended by some economists, or from a saner concept of "defense" on which we are spending $40 billions annually. We have reviewed already the latter expenditure. General Taylor says the Defense Department errs in their "weaponry bookkeeping," which is a relic of the last war instead of keying into any possible war of the future. Other people compare the whole defense program to the act of a fearful householder in purchasing a gun. The man is now defended against "hairy intruders," but his gun does not shield him from pneumonia, unemployment, adultery, conscription into the army, or ennui. That is reasonable enough so long as our man looks upon his gun as just one of the precautions of life—to be used in case of special emergency. But if he spends half his waking hours and half his energy contemplating and polishing this gun, neglecting every other aspect of existence, then we judge that an obsession has overset the balance of his mind; what to him is a simple case of "defense" is in reality the monomania of an inert and overpowered brain.

But systematic, scientific, documented attacks on the "bookkeeping" of our postwar defense budgets, let alone their basic philosophy, have hardly begun in this country, though one hopes for much from the 1960 elections. And it is hard to guess when, or if, the major parties will discard their standard anathematizations of a national sales tax. Will it suffice to keep in mind that the wherewithal to modernize Africa is going to come from someplace—ultimately, out of our wallets or out of our hides—under the auspices of Free Men or the auspices of Despotism?

The last word cannot lie with Strategy and Fear. Without nobility and pride of self, and the highest moral standards that we know, we can build nothing which will memorialize the dreams and sacrifices of our forefathers as they deserve to be memorialized. Unless we Americans, within ourselves and within the Community, find the path to an inner life of greater joy and intensity—a search to the core of spiritual and political meanings—no program, however solid or melodramatic, will really suffice to lift American public policy out of the ruts of stopgap improvisation into a potent, flexible instrument that surges forth against the Republic's enemies. We may erect a dam here, or send a few hundred thousand tons of surplus wheat there, or open credit accounts for this or that government at the Federal Reserve Bank—but unless these individual acts are embraced and exalted by a resolute and truly responsible image of what we believe ourselves and the Republic to be, they will not possess the *force* coming from the concentration of intellect and passion that alone can dub a deed with the title Progress.

Perhaps it is disappointing that a discussion which began mundanely enough with specific proposals for Big Dams and Big Fellowships should drift off into these hortatory intangibles. But, as everyone knows, it is these intangible matters of the wills and spirits of individuals of which the history of man is made. As we have said, our own time is an innovating time: war and peace, for example, do not mean today what they meant only twenty years ago; it is no longer possible for a nation to tend its own garden, while in another part of the world another nation goes destitute; even in our own country, so interdependent have we become—through the "cooperative phenomena" of the Technological Revolution—that we must exercise conscious, *and conscientious*, direction of all kinds of forces which only a generation or so ago we could leave to sort out by themselves.

None of this means that America is doomed like an old-fashioned bibelot to be devoured by "pauperization," the "population boom," the "yellow peril," "Communization," or any of the rest of it. It means only that we must invent new structures to accommodate to the new conditions, wherein to press forward our national destiny of emancipating mankind from the dull, crippling, soul-exhausting ordeals imposed upon so large a proportion of the race by cruel, mindless hostilities in the environment. Fortunately, God has already blessed us with a goodly number of truly responsible citizens who are rejoicing in the opportunity to gamble their intelligence and their toughness for the prize of wondrous new glories of the imagination. The children, scientists, and musicians of America, for example, have never been wholly taken in by the seductions of filter-tips in flip-top boxes and all the rest of this crazy hugger-mugger on which millions spend billions every day. Children, scientists, and musicians want to *live*—to live in a little style, and specifically to live into the Age of Space of which the glorious dawn has arisen in our own day.

But who *can* resist the Age of Space? Even our *homme moyen sensuel*—our soap manufacturer, our used-car salesman, our soldiers, lawyers, and journalists—we are all being drawn out of ourselves, as old warriors in damp fortresses in north Europe were drawn out of themselves toward the dusty hills around Jerusalem. And that is the way it must be—and thank God for it. We must follow the little boy in his space helmet; the clear-eyed, impatient mathematician; the violin player. We must rebel at littleness, at petulance, at self-pity and ignorance and bullying. We must not permit men to die of hunger when we are standing on the means to feed them. We must not permit men to be beaten until they scream in anguish. We must cease polluting rivers because a proper decontamination unit is an "impractical notion," according to some paper firm's controller; we must cease desolating our lakes, destroying our topsoils, forests, valleys, fish and animal reserves; we must cure our cities of their inner cores of decay and their belts of slums, and free our industrial workers of the tedium of the assembly line; we must cease smashing down every old monument a real estate finagler chances to covet; we must cease defacing our countryside with toothpaste advertisements; baiting and tormenting our minorities because it is an "inherited way of life"; drugging our minds with ninth-rate fatuities and cynicisms;

sitting by complacently while our orchestras, schools, libraries, museums, and universities founder in oceans of debt like dirty, sea-weary galleons.

We must fly high, very high, very much higher than we now are flying if we desire to retain the power to fly at all. The Republic must survive for very many more centuries if it is to justify the love and the pain which our national heroes have lavished on it. We of this generation have not yet proved ourselves the equal of those heroes. We do not glory in our strength as they did, using it as all truly strong men use their strength, to heal and liberate the weak and the unfortunate. We have still to become, as Milton saw England becoming in the darkest hours of the Civil War: "A Nation not slow and dull, but of a quick, ingenious, and piercing spirit, acute to invent, subtle and sinewy to discourse, not beneath the reach of any point the highest that human capacity can soar to."

GOD PRESERVE THE REPUBLIC!

Index

Abako Association, 139, 141, 142–144
Aberdare Mountains, 179
Abidjan, increase of port facilities of, 161
Abyssinia, Plateau of, 5
Abyssinian Coptic Church, 201
Accra Conferences of 1958, 260
Achimota, 208
Action Group, Nigeria, 226, 228
Addis Ababa, 4, 201
Adloff, Richard, 163
Adowa, Battle of, 200
Affluent Society, The (Galbraith), 295
Africa: assault of Victorian Europe on, 9–10; birth and death rates in, 14; BLACK: 4, 7, 8, 11, 12, 13, 23, 93, 158, 207, 254, 258, 260, 263, cash cropping in, 20, French rule in, 158, hydroelectric potentials, 23; CENTRAL: 93, 125ff.; Chinification of, 267–271, program for, 274–300; diet deficiencies in, 20; EAST: 5, 172–204, Arabs in, 175, deserts of, 173, economic investment and practice in, 162–165, history and physiography of, 174–177; education in, 20, 282–283; effects of World War II on, 10; expanding population of, 3; FRENCH: 10, 125, 173, agricultural subsidies for, 165, effects of World War II on, 159f., evolution and assimilation in, 158, French Community in, 152–171, French economy and, 164–165, malnutrition in, 163, multi-deterioration process in, 165, political life of, 166–171; FRENCH EQUATORIAL: 5, 11, 126, 157, 158, 264, economic development in, 161, erosion in, 163–164, for French Community, 156, 160, lumber exports, 163; FRENCH NORTH: pauperization, 21; FRENCH WEST: 5, 11, 157, 158, economic development in, 161, for French Community, 156, 160, imports of, 163, iron-ore production of, 161, population increase in, 14; as future hostile element, 152–153; "gross product" of, 16–17, 18–19; history of French Empire in Black, 156–159; illusion of economic advances in, 16–20; impact of Technological Civilization on, 1–3; impoverishment of, 14–16; industrialization of, 285–287; malnutrition in, 22, 284; modern politics in, 230;

modernization of, 14, 16–18; need for business, 242–247; overpopulation of, 12–16; per capita income in, 18, 19; physiography of, 4ff.; politics in, 20–21; population concentrations of, 20; population expansion of, 20; "Potemkin" cities and industries of, 18; problems of health and pest control in, 283–285; prospects for, 257–273; receding from economic "hump," 22; relations with U.S.A. and West, 206, 232–256, 275–300; and slave traffic, 7–8, 9; sociologists', 172–174; SOUTH: 5, Act of 1909, 49, English-speaking population of, 86–88; SOUTHWEST: 4, 173, 291, administration of, 77, Afrikaners in, 79, apartheid in, 80–81, brutality of German regime in, 77–78, German influence on, 77–79, German support in, for Union of South Africa, 78–79, history of, 77–79, pass system in, 80, petitions annexation to Union of South Africa, 78–79, physiography of, 76–77, "Police Zone," 77, population increase in, 14, "Tribal Areas," 77, and Union of South Africa, 79–82, and United Nations, 79–82; sub-Sahara of, 4; and Technological Revolution, 1–3, 10–11, 12, 14, 23; tourists', 172–174; unemployment in urban concentrations of, 18; varied geography of, 1–26; WEST: 7, 11, 15, 229, 260, 263, 287, cash cropping in, 15, environment and conditioning of, 8–9, 23–24, proletarianizing of, 51–52

African Democratic Rally (RDA), of French Africa, 168–170

African Elected Members' Committee of Kenyan Legislature, 177

African middle class, in Portuguese Africa, 120–121

African Mineworkers' Union, Northern Rhodesia, 106

African National Congress, 61, 69, 70, 72, 73, 104, 188, 266; of the Rhodesias, 109

African Regroupment Party (PRA), of French Africa, 168

African uprising, possibilities of, 70–74

Afrikanerdom, 28–46, 147, 291–293; brutalities of, 292–293; and High Commission Territories, 84–86; history of, 29–34; isolation of, 35–36; oppression by, 47–75 *passim;* in Southern Rhodesia, 94, 105

Afrikaners, 27–75, 265; attitude toward High Commission Territories, 83–84; domination of, 47–75 *passim;* emigration to High Veld, 30ff.; German support for, 78–79; mentality of, 27ff.; racism of, 47–75 *passim;* in Transvaal, 50; tyranny of, 32–33, 34. *See also* Afrikanerdom

Age of Exploration, 118

Albert National Park, 148

Alexander the Great, 6

Alexandria, Church of, 201

Algeria, French "imperial defensives" in, 161; French investment and economic practices in, 161

Algeria (Tillion), 21

Algerian war, 159, 165

All-Africa People's Conference, of December 1958, 123

Aluminium Limited, of Canada, 215

Anglo-American Corporation, 65, 75

Angola, 4, 11, 126; African middle class in, 120–121; cash crops of, 117–118; emigration of youths to Bechuanaland and Northern Rhodesia, 116; increase of exports of, 16; investigation of conditions in, 123; labor emigration to Union of South Africa, 116–117; lack of liberalism in, 122–123; land area, 111; population, 111, 113; resources, 111–113

Antelope Mine, 101–102

Apartheid, 38, 39, 42, 44, 52, 54, 56–57, 63, 70, 76, 80–81, 85, 88, 97, 99, 108, 290. *See also* Afrikanerdom; Afrikaners

Arabs, in East Africa, 175; slave expeditions of, 181

Aristotle, 219

Ashantehene, 212, 213

Ashanti, 216, 217; Confederacy, 207, 212

Aurelius, Marcus, 236

Awolowo, Obafemi, 223, 226, 227

Azikiwe, Nnamdi "Zik", 225, 226, 227–228, 230

Baganda, 174, 196

Bagehot, Walter, 200

Baker, Samuel, 174

Balewa, Abubakar Tafawa, 223

Banda, Hastings, 104, 109, 170

Bandung Conference of 1955, 260, 261

Bantu, 6, 31, 44, 47, 68, 89, 94, 95, 174, 175, 284; enslavement of, 33; "ethnic groups" of, 51; German brutality toward, 78; migration of, 30, 31

Bantustan, 63, 64, 68, 87

Barotse, 93

Basutoland, 5; British administration of, 84–85; constitution granted to, 88; physiography of, 84

Bechuanaland, 4, 34, 77, 93, 173, 297; British administration of, 84–85; Crown land in, 86; migration of population of, to Union of South Africa, 87; physiography of, 84

Beira, Mozambique, 113

Belgian Congo, 4, 5, 97, 124–151, 177, 199, 285, 286, 287–288, 290; administration and control of, by Société Générale de Belgique, 130–132; Belgians' mandate in, 143–145; bureaucracy in, 130–132; colonization of, 77; Decree of January 13, 1959, 139, 140; doctrine of racial mind in, 135–136f.; economic expansion of, 132–133; economic investment in, 161; economic and living conditions in, 133–134; history of, 127–130; hydroelectric potential of, 145–146; increase of exports of, 16; independence promised to, 11; multideterioration process in, 165; nationalism in, 139; new proletariat in, 133; paternalism in, 124–126; physiography of, 126–127; political administration of, 131–134; population of, 126–127; sexual antagonisms as racial, 137–138; stock breeding and raising in, 149–151; urbanization of, 132–134; wages in, 134

Belgian Ten-Year Plan of 1949, 130

Benin, King of, 224

Berle, Adolf A., Jr., 243, 246

Berlin Conference, 220

Bismarck, Otto von, 77, 170–171

"Black Federations," 263–265

Blackstone, William, 200

Blantyre riots of 1959, 100

Blood River, Battle of, 30–31

Blum, Léon, 159, 168

Boer War, 35–36, 37, 84

Bolton Report, 249

"Borrowdale incident," 102

Botha, Louis, 37, 85

Bradley, Omar, 248

Brazza, Savorgnan de, 157

Brazzaville Conference of 1944, 159

British Commonwealth of Nations, 36, 87, 263, 275, 281, 287, 288, 289. *See also* Great Britain

British East Africa, 170

British Empire, 90–93

British Guiana, 30

British Somaliland, 203

British South Africa Company, 93

Browne, Sir Thomas, 171

Bryce, Viscount, 256

Buganda, Uganda, 196

Bukavu, Kivu province, B.C., 140

Burckhardt, Jacob, 258

Burke, Edmund, 200

Burns, Sir Alan, 82

Bushmen, 6, 14, 30, 48, 77–78

Cabinda, 126

Cairo, Egypt, 93; and Somalia, 203; Conference of 1958, 260

Cameroons, 5

Cannibalism, 137

Canterbury Tales (Chaucer), 279

Cão, Diego, 7

Cape of Good Hope, 4, 5, 7, 9, 35, 50; Dutch settle at, 31

Cape Colony, 182

Cape Malays, 51

Capetown, South Africa, 53–54, 92, 173

Capital, shortage of, 262
Capital (Marx), 90
Capital Formation and Foreign Investment in Underdeveloped Africa (Wolf and Sufrin), 245
Capital starvation, in Portuguese Africa, 112–113
Capitalism, democratic, 241; new and old, in U.S.A., 243–256, 262–263
Caprivi, Leo von, 169
Carothers, J. C., 188, 189
Cash cropping, 15–16, 20, 117–118
Central Highlands, Kenya, 180
Central Lakes, 149
Chad, chooses French Community, 160
Chaka, King of Zulus, 31
Chamberlain, Joseph, 36
Chase Manhattan Bank, 146
Chiang Kai-shek, 202
China, 249, 253–254, 260, 261, 264, 294, 295; and Chinification, 267–271; Communist movement, 248
Chinification of Africa, 267–271
Chipembere, H. B., 105
"Cocoa Islands," São Tomé and Principe, 118–119
Colonial Development and Welfare program, 287
Comité Spécial du Katanga, 130
Commission for Technical Cooperation in Africa South of the Sahara, 281–282
Communist Party of France, 158, 160, 166
Conakry, increase of port facilities of, 161
"Confederation of Color," 152–153, 261–262, 263
Conference of Berlin, 1884–1885, 127
Congo basin, 127–129, 173
Congo estuary, 128
Congo Free State, 8, 127; Belgium acquires, 129; competition for, 127–130
Congo Republic, 156, 165, 170, 285
Congo River, 5, 7, 126, 148, 149, 157
Congo, self-government for, 132
Conrad, Joseph, 271

Conservative Party, of Great Britain, 89
Constitution of October 4, 1959, 11
Convention People's Party, Ghana, 210
Coolidge, Calvin, 241
"Copper Belt," 126, 133
Corporal punishment, in Portuguese Africa, 118
Curzon, Marquess of, minute of, 144
Cyrenaica, 7
Czechoslovakia, 221

Dahomey, chooses French Community, 160
Dahomeyans, riots against, 163
Daily Worker, 208
Dakar, 160; increase of port facilities of, 161
Darlan, Jean François, 159
Darwin, Charles, 13
"Day of the Covenant," 30
de Beers Diamond trust, 65
Delamere, Lord, 176, 178
Denmark, 152–153
Deportation, in Portuguese Africa, 119–120
Devonshire White Paper, 183–184, 186
Diamonds of Angola Company, 113
Diaz, Bartholomeu, 7
Dillon, Read, 146
Dingaan, King of Zulus, 31
Disraeli, Benjamin, 36, 234
Divine, Father, 208
Dominion Party, Southern Rhodesia, 108
Drake, Francis, 25
"Dual Mandate," 94–95, 96, 226
Dulles, John Foster, 261
Dutch East India Company, Cape Colony, 29–30, 31, 32

East Africa High Commission, Central Legislative Assembly, 195
East African Federation, 195, 196, 197, 199, 288
East African groundnut scheme, 286
East Coast fever, 23
East Germany, 221
East India Company, 91

Eastern Region, Nigeria, 224, 225, 229
Edict of Nantes, Revocation of the, 29
Egypt, 6–7, 157, 259–260; and Uganda, 197
Eisenhower, Dwight D., 215
Elisabethville, B.C., 133, 141
Elizabeth II, 88, 190, 209, 211, 216, 225
Emby, 185
Entebbe, Uganda, 197
Equator province, B.C., 5, 126, 131
Eritrea, 202
Esser, Carl, 149–151
Ethiopia, 5, 11, 173, 200–204, 211, 260; Communist aid to, 202; contribution to Korean War, 25, 200
Eurafrica, 170; problem of, 155f.
European Economic Community, and French development, 165
European Mineworkers' Union, Northern Rhodesia, 106
Exploration, Age of, 7

Fabian Society, 194
Facing Mount Kenya (Kenyatta), 188
Faidherbe, Louis Léon César, 157, 171
Fashoda Incident, 157
Federation of the Rhodesias and Nyasaland, 11, 89–110; economic expansion, 106; Federal Parliament of, 108; formation and structure of, 98–101; founded, 96f.; motive for, 98–99
Fingos, 51
Firestone Rubber Company, 211
Fisher, Ed, 236
Ford, Henry, 243
Formosa, aid from U.S.A., 202
France, 152, 293; investment and economic practices in Africa, 161–166; investment in French Community, 161. *See also under* French
Frankel, S. H., 16, 18, 276
"Free France," 159
"Freedom Day," 185
French Community, 156, 160, 263, 275, 281, 287, 289
French Constitution of 1946, 159–160; of 1958, 160

French Empire, in Black Africa, 156–159
French Guinea, 221; against French Community, 156
French Huguenots, at Table Bay, 29
French Investment Fund for Economic and Social Development in the Overseas Territories (FIDES), 162–165, 287
French "Labor Code" of December, 1952, 160
French Revolution, Wars of, 30
French Union, 160
French West Africa (Adloff and Thompson), 163
Friedman, Milton, 259
Fulanis, 230
Fulbright, Senator J. W., 250

Gabon, 156, 158; chooses French Community, 160
Galbraith, John Kenneth, 241, 246, 295
Gama, Vasco da, 7
"Garden Route," Capetown, 173
Garveyites, 209
de Gaulle, Charles, 160, 165, 168, 221
"De Gaulle Constitution," 156, 167, 168
German East Africa, 196
German Navy League, 293
Ghana, 61, 100, 125, 157, 194, 260, 262, 263, 275, 285; Assembly, 217, 218; cocoa blight in, 18; cocoa crop of, 213–215; Cocoa Marketing Board, 213, 216, 221; Constitution of, 219; economy of, 213–217; finances of, 213–215; government of, 217–222; and Guinea in Federation, 221; increase of exports of, 16; and Nigeria, 205–231; Official Gazette, 218; physiography of, 207; politics in, 212–213; Preventive Detention Act, 217; resources of, 212–217
Ghana (Nkrumah), 207–208
Goa, 157
Goering, Hermann W., 78
Gold Coast, 207
Goma, B.C., 138

Gomez, Monsignor Ferreira, 121
Gondar, Ethiopia, 173
Grand Central City, N.Y., 249
Grant, J. A., 174
Great Britain, 152, 293, 295; and the Afrikaner problem, 36–37, 87–88; Blue Books, 90; Charter Act of, 91; Civil War, 300; Colonial Office, 10, 87, 99, 105, 108, 179, 182, 184, 185, 197, 206, 223, 225; House of Commons, 104; and Orange Free State and Transvaal, 34–36; returns Transvaal to Afrikaners, 92; and the Rhodesias, 92–96; Royal Commission of 1955, 180; Royal Commission reports, 90; at Table Bay, 29–30
Great Central Plateau, 4–6, 7, 76
Great Fish River, 30
Great Trek, 30, 32, 33, 34
Griffith, Sir William, 213
Gross National Product, in Union of South Africa, 19
Gueye, Lamine, 168
Guinea, 146, 263, 285; Coast, 5, 8, 165, 173, 207; forests of, 158; and Ghana in Federation, 221; urbanization and unemployment in, 163; withdrawal from French Community, 165
Guinea, Gulf of, 4, 7, 118, 207

Haig, Earl, 255
Hailey, Lord, 23, 101
Haiphong, bombardment of, 159
Hamite, 6
Harris, Marvin, 117, 119
Harvard University, 283
Hastings, Warren, 90–91
Hausa-Fulani, 227
Haushofer, Karl, 170
Helwan steel works, 259
Hemelrijck, Maurice van, 140
Henry J. Kaiser Company, 215
Hereros, massacre of, 78
Hertzog, J. B. M., 37, 98
High Commission Territories, administration of, 84–85; and Afrikanerdom, 84–86, 291; and Union of South Africa, 84–86
High Veld, 30, 33, 34

Hitler, Adolf, 39, 169, 170, 248, 294
Hodgkin, Thomas, 169
Hola debates, 191
Hottentots, 6, 30, 48, 77–78
Houphouet-Boigny, Félix, 167–168, 169–170, 221, 260
Hoyle, Fred, 277
Huddleston, Father, 41, 74
Hunger, and color, 155
Huxley, Elspeth, 178
Hydroelectric projects, 165–166

Ibo, of Nigeria, 224, 227
Iboland, Nigeria, 225, 229
Iceland, 152
Idées Napoléoniennes (Napoleon III), 167
"Ilbert Bill," 91
Imperial British East Africa Company, 181
"Index of specific population," 22
Indian Ocean, 5
Indo-China, French "imperial defensives" in, 161
Industrial Revolution, 239
Industrialization, of Africa, 285–287
Inga Falls project, 145–147, 166, 285, 297
International Bank, 202
International Court of Justice, 81
International Red Cross, 123
Iron Curtain, 74, 202, 221
Islam, effect of, on Africa, 7
Ituri forest, 21
Ivory Coast, 207, 221, 260, 262; chooses French Community, 160; coffee and cocoa culture of, 164; politics in, 166, 168; urbanization and unemployment in, 163

Jadotville, B.C., 133
Jameson Raid, 35
Jaurès, Jean Léon, 168
Jefferson, Thomas, 239, 273
Johannesburg, Transvaal, 50, 53, 67, 68, 75, 122; bus boycott in, 70–71; Msomi gang, 60

Kabaka of Uganda, 196–197
Kagera Park, 149
Kalahari Desert, 77
Kalb, Bernard, 22

Kampala, Uganda, 197
Kano, Nigeria, 230
Kaokoveld, 77
Kariba Dam, 40, 97, 146
Karroos, Little and Great, 4
Kasai province, 149
Kasavubu, Joseph, 142–143
Katanga province, B.C., 4, 5, 97, 112, 133
Kavirondo region, Kenya, 180
Kellogg-Briand Pact, 291
Kenya, 5, 11, 174, 175, 203, 222; African Union, 188, 189, 190; Chambers of Commerce, 178; Constitution of 1927, 184; Constitution of 1958, 193; Council of State, 193; Federation of Labor, 177; Highlands, 181–182; history of, 180–185; immigration of Asians into, 187; Land Commission of 1934, 186; Legislative Council, 182, 184, 187, 193, 288–290; physiography and resources of, 179–180; politics and history of, 182–193; population explosion in, 180; problems of, 288; prospects for, 193–197; Protectorate, 181; wage scale for farm Africans in, 186–187; *Weekly News*, 187
Kenyatta, Jomo, 187, 188–189, 209
Keppel-Jones, Arthur, 33, 41
Keynes, John Maynard, 296
Keyser, A. G., 187
Khama, Seretse, 87
Khartoum, 157
Khrushchev, Nikita, 254
Kiama Kia Muingi (KKM), 194–195
Kikuyu, 181–182, 185–187, 188, 191, 194
Kilimanjaro, 196
King Kong, 61
King Ranch, 150
Kipande institution of labor passes, 187
Kisenyi, Ruanda-Urundi, 172
Kivu, Lake, 172
Kivu province, B.C., 5, 133, 140, 148
Kivu Social Foundation, 287
Konkoure River dam project, 165, 166, 221, 285
Korean War, 249, 268; Ethiopians in, 200
Kruger, Paul, 34–35, 41, 84, 93

Kruger National Park, 173
Kuilu project, 285
Kuilu scheme, of Congo Republic, 165
Kuznets, Simon, 18
Kwashiorkor, 284

Labour Party, of Great Britain, 89, 209
Lagos, Nigeria, 21, 224
"Lari massacre," 190
League of Nations, 79, 82–83; African Mandates of, 10, 76
Lenin, Nikolai, 245
Leopold II, King of the Belgians, 8, 124, 127–129, 130, 157
Leopoldville, B.C., 21, 141, 145, 280; population of, 133, 135; riots of January, 1959, 117, 141–143, 144
Lesser Rift Valley, 126
Liberal Party of the Union of South Africa, 41, 43
Liberia, 11, 206, 211, 221; American oil tankers registered under, 246
Lincoln, Abraham, 75, 273
Lincoln University, Pa., 208, 225
Livingstone, David, 92, 171; explorations of Belgian Congo, 127–128
Lloyd George, David, 36
Lobengula, King, 94
Lobito, Angola, 113, 118
Locarno Pact, 291
"*Loi-cadre*" of June, 1956, 160
London Conference of Commonwealth Ministers, 211
London School of Economics, 187, 208
Louis XIV, of France, 159
Lourenço Marques, Mozambique, 113, 119, 122
Louvain University Medical Foundation, B.C., 287
Luganda, 196
Lugard, Lord, 94
Luluabourg, B.C., 138, 141, 149
"*Luso*-populations," in Portuguese Africa, 119–120
Luthuli, Chief Albert, 61, 69–70, 71, 73, 74
Lyautey, Louis H. G., 287

MacArthur, Douglas, 248
Majuba, 34, 92

Makarere, Uganda, 186
Malan, D. F., 37, 38, 44, 62, 80, 86
Mali Federation, 7, 157, 160, 168
Malinowski, Bronislaw K., 107
Malnutrition, 22, 284; in French
   Africa, 163
Malvern, Lord, 107, 108
Marshall, George C., 248
Marshall, S. L. A., 25
Marx, Karl, 90
Masai, 174; decline of, 180, 181
Masailand, 181
Mashona, 93, 94
Matabele, 14, 92, 93, 94, 96
Matadi, B.C., 7, 128, 141, 145, 148;
   riots in, 142
Matadi-Stanley Pool railway, 128, 130
Mau-Mau, 137, 178–179, 185, 188, 189–
   193, 194, 197, 288
Mauretania, 7; chooses French Com-
   munity, 160
Mboya, Tom, 177, 184, 186–187, 194,
   195, 263, 288
Meru tribe, 185
Middle Congo, 158; chooses French
   Community, 160
Milner, Lord, 96
Milton, John, quoted, 300
Mombasa, 179
Mombasa-Lake Victoria railroad, 181
Montoire Conference, 170
Morgenstern, Oskar, 252
Moro Naba, 159
"Mountains of the Moon," 148
Mountbatten, Earl, 144
Mozambique, 4, 7, 11; African middle
   class in, 120–121; cash crops of, 117–
   118; imbalance of population of, 15;
   investigation of conditions in, 123;
   labor emigrations to Union of
   South Africa, 116–117; lack of lib-
   eralism in, 122–123; land area, 111;
   migration of tribesmen of, to Nyasa-
   land, 117; population of, 111, 113;
   port cities of, 113; resources of, 111–
   113
Msomi gang, 60
Multiracialism, 288–290
Mussolini, Benito, 259
Mutesa, King of Baganda, 174, 175

Nairobi, 176–177, 178, 179, 188, 189;
   slums of, 178–179
Namib, 4, 76
Namier, Sir Lewis, 167
Napoleon I, 30
Napoleon, III, 167
Nasser, President Gamal Abdel, 259–
   260, 286
Nasserism, 259–261
Natal, 7, 35, 50; Asian population of,
   48
National Association for the Advance-
   ment of Colored People, U.S.A., 208
National Council of Nigeria and the
   Cameroons, 225
Nationalism in Colonial Africa
   (Hodgkin), 169
Nationalist Party of the Union of
   South Africa, 37, 38, 42, 50, 53, 80
Ndebeles, 51
Ndola, N. Rhodesia, 97
Negro race, subraces of, 6–7
Nehru, Jawaharlal, 144
New York Times, 22, 101
Ngurus, displacement and migration
   of population, 117
Niger basin, 157; development of, 162
Niger River, 9
Nigeria, 5, 7, 13, 61, 100, 194, 196;
   cocoa crop of, 213; Federal House
   of Representatives, 227; Federation
   of Ghana and, 222–231; and Ghana,
   205–231; physiography of, 224; rural
   economy of, 229–231
Nightingale, Florence, 36, 273
Nile River, 149, 157; source of, 174
Nilo-Hamite, 6
Nilote, 6
Nkrumah, Kwame, 146, 147, 170, 177,
   206–223, 260, 263, 288; early life and
   education of, 207–208; education in
   U.S.A., 208; in England, 208–210;
   politics of, 209–223 *passim*
Nkrumbula, H. M., 105
Norris, Senator George, 277
North Atlantic Treaty Organization,
   248, 250, 276
Northern People's Congress, Nigeria,
   227, 228
Northern province, Kenya, 179, 203

Northern Region, Nigeria, 224, 226–227, 229

Northern Rhodesia, 4, 11, 97, 126, 193, 290; African National Congress, 105; "Copper Belt" in, 97, 108; economic expansion of, 97–98, 106; emigration of labor from Angola to, 116; Legislative Council, 105

Northern Territories, 212, 217, 218

Nyanza province, Kenya, 179

Nyasa, Lake, 5, 92

Nyasaland, 4, 11, 93, 97, 170, 193, 290; African National Congress, 104; as British protectorate, 98; Congress, 109; Legislative Council, 105; migration of tribesmen to, 117; population of, 98; "protectorate status," 108; "trouble," 103–105

Nyerere, Julius, 196, 198

Ogaden, Ethiopia, 5, 179, 203

Ogowe River, 157

Okovangoland, 77

Oppenheimer, Sir Ernest, 65, 66

Oppenheimer, Harry, 65–68

Orange Free State, 4, 30, 34, 66

Organization of American States, 276

Ouagadougou, 157

Ovamboland, 77

Overpopulation, 163

Padmore, George, 209

Palmatorio, 118

Parerenyatwa, Samuel, 101–102

Paton, Alan, 41, 74

"Pauperization," 254

Pedro, Chief, 25

Perham, Margery, quoted, 192–193

Pétain, Henri Philippe, 159, 170

Philosophy of the Revolution, The (Nasser), 259

Pistorius, P. V., 39, 41, 74

Plato, 45, 171, 234

Point Four program, 161

Pointe-Noire, increase of port facilities of, 161

Polarization, of mankind, 153–154

Pondas, 51

Popular Front, in France, 158, 166

Portugal, 293; administration of Angola and Mozambique by, 111–123; labor agreement with Union of South Africa, 114

Portuguese, the, 7. *See also* Portugal; Portuguese Africa

Portuguese Africa, 111–123, 158, 173, 262, 266; African middle class in, 120–121; "assimilated" Africans in, 114, 120; boycott of goods of, 291; compulsory labor in, 113–116; corporal punishment, 118; *indigenas* and *assimilados*, 120; labor and trade agreements with Union of South Africa, 116; Latin paternalism in, 123; "*luso*-populations" in, 119–120; "social equality" in, 119

Portuguese Guinea, 118

Portuguese labor code of 1899, 114–115

Portuguese "overseas provinces," 11

Pretoria, 35, 62

Pretorius, Andries, 30

Prince of Wales's College, Achimota, 208

Rand, the, 64

Rand Daily Mail, 39, 40

Red Sea, 5, 157

Republic, The (Plato), 234

Rhodes, Cecil, 34, 38, 67, 92–93

Rhodesias, 34, 113, 146, 222, 250, 266, 276, 290, 293; expansion of, 120; history of, 92–96. *See also* Federation of the Rhodesias and Nyasaland; Northern Rhodesia; Southern Rhodesia

Riesel, Victor, 267

Rift Valley System, 5, 9, 126, 177, 179

Rinderpest, 23

Ripon, Marquess of, 36, 91

Robinson, Mrs. Joan, 23

Rockefeller, David, 146, 246–247

Rockefeller, John D., 247

Rockefeller, Winthrop, 282

Rockefeller Foundation, International Health Division, 284

Roman Catholic Holy Ghost Fathers, 284

Roosevelt, Franklin Delano, 75, 205, 232–233, 273, 277

Rosebery, Earl of, 36, 90
Royal African Frontier Force, 216
Ruanda-Urundi, 5, 149, 172
Ruark, Robert, 190, 191
Rudolf, Lake, 5
Russell, Sir John, 22
Russia, 153, 248, 252–253, 264, 294. *See also* Union of Soviet Socialist Republics
Russian Revolution, 219

Sabena Airlines, 148
Sahara Desert, 6, 157
St. Augustine, 171
St. Louis, Senegal, 157
Salazar, Antonio de Oliveira, 121, 122
Salisbury, Federation of the Rhodesias, 93
Sand River Convention, 34
São Tomé and Principe, 118–119
Sardauna of Sokoro, 227
Scott, John, 293
Scott, Michael, 78, 81–82, 83
Selassie, Haile, 25, 200–204, 260
Senegal, 156, 157, 262; chooses French Community, 160; in Mali Federation, 168; opts for Mali, 160; peanut exports of, 164; politics in, 166; rice importations of, 163; urbanization and unemployment in, 163
"Senegalese" communities, 158
Senghor, Leopold, 168
Shaftesbury, Earl of, 36
Shangaan, 51
Shark's Point, 148
Shibalos, 117
"Shifting cultivation," 15
"Short-fall" system, in Union of South Africa, 57–58
"Single-strap" society, 20
"Slave Coast," 7
Slave Emancipation Act of 1833, 30
Slave traffic, 175, 181; Arab, 8; European, 7–8, 9
Smuts, Jan Christian, 37, 42, 79, 85, 98
Social antagonisms, polarizing, 153–154
"Social equality," in Portuguese Africa, 119
Socialism, 249

Socialist Party, of France, 158, 166
Société Générale de Belgique, administration and control of Belgian Congo by, 130–132, 149
Somalia, 5, 40, 179, 260; and Cairo, 203–204; independence of, 203
Something of Value (Ruark), 190, 191
Sophiatown, Johannesburg, 53
Sotho, 51
South Africa: A Short History (Keppel-Jones), 33
South Africa Act of 1909, 36
South Africa Institute of Race Relations, 57
South African Customs Union, 85
South-East Asia Treaty Organization, 276
Southern Rhodesia, 4, 87, 184, 198, 290; African National Congress, 40, 104; Afrikanerdom in, 94, 105; Antelope Mine area of, 101–102; apartheid in, 97, 99, 108; Dominion Party, 108; economic expansion of, 96–97, 106; founded, 93–94; racist regimes of, 11–12; United Federal Party of, 108; white population of, 101
Spain, present polity of, 154–155
Speke, John Hanning, 174
Stalin, Joseph, 247–248
Stanford University, Calif., 249
Stanley, Sir Henry M., 127
Stanley Pool, 128, 145
Stellenbosch University, 67
Strachey, John, 241
Stresemann, Gustav, 169
Strijdom, J. G., 38, 62
Strikes, in Union of South Africa, 72
Sudan, 5, 167; chooses French Community, 160; opts for Mali, 160
"Sudanese" belt, 158
"Sudanese" plains, 156
"Sudanese" savanna, 207
Suez Canal, 260
Sufrin, Sidney C., 245
Swaziland, 86; alienated from African, 86; Kruger rule of, 84; physiography of, 84
Swazis, 51
Sybil (Disraeli), 234

Table Bay, 4, 29
Table Mountain, 29
Tanganyika, 5, 174, 180, 194, 195, 196, 197, 222; group farming in, 199; multiracial principle in, 198
Taylor, Maxwell, 297
"Taylor System," 8
Technological Revolution, Africa and the, 1–3, 10–11, 12, 14, 23, 153, 169, 180, 230, 240, 249, 254–255, 267–268, 293, 298; in the U.S.A., 2–3
Tembus, 51
Tennessee Valley Authority, 277, 285
Thompson, Virginia, 163
Thomson, Joseph, 178, 181
Tib, Tippoo, 8
Tillion, Germaine, 21, 161, 254, 281
Time magazine, 293
Tocqueville, Alexis de, 159, 234
Togolanders, riots against, 163
Touré, Sekou, 167, 221, 263
Trajan, 7
Transvaal, 4, 30, 34, 113; discovery of gold and diamonds in, 9; opening of mines of, 31, 33; returned to Afrikaners by Great Britain, 92
Die Transvaler, 67
Trotha, General von, 78
Trypanosomiasis, 23
Tshekedi, Regent of Bechuanaland, 87
Tubman, William, V. S., 221

Ubangi-Shari, chooses French Community, 160
Uganda, 5, 174, 186, 195, 199; pauperization and urbanization in, 196–197; and U.S.S.R., 197
Ugandan National Movement, 197
Ujiji, B.C., 127
Unemployment, in urban concentrations, 18, 21
Union of South Africa, 27–75, 81–82, 172, 220, 250, 293; Act to Amend the Suppression of Communism Act, 55; anti-Semitism in, 67–68; Appeal Court, 50; Asian population of, 48; Cape Province Coloreds, 48–50; constitution of, 36; created by Act of 1909, 85; Criminal Laws Amendment Act, 55; emigration from Angola and Mozambique to, 116–117; food imports in, 20; gold mining in, 64–65; Government, 32, 37–38; Great Debate, 48; Gross National Product of, 19; and High Commission Territories, 84–86; labor and trade agreements with Portuguese Government, 116; miners' strike of 1946, 66; Ministry of Native Affairs, 214; Native Reserves, 20, 47, 63–64; Parliament, 49, 80; Pass Laws of, 52–53; political parties of, 37–38, 40–42, 43; population structure of, 27, 47–52; Prisons Bill, 40; problems of, 292–293; prospects for, 265–266; Public Safety Act of 1953, 55; racial issues in, 28–46, 47–75 *passim*; racist regimes of, 11–12; the Rand, 64; Senate of, 50; "short-fall" system in, 57–58; and Southwest Africa, 79–82; strikes in, 70–71, 72; Suppression of Communism Act of 1950, 55, 60, 72; "Treason Trial," 60–61; United Party, 37, 38, 40, 42, 43, 55, 66, 67; and the U.S.A., 75; urban, 58–59; white population of, 50; in World War II, 38
Union of Soviet Socialist Republics, 260, and Uganda, 197. *See also* Russia
"Union of West African Socialist Republics," 209
United Federal Party, of Southern Rhodesia, 108
United Gold Coast Convention, 209–210
United Nations, 10, 25, 73, 203, 261, 276, 291; Charter, 289; Demographic Yearbook, 1958, 14; Fourth Committee, 122; General Assembly, 81–82; impotence of, 82–83; Mandate System, 76; and Southwest Africa, 79–82; Trusteeship Council, 81, 82; and Union of South Africa, 81–82
United States and Africa, The (Columbia University American Assembly Report), 202
United States of America, and Africa, 206, 220, 232–256, 275–300; Atomic Energy Commission, 296; Bureau for

African Affairs, 281; capitalism old and new in, 243–256, 262–263; Civil War, 229, 240; Congress of, 263, 283; "de-communitization" in, 235; Department of Defense, 252, 296, 297; Development Loan Fund, 250; "Europe-centricity" of, 247–251; failure of policies of, 278; Federal Reserve Bank, 298; Gross National Product of, 255; investment in Africa, 245–246; and the New Imperialism, 294–300; Office of Dependent Area Affairs, 281; Point Four program, 278; Senate, 288; and South Africa, 75; State Department ostrich policies, 268; Technological Revolution in, 2–3
"United States Institute of African Affairs," 281–293
Upper Volta, 159; chooses French Community, 160; opts for Mali, 160
Urbanization, 18, 21; of Belgian Congo, 132–134; in Senegal, Guinea, and Ivory Coast, 163

Venda, 51
Vereeniging, Treaty of, 36
Versailles Treaty, 78
Verwoerd, Hendrik Frensch, 37, 38, 39, 50, 62–64, 65, 66, 67, 72
Vichy, France, 10, 159, 166
Victoria, Lake, 174, 175, 179, 180
Victoria, Queen of England, 129
Volta River project, 219, 221
Voortrekkers Monument, 173

Washington, D.C., 236
Watusis, 149
Waugh, Evelyn, 271
Wedemeyer, Albert C., 251

Welensky, Sir Roy, 103–104, 105, 108–109
"West African Confederacy," 209, 221
West African Federation, 170
Western Region, Nigeria, 223, 224, 226, 227, 228
White Highlands, Kenya, 180, 188, 200
William II, 257
Wilson, Charles, 237
Wilson, Woodrow, 202, 205
Windhoek, Southwest Africa, 76, 78
Witswatersrand, 33; University of, 40
Wolf, Charles, Jr., 245
Work population controls, in Portuguese Africa, 117
World Bank, 215
World Health Organization, 284
World War I, 78, 157, 180, 183, 195, 196, 202, 283
World War II, 79, 89, 90, 132, 153, 158, 161, 208, 233, 245, 295; effect of, on Africa, 10; effect of, on French Africa, 159f.
World War III, 252, 254

Xhosas, 51

Yalta Agreements, 89
Yao, 93
Yoruba, of Nigeria, 224, 227
Youlou, Prime Minister, Congo Republic, 156

Zambesi, 92; River, 7
Zambia African National Congress, 109
Zanzibar, 8, 127; Sultan of, 179, 180–181, 197
Zulu, 30–31, 51, 93

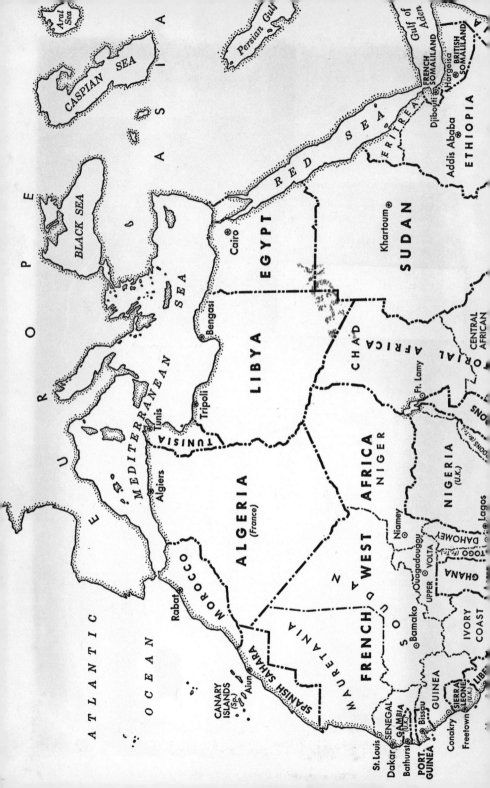